HAMILTON

It's Happening

HAMILTON
150TH BIRTHDAY
1996

T he official logo for Hamilton's Sesquicentennial is the brainchild of municipal employee and graphic artist Richard Freedman.

The Sesqui logo design began with the basic concept of the Hamilton Harbour as one of the great inland harbours, the reason for being for the City of Hamilton. This is represented by a blue field for water and three schooners symbolizing early historic shipping, pleasure craft and boat racing.

The second component is the green field with the stylized trees representing the Niagara Escarpment, Hamilton's second most prominent feature.

The trees evolve into balloons which represent the aura of a birthday celebration. The colours blue and green were selected to co-ordinate with the present City logo. The brighter colours were meant to transmit a festive birthday celebration. The overall shape is a visual pun of a birthday cake.

The artist feels that all of these elements combine the past and the present, making a fitting logo for the city's Sesquicentennial.

••••••••••••••••••••••••••••••••••••••

Canadian Cataloguing in Publication Data:

Sleightholm, Sherry
HAMILTON: It's Happening

Includes index.
ISBN 1-895208-02-5

1. Hamilton (Ont.).   2. Environmental policy -
Ontario - Hamilton.   3. Hamilton (Ont.) -
Economic conditions.   I. Davie, Michael B.
II. Ruberto, Bruno.   III. Title.

FC3098.3.S54 1996   971.3'52   C96-930698-9
F1059.5.H25S54 1996

Published 1996

Advertising Sales:
Joe Kelly and Amalgamated Industries

Printed in Hamilton, Ontario, Canada
by W.L. Griffin Printing Limited

Colour separations by SE Graphics Ltd.

ABOVE: *The city as seen from Sam Lawrence Park on the Mountain.*
– Photo by Dennis McGreal

HAMILTON

It's Happening

BRaSH Publishing Incorporated
Hamilton, Ont., Canada

ABOVE: *A look at the city from the harbour.*
– Photo by Dennis McGreal

From The Editor

As publisher and editor of Hamilton, It's Happening, I would be remiss if I did not take the opportunity to thank some of the many people who contributed to this fine book.

I'll begin with author Sherry Sleightholm, who once again produced an outstanding text. Sherry and I last teamed up to deliver the award-winning book, Hamilton, A View From The Top, and it was a pleasure working with her once again.

Much of the other copy in this book comes in the form of company profiles, and credit there belongs to Michael B. Davie for his insightful features on members of our business community.

A coffee table book wouldn't be much at all without pictures – and there are more than 250 of them, all crisp and in colour, in this book.

On that front, I'll begin by thanking Dennis McGreal, who contributed the bulk of the book's editorial pictures. Like a true photographer, Dennis refused to hand over anything but the best for these pages and he can certainly be proud of his work.

Also, thanks to David Gruggen and Joe Bucci for their profile shots, and to Bob Chambers for his spectacular cover photo. All of their efforts, and those of others, are duly noted throughout the book.

My thanks also to Peter Bailey for his much-appreciated help with the final edit on the book.

I wouldn't be thanking anyone had I not been given the opportunity to produce this book in the first place, and for that honour I must acknowledge Hamilton Sesquicentennial Celebrations Inc.

Thanks to co-chairs Vincenza Travale and Milt Lewis for showing faith in my abilities, and an extra special thanks to Sesqui's executive director Carmen Rizzotto, the person I turned to for advice and guidance on a day-to-day basis.

Thanks also to Mayor Bob Morrow, who once again provided unflagging support along the road to the producing of a book that shows Hamilton as the outstanding city that it truly is.

Finally, thanks to my wife Cathy and our sons Matt and Mike, who provided their own special support as I laboured into the wee hours of the morning for the past year to complete this project.

– Bruno Ruberto

A Sesquicentennial Message

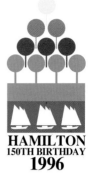

HAMILTON 150TH BIRTHDAY 1996

HAMILTON SESQUICENTENNIAL CELEBRATIONS INC.

Honourary Chairperson

His Worship,
Mayor Robert M. Morrow

Directors

Milton J. Lewis, Q.C.
Vincenza Travale
Co-Chairpersons
Ted Urbanowicz, C.A.
Treasurer

Honourary Patrons

The Honourable
Lincoln M. Alexander
P.C., C.C., K.ST.J., O.Ont., Q.C.

Bertram N. Brockhouse
Nobel Laureate (Physics, 1994)

The Right Honourable
Ellen L. Fairclough
P.C., C.C., F.C.A., LL.D., U.E.

D. Morgan Firestone

The Right Honourable
Ramon J. Hnatyshyn
P.C., C.C., C.M.M. C.D., Q.C.

Sir Edwin Leather
K.C.M.G., K.C.V.O., LL.D.

Brigadier General
W. Denis Whitaker
DSO, CM, ED, CD, LdeH

Executive Director

Carmen D. Rizzotto

Corporate Liaison

Frank P. DeNardis

Executive Secretary

Susan K. Reeder

Volunteer Members

Advisory Body

Sub-Committees

Corporate Sponsors

Official Registration as a
Charitable Organization
1015635-59

During Hamilton's Sesquicentennial Year, the focus of our celebrations has been on 150 years of Hamilton's people and their achievements and on the hope that we have in this community for a bright and prosperous future.

Our optimism stems from an understanding of our current reality. Hamilton in 1996 is a city built firmly on a manufacturing base and yet, a city that has enhanced this base through environmental renewal and excellence in health, education and entrepreneurial fields.

This book was commissioned by Hamilton Sesquicentennial Celebrations Inc. to capture the spirit of renewal that permeates Hamilton in 1996, to tell the story of the changes and the enhancements and to acknowledge and recognize some of the people who are leading Hamilton toward a successful entry into the 21st century.

We congratulate all who have participated in the efforts to renew and revitalize our community and all who have contributed to the production of Hamilton, It's Happening, especially Bruno Ruberto and Sherry Sleightholm.

We hope that you will enjoy our Sesquicentennial commemorative book.

• Vincenza Travale

• Milton J. Lewis

• Frank P. DeNardis

• Carmen D. Rizzotto

• Ted Urbanowicz

Foreword

● ●

During our Sesquicentennial year, we celebrate our city's proud past, a present with many great success stories and we look optimistically to the future.

In 1996, we can boast of successful economic diversification and also of our United Nations designation as a "model sustainable community."

We're also a caring, sharing and giving community. We are very Pan-Canadian in our outlook and we have ties around the globe. We have contributed to our country and the world and want to do more and be better still in the future.

This book serves as a great opportunity to remember our "Sesqui" year and all the events, large and small, that have been part of it.

Robert M. Morrow
Mayor
City of Hamilton

ABOVE: *Mayor Robert Morrow is pictured with council members in the City Hall lobby. The 16 aldermen during Hamilton's Sesquicentennial year were as follows:*
- *Mary Kiss, Marvin Caplan, Ward 1*
- *Vince J. Agro, Wm. M. McCulloch, Ward 2*
- *Bernie Morelli, Don Drury, Ward 3*
- *Geraldine Copps, Dave Wilson, Ward 4*
- *Fred Eisenberger, Chad Collins, Ward 5*
- *Tom Jackson, Bob Charters, Ward 6*
- *Henry Merling, Terry Anderson, Ward 7*
- *Don Ross, Frank D'Amico, Ward 8*
– Photo by David Gruggen

I n 1846, Hamilton, the head of the lakes, housed a population of 6,832 "souls" – or so
they were deemed in the incorporation census. The stiff nomenclature may have been
scrupulously accurate; at least according to the day's residents of neighbouring Dundas and
Ancaster, who charged that the numbers had been flagrantly inflated by adding names of
the dear departed resting in local cemeteries.

With the incorporation came an extension of the urban boundaries to Paradise Road on the
west and Emerald Street on the east, along with a north and south perimeter of the harbour and
Aberdeen Avenue. Colin Campbell Ferrie, who had served as the first president of the Board
of Police, assumed the mayoral chain of office.

We have come a long way since then; through two world wars and a Depression; through
industrialization, with machinery fuelled by steam, brute strength and sweat; to technological
innovation driven by space-age computer chips, brain power and suits.

This is a celebration of that journey. And here's to the next 150 years!

BELOW: *A panoramic view of the harbour with the city in the background.*
PAGE 10: *Two downtown landmarks, the Queen Victoria statue and the CIBC building.*
– Photos by Dennis McGreal

CONTENTS

The Environment .... *Chapter* **1**

Health Care .... *Chapter* **2**

McMaster University.............................. *Chapter* **3**

Sports & Recreation .... *Chapter* **4**

Arts & Entertainment .... *Chapter* **5**

Sights & Sounds .... *Chapter* **6**

Local Landmarks .... *Chapter* **7**

Industry & Technology .... *Chapter* **8**

Renaissance Project .... *Chapter* **9**

Prologue

• •

I arrived here in 1974 – armed with a Journalism Degree and a portfolio of clippings from a two-year stint at the Toronto Sun. Media veterans are a cynical bunch. I was regaled with lurid tales of Steeltown; how it was the boondocks of urban sophistication and a backwater of intelligentsia. Oh, the stories they told.

For my irascible cronies in the fourth estate, civilization ended at Mississauga and Scarborough. And like the good ship Santa Maria, (sailed by Christopher Columbus), I would fall off the face of the earth. Well, I did find the new world. And for me it was a far sight better than the old.

By virtue of their size, many municipalities lack a distinct persona, as if you were adrift in a sea of strangers; a fathomless crowd which surges out of subways, and lurches up concrete stairs. But far from the pervasive anonymity which characterizes the latter 20th century, Hamilton is a region of "real people."

They chat at the Farmers' Market and swap stories at Tim Hortons. They are the steelworkers, and the McMaster University professors, the nurses and the environmental scientists. They are the housewives wheeling baby buggies, and the auto mechanics with their grease-splattered overalls.

They are Italian and Portuguese; people of colour, people of all faiths; people of athletic prowess, and people surmounting physical challenges. It was here that I found the diverse, multi-cultural and cosmopolitan society as it was meant to be, with a smorgasbord of ethnic flavour.

But more than that, it is a place with a palpable spirit of camaraderie – one best exemplified by our last-ditch attempt to save the Tiger-Cats, the beloved black and gold of pigskin fame. With the threat of loosing the franchise, and an ultimatum imposed by the Canadian Football League bosses, Steeltown showed its true colours. And like a Hail Mary pass, with seconds remaining on the clock, loyal fans scrimmaged at the Tabby box office, snapping up 15,000-plus season tickets and pledging more than a million dollars in corporate support. Touchdown!

We are so much more than rolled steel, apple fritters and Oskee Wee Wee. Some say we share the best of all worlds.

"Home, Sweet Home" is the reality of the working class wage earner. Often the rents in other metropolitan cities far exceed the mortgage payments of families here in the heart of the Golden Horseshoe. Affordable prices mean you need not be restricted to a cramped Main Street garret, a bachelor condominium, or a 35-foot frontage.

Members of our home builders' industry are among the most respected professionals of their kind in Canada. With a rich 54-year history, our local builders' association pre-dates its national counterpart by a full year.

Their craftsmanship is the stuff of glossy magazine centre-spreads; with spiral oak staircases, gas fireplaces, Great Rooms, ground floor dens, country porches and harvest kitchens.

There is no dearth of picturesque properties in the area – be it in the scenic meadows, coursing waterfalls and open farmlands of Flamborough, or on the shore of Lake Ontario at the foot of Bay and John streets, with its panoramic vistas of sailboats slicing the whitecaps or yachts cruising to port. And it all lies within minutes of an historic and vibrant business core.

You can linger at lookouts such as the perch at the crest of Sydenham Road, soaring above the precipice of the escarpment with a sweeping view of the Valley Town of Dundas, or you can wander the Bruce Trail, cutting a swath across the region. But you can never weary of the pilgrimage down the Mountain, and that line of sight that stretches all the way to Toronto.

Across Canada, in the 1990s, an average trip to and from the office consumed 59 minutes – 60 seconds shy of one hour. During a working career, some travel 235,200 kilometres, equal to about six times around the globe.

It's not so much the physical toll of this lifestyle; though that too is costly. It is more the emotional duress; the frayed nerves, the clogged arteries and the clock ticking. Raised in such a milieu, where a seething crawl of angry motorists, shaking their fists and railing at the gods, was as common as the sunrise, I was unprepared for the Ambitious City, where you can scoot from one end to the other in a quarter of an hour.

No sooner had I settled here in Hamilton-Wentworth, than one acquaintance impetuously relocated from a rural hinterland to the Mountain. He complained about a former 15-minute commute – a daily trek down country roads, lined with cow pastures and century homes – to his office in the core. He proudly announced that the drive had now been cut in half.

I guess it takes an "adopted" daughter to truly appreciate the splendour of one's surroundings. And so, in the words of Ralph Waldo Emerson: "Though we travel the world over to find the beautiful, we must carry it with us or we find it not."

In 1996 we salute the beauty within us, and the beauty in our own backyard. Because, as you will see for yourself, there is no place like home.

– Sherry Sleightholm

Chapter 1

The Environment

The best circulating books of the 1990s are no longer romances or even whodunits, but the series of Round Table and Special Task Reports, all printed on stacks of recycled paper. For this is the age of ecological awareness.

The concept of a Round Table harkens back to the days of King Arthur and his knights; where all the participants spoke with equal authority.

You may also remember the literati at the Round Table in New York's Algonquin Hotel back in the 1920s; people such as Dorothy Parker and Robert Benchley, the irreverent and wry-witted critics, who set the stage for the future. There was no more sophisticated place to be than with those urbane prodigies, on the cutting edge of their era.

Seventy years later, our National and Ontario Round Tables on Environment and Economy deal not with whimsical repartee, but with ominous realities. Experts from all walks of life wrestle with the crisis in 20th-century development; a debate laced with the jargon of sustainable development.

In October 1993, the United Nations named Hamilton-Wentworth as one of its 21 model municipalities for sustainable development. The designation, which arose from the June 1992 Earth Summit in Rio de Janiero, set the stage for our region to act as a prototype for development that will benefit the present, without compromising the future.

We are the first and only city in Canada to receive the honour as a Local Agenda 21 Model Community Programme (a moniker to denote a course of global action for the 21st century). We are one of only two such cities across North America, and one of only 21 around the world participating in the UN's master plan. (Some of the other top guns in this test flight include Quito,

Ecuador; Hat Yai, Thailand; Manus Province, Papua, New Guinea; Buga, Colombia; Johnstoneshire, Australia; Hamilton, New Zealand; and Santos, Brazil. Communities in England, India, South Africa and Kenya will be targeted in the future.)

The UN established a stringent set of criteria for candidates; among them a "multi-stakeholder approach," or widespread community support; inter-disciplinary analysis; an action plan and reporting mechanisms.

The three-year project, monitored by the International Council on Local Environment Initiatives (ICLEI), dovetailed with the region's own long-range goal called Vision 2020 – a 30-year ecological blueprint for environmental renewal which impressed and swayed the selection committee.

"We filed that report with a number of people," recalls then Regional Chairman Reg Whynott. Fortuitously, the UN had initiated a search for communities with long-range environmental plans. "They were looking for examples. And it was their decision to select us as the model for Canada."

Mr. Whynott campaigned on that clean-up strategy when he ran for the Regional Chair in 1988.

"One of the issues we found in our survey of the community was the future of our environment." A trio of signatories – Reg Whynott, Federation of Canadian Municipalities representative Grant Hopcroft and ICLEI Secretary-General Jeb Brugmann – proclaimed the UN's Memorandum of Understanding at the Greater Hamilton Technology Enterprise Centre.

In 1996 we will tender a report to a UN Conference on Human Settlements. And thus the eyes of the world will be upon us. In the ecological scientific struggle, we will have become the slide under the microscope.

PAGES 12-13: *Another day draws to a close as the sun sets on Hamilton Harbour.*
– Photo by Dennis McGreal

FACING PAGE: *A family outing turns into feeding time for the waterfowl at Bayfront Park. More than $9 million in remediation work has turned 16 hectares of formerly vacant North End land into versatile greenspace, with 1,800 metres of shoreline integrating fish habitat, native vegetation and facilities. Among the park's other features are a public boat launch, fishing areas, a 250-space parking lot and pedestrian and bicycle trails leading to Pier 4 Park.*
– Photo by Dennis McGreal

RIGHT: *The region is home to numerous scenic waterfalls, including this one, cascading over the escarpment near the Bruce Trail in Ancaster.*
– Photo by Vic MacBournie

The residents of Hamilton have a rich tradition of supporting those in need and for providing amenities and services that make this city great. Whenever there has been a challenge we have had a leader to spearhead the cause.

In 1950, Ken Soble rallied our community behind his dream of raffling off a house to raise money for flood victims in Winnipeg. The "Dream Home" lottery was the first of its kind – and its success made Hamilton the nation's largest contributor to the flood relief campaign.

In 1971, the Jaycees successfully headed a community campaign to put Astro Turf in Ivor Wynne Stadium.

In 1972, Jack MacDonald was Chairman of a successful Grey Cup Week in Hamilton. With just two hotels, the old Armoury, a bunch of tents and thousands of volunteers, Jack pulled off a miracle. The same enthusiasm will make the 1996 Grey Cup Celebrations just as successful.

Sports, Education, Health Care, Culture and the well-being of our citizens have all benefitted from the leadership of many dedicated individuals.

In keeping with the tradition of giving and caring, Peter DeSantis, President of Homes By DeSantis, is building the "Sesqui Super Home On Paradise" to be raffled in a fund-raising lottery.

Mr. DeSantis chose the occasion of Hamilton's 150th birthday to again lead the citizens to financially support health care, cultural and recreational facilities.

"The fight to keep our community healthy in body and mind is never-ending," says Mr. DeSantis. "It is a fight that is getting harder and harder to win, but through efforts like the Sesqui lottery, we are winning the battle."

Among the many beneficiaries of the home lottery are the Hamilton hospitals.

"For many years, Peter DeSantis has been a great supporter of health care and we are grateful for his continuing support," says John Bienenstock, vice-president, Faculty of Health Sciences at McMaster University.

Hamilton Mayor Bob Morrow echoed those sentiments, saying: "Peter DeSantis exemplifies the same spirit and vision of all the great builders of this community who have helped make Hamilton a special place to live, work and play."

Mr. DeSantis had the home designed by Fabiani Architects specifically for this lottery. Every detail was planned with the future and the environment in mind.

The Sesqui Home, which features a cut stone exterior provided by Arriscraft, includes extensive use of steel from Dofasco and Stelco, says Mr. DeSantis. Sidus Systems has created and provided a computer brain that truly exemplifies the

• Builder Peter DeSantis stands at the site of the Sesqui Super Home on Paradise. The home is being built by Homes By DeSantis as a fundraiser.
– Photo by Joe Bucci

"home of the 21st century," he adds.

The Sesqui Home utilizes the energy-saving and environmental products of the Green Venture community-based organization, and features the latest technology in the home-building industry.

Mr. DeSantis received unprecedented support from the Hamilton-Halton Home Builders' Association, national and local suppliers and countless friends and volunteers in building this fine home.

This support comes as no surprise,

says Tom Cochren, past president of the Canadian Home Builders' Association.

"Peter has always been an outstanding member of our association and few builders have contributed as much to the quality, security and the affordability of housing in Canada," adds Mr. Cochren.

The Sesqui Home is just another example of Peter DeSantis' continuing contribution to this community, and his efforts will not go unnoticed.

"Peter's contribution to charities and civic causes is noteworthy and a source of pride to the entire community," says Nicholas Zaffiro, a well-known Hamilton lawyer and community leader.

The DeSantis-built "Super Home" will be a great legacy to both its builder and to Hamilton's Sesquicentennial.

• Philip Environmental is committed to the highest standards of environmental leadership and compliance in all areas of its operations.

Where others see refuse, the Fracassi brothers see revenue. Together, they've built their company, Philip Environmental, into the nation's largest recycler of industrial by-products and one of the fastest-growing firms in Canada.

"There's really no such thing as waste, just materials we can recycle and resell," notes Allen Fracassi, company president and chief executive officer. "We always ask: 'What can I do with it?' – rather than 'How can I get rid of it?'"

That philosophy is shared by his brother Philip, company executive vice-president and chief operating officer, who observes that "one company's waste is another company's raw material."

The Fracassi brothers had shared a childhood of hard work in a family which immigrated to Canada from Italy in 1965.

They laboured after school and weekends in their backyard, maintaining trucks owned by their father, Enzo Fracassi, who ran a haulage firm from their home.

After his father's business went bankrupt in the late 1970s, Allen Fracassi borrowed $10,000 from his fiancee and $10,000 more from Toronto Dominion Bank and bought the trucks.

Allen Fracassi soon realized that scrap steel contained in waste sands could be screened out and resold – and he set up a backyard screening operation. The early emphasis on waste reuse and recycling was born of necessity: Although the firm began in the early 1980s as an industrial waste handling-disposal firm, it didn't acquire its first landfill site until 1988.

To avoid paying other landfill site owners' steep fees to dump wastes, the company tried to divert as much material as possible away from landfill. It sold the foundry sand it was hauling to cement factories as a substitute raw material.

• In 1995, Philip Environmental's Metals Recovery Group recycled more wire and cable than any other firm in North America. Outokumpu American Brass was among the U.S. companies who benefitted from Philip Environmental's recycling expertise last year. Shown above is Philip's Mladin Miceta, Assistant Operations Manager, with Outokumpu's Ed Galenza, right.

"We did it partly to cut costs," explains Allen Fracassi, noting that his company was then able to profit in two ways – from waste haulage fees and from the revenue raised through the sale of waste as raw material.

"By recycling and reselling a lot of the waste materials, we earned additional revenue and cut the landfill expense."

From these entrepreneurial roots and talent for converting waste into raw material, the company named after the brothers' grandfather would grow into a diversified recycling giant.

Philip Environmental also provides extensive consulting services, analyzing the customer's production process to find ways in which waste generation can be minimized. And for remaining waste that can't be eliminated from the production process, the firm uses its technology to help the customer reuse or recycle as much of this waste as possible.

Much of this new technology is installed by Philip Environmental at the customer's site, where waste is reduced, reprocessed and recycled prior to transport. All told, Philip Environmental is able to divert 70 per cent or more of the waste it handles from disposal.

Philip Fracassi says the company takes pride in offering a full range of services. "We don't allow our people to wear blinders. They can't just focus on removing waste materials from a customer site. They have to consider all aspects of serving the customer, including transportation services and consulting services to reduce the amount of waste generated."

This approach has allowed Philip Environmental to establish enduring relationships with its customers, ensuring wherever possible that customers realize lower energy or disposal costs by reducing or altering the waste they generate.

And this approach is helping drive the phenomenal growth of a firm which by 1995, had annual sales revenue of over $700 million – up from less than $60 million in 1988. Revenue has been growing by a staggering 2,700 per cent annually.

Philip Environmental has also grown into a major employer. In 1989, it had 350 employees. By the mid-1990s, it had a North American workforce of more than 3,000 employees – about one-third of them in the Hamilton area.

The company boasts the largest chemical by-product recycling facility in the United States which processes solid and liquid residues into a fuel supplement. Cable and wire processing operations in Hamilton recover valuable copper, aluminum and plastics.

Other major factors driving Philip Environmental's growth include Allen

Fracassi's ability to foresee environmental trends, his financial acumen enabling the firm to become publicly traded on several stock markets – and his emphasis on steady expansion through acquisition.

In 1993 alone, the company acquired Nortru, a recycler of waste oils, sludges and solvents with operations in Detroit and Texas; Burlington Environmental, with five chemical recycling plants in the Pacific Northwest and an environmental consulting division with field offices across the U.S.; Waxman Resources, the Hamilton-based innovative recycler of plastics and cable; and Hamilton-based I.W. & S. Ferrous, the second-largest ferrous scrap recycler in Canada.

In 1994 Philip Environmental acquired control of Rockcliffe Research, managing the renowned Wastewater Technology Centre in Burlington, and founded Philip Utilities. And in 1995, Philip Utilities began a $187-million contract to operate several sewage and water treatment plants of Hamilton-Wentworth region.

Under this private-public partnership – the first of its kind in Canada and largest in North America – the first $700,000 in savings are passed on to the region and the next $1 million in savings goes to Philip. It eventually retains 60 per cent of the savings and the region 40 per cent.

"In the case of municipal systems, we're quite convinced we can operate plants more efficiently, so we can guarantee cost savings," says Allen Fracassi, noting the private sector is more efficient in general because it is driven by a profit motive and an understanding that firms must be accountable to retain contracts.

And the potential for such private-public partnerships is enormous, adds Mr. Fracassi. "The building and operation of water and sewage works constitute the fastest-growing market in the world . . . something like $150 billion annually,

it's a very, very big figure. It's growing faster than even telecommunications and the computer industry," he explains.

Also in 1995, Hamilton was chosen as the site of a $25-million plant which utilizes plasma torch technology to recover valuable metals in electric arc furnace residue created through steel production.

It is another example of a deep com-

• AFC Industries, the Army Corps of Engineers, and Philip Environmental had a common goal – to clean up the Winfield Locks site in Red House, West Virginia. Together, they solved an environmental problem safely, economically and with the complete support of the community.

mitment to research and development of new technologies – in this case allowing extraction of zinc, lead and iron products from industrial by-products.

"This process clearly represents our approach to treating industrial by-products as raw material," says Allen Fracassi.

"We are able to produce materials with valuable reuse applications and provide viable alternatives to disposal."

He envisions Philip as an industrial services company offering services in three key areas: By-product processing, metals recovery and environmental services. In fact, the Fracassis prefer to describe their core business as 'fully integrated resource recovery and industrial services' rather than waste management, which only occurs when by-products can no longer be recycled, reused or refashioned into new products.

While Allen Fracassi continues to demonstrate a knack for acquiring good-fit companies, Philip Fracassi brings operations experience and leadership to the company, developing the company from within while managing a diverse group of operations.

"We work in tandem," Philip Fracassi says of the successful, brotherly, entrepreneurial management arrangement. "While Allen works on acquisitions, my focus is on developing what we've got and enlarging it – I like to keep very focused on our margins," he notes. "And we both recognize the need to focus heavily on technology, to make sure we never fall behind and that we're the ones leading the way with the right technology."

Philip Environmental is also leading on the social front, helping companies achieve new societal dictates for cradle-to-grave responsibility for waste. And Philip has worked directly with community groups to solve pollution problems left by industry from another era.

The company's community involvement runs deeper: Sponsoring students' excursions to conservation areas, theatre and sports events, the firm virtually adopted Robert Land School, located in Hamilton's North End where the Fracassi brothers grew up.

Clearly, Philip Environmental has never lost touch with its roots and continues to invest substantially in the economic and social vitality of its home city.

'We won't have a society if we destroy the environment.'
— Margaret Mead

They are the modern acronyms of a city in transition; pet names such as BARC and RAP; not to mention significant letters like RBG and HRCA. Together they speak volumes to environmentalists across the globe; because this is the story of a municipality that has re-written its history.

And it all starts here in the erstwhile murky waters of Cootes' Paradise, where pioneers once paddled birchbark canoes and let down their fishing lines to snag schools of trout. A century-and-a-half later it is a mammoth scientific laboratory, the likes of which the world has seldom seen.

It's a community initiative, and a microcosm of Hamilton's quest to paint the town green. And it is a study in partnership – pooling the resources of professors, politicians and lay people.

No one is as ardent a believer as the recently converted. Like a blind person miraculously restored to sight, the city focused on Vision 2020; a policy paper drafted by the Regional Chairman's Task Force on Sustainable Development.

The dogma, spelled out by the community, concentrated on four precepts. Key among them were the basic human needs – the right to clean air and water, food; shelter, education and employment. But, like psychologist Abraham Maslow's pyramid of self-actualization, other platforms were devoted to loftier desires; and none so much as an ecological integrity, mindful of preservation – a place to pass on to our descendants. For we are the custodians of tomorrow.

In the watershed year of 2020, the report envisions a region with a vibrant urban core, nestled amid family farms, hamlets and a network of natural terrain; a pristine ecosystem that would stand as a Walden Two of the environment. That prototype triggered a pair of documents which translated a Utopian concept into the cold, hard reality; namely Directions and Detailed Strategies for creating a sustainable Region.

Taking a much closer look, the hundreds of recommendations scrutinize every modern phenomenon, from the phasing out of pesticides to promoting bicycle paths and public walkways.

In 1994, Regional Council passed a new Official Plan called Towards a Sustainable Region.

And thus was laid the ground work for the citizenry.

Nowhere is that vision more evident than in Project Paradise, here on the western reaches of Hamilton Harbour. Seven years in the planning, the goal is to restore a healthy and self-sustaining marsh ecosystem for fish and wildlife.

Oriented from the east to the west, these wetlands drain 250 square kilometres – from the largest tributary of Spencer Creek to Grindstone Creek, parts of Flamborough and the Beverley Swamp. The sprawling mass of marsh, with a stable of nationally significant species and Carolinian forest, is designated as Class 1 wetlands under the Ontario Ministry of Natural Resources (OMNR) criteria.

And as such, it is a critical piece in the ecological puzzle, especially lying within an industrial cityscape. During the spring migration, it is a birder's heaven; they stand with binoculars glued to their eyes, fingers pointing skyward. Much like a human kidney, the marsh filters nutrients and sediments as well as stores and regulates water. Its health is a measure of the area's environmental well-being; a prognosis for the future.

Project Paradise is part of RAP, or the Remedial Action Plan for Hamilton Harbour, one of 43 areas of concern along the Great Lakes, based on an International Joint Commission (IJC) initiative that dates back to the mid-'80s.

Sad to say, the harbour was red-flagged as being among the Number One hot spots identified by the IJC.

ABOVE: *A Canada goose nurtures a newborn in an open field in one of the region's many conservation areas.*

FACING PAGE: *Albion Falls, located in the Red Hill Valley in Hamilton's east end, is one of the 'Ribbon Falls,' named because their height is much greater than their width.*
— Photos by Dennis McGreal

Morgan Firestone has touched the lives of many people in countless ways through charitable contributions totalling millions of dollars.

The Ancaster resident is a scion of the Firestone tire dynasty, the multi-national Akron, Ohio-based empire founded by his grandfather Harvey Firestone in 1900.

After being educated at Princeton University and serving as a U.S. Army second lieutenant in the Korean War, Morgan Firestone spent the mid-1950s through mid-1960s working as a Firestone company salesman in Minnesota, store supervisor in Florida and finance manager at the Akron head office.

In 1966, Mr. Firestone left Akron for Hamilton, where he would serve for the following three years as the president of Firestone Tire, the Canadian branch operation based in Hamilton.

As his 40th birthday approached in 1970, Mr. Firestone realized he loved Canada but didn't particularly like tires or large corporations. So, he left Firestone, took his multi-million-dollar trust fund with him, and founded Firan Corp.

From the beginning, Mr. Firestone, the founder, chairman and chief executive officer of Oakville-based Firan, has built an oddly successful company by investing in unrelated businesses he happens to find interesting. The company employs 1,200 people around the world.

The broadly diversified firm became the leading Canadian manufacturer of motor homes after acquiring Glendale Recreational Vehicles of Strathroy, Ontario; Travelaire Canada of Red Deer, Alberta and an Indiana RV manufacturer now known as Firan Motor Coach.

An aging baby boomer market in Canada and the United States has given Firan's RV business promising growth potential, especially with exchange rates favouring Canadian exports.

Firan is also a leading producer of electronic systems for air traffic control applications worldwide. Washington-based Denro unit is the world's largest supplier of ATC communications switching systems while London, England-based Fernau Avionics produces ground-based ATC navigation systems and Toronto-based Graphico makes printed circuit illuminated cockpit panels for civil aviation and printed circuit boards for the North American electronics market.

• *Morgan Firestone, who founded the St. Joseph's Hospital Foundation to fund worthy projects at the hospital, is shown with former U.S. President George Bush at a hospital fundraiser.*
– Photo by Creative Visions

• A co-operative effort between the Town of Ancaster and Firan Foundation resulted in the building of the Morgan Firestone Arena in Ancaster.
– Photo by David Gruggen

Publicly traded Firan's sales revenue increased to nearly $250 million in the mid-1990s, up from less than $70 million when the decade began, while profit approached about $4 million annually.

While the company is unquestionably successful, Mr. Firestone's success can also be measured in terms of his deep and abiding commitment to charitable causes.

In 1970, just as he was getting Firan off the ground, Mr. Firestone founded the St. Joseph's Hospital Foundation in Hamilton to fund worthy projects at the hospital. Then, in 1978, he founded the Firestone Chest and Allergy Unit at St. Joseph's Hospital to assist in new respirology research. It is now an internationally renowned respirology unit.

"I am pleased that the Unit has had a positive effect for the many patients who attend clinics," says Mr. Firestone, adding that "I'm very proud of the research that has taken place for the benefit of the thousands of people who are affected by allergies and respiratory diseases."

In 1984, Mr. Firestone became

Honourary President, St. Joseph's Health Care Foundation. During the early 1990s, he raised funds for the Unit by chairing dinner events featuring such famous speakers as former British Prime Minister Margaret Thatcher, former U.S. President George Bush, former U.S.S.R. leader Mikhail Gorbachev and former New York Governor Mario Cuomo.

Mr. Firestone established Firan Foundation in 1983 with his portion of the family charitable foundation that had been known as the Firestone Foundation.

Firan Foundation has contributed funding for several construction projects to expand and develop McMaster University. Mr. Firestone is a member of McMaster's Board of Governors and chairman of the university's Business Advisory Group for the Faculty of Health Sciences.

The foundation has also financed a colour catalogue of permanent art of the Art Gallery of Hamilton, a fitting action given Mr. Firestone's instrumental role in contributing funding in 1975 towards the gallery's construction.

Firan Foundation has also supported the Canadian Equestrian Olympic Team and the E.P. Taylor Equine Research Fund. In 1994 Mr. Firestone founded the Firestone Golf Classic for Kids Help Phone. He's also been a regular contributor to the Catholic Youth Organization, Sister Servants of Mary Immaculate, Sisters of Social Service, educational programs and the Hamilton AIDS Network, Good Shepherd Centre, Bach Elgar Choir, Big Brothers, Hamilton SPCA and other worthy causes too numerous to mention.

Not surprisingly, Mr. Firestone has been named Honourary Patron of Hamilton's Sesqui Celebrations. He has donated a motor home to the Sesqui Super Home on Paradise Lottery. He also sponsored the 1996 Sesquicentennial Morgan Firestone Pro-Am Golf Classic.

The magnitude of Mr. Firestone's ongoing contribution to the Hamilton community is indeed an inspiring example of the extent to which a successful businessman can use his resources to improve the lives of his fellow citizens.

• The Fortinos store at Upper James and Rymal Road on the west Mountain.
– Photo by David Gruggen

Since its inception in 1961, Fortinos' approach with customers has been best summed up by its slogan: "Your supermarket with a Heart!"

Indeed, Fortinos' skill for meeting the needs of its customers was recognized by National Grocers when it bought the Hamilton-based chain of grocery stores in 1988 – and decided not to tamper with the Fortinos success formula. Instead, National Grocers kept the Fortinos name and allowed the stores to continue to operate independently – and franchise out into a chain of 17 grocery stores by 1996.

This hands-off approach by the new owner was also a sincere – and well-deserved – compliment to John Fortino, who started it all in 1961 with the purchase of a small store at Dunsmuir and King streets in the heart of Hamilton.

From the beginning, Mr. Fortino sought to give families a break with weekly specials offering exceptional value and variety. His friendly, family-style operation, his sincere interest in his staff and his open approach generated success by building customer loyalty.

As Mr. Fortino would recall: "I don't like to be thought of as the boss or be called 'Mr. Fortino.' I like to keep friendly with people . . . we are like a family."

In 1972, the award-winning Canadian entrepreneur brought his customer-first philosophy and commitment to quality fresh foods to a second location at Mohawk Road E. and Upper Ottawa St.

Mr. Fortino took a decidedly hands-on approach, working 80-hour workweeks, personally running the store, washing the floors at closing time, unloading his truck at 3 a.m. – and finally allowing himself a few hours sleep before making a routine early morning drive to the food terminal.

A year later, he opened a third store, a large full-service supermarket on the West Mountain on Limeridge Road.

Years of steady growth followed, leading to the 1982 opening of the Fortinos office and warehouse complex on the East Mountain at Nebo Road.

The 1980s were years of continuous growth which saw the opening of stores elsewhere in Hamilton and in Burlington and Brampton. The chain had grown to eight stores by 1988 when it was purchased by National Grocers.

In 1991, Fortinos opened a new head office and distribution centre on Glover Road in Hamilton, more than three times the size of its older complex.

Franchising was also emphasized in the 1990s as Fortinos went through yet

another period of rapid growth, opening stores in Woodbridge, Etobicoke, Markham and North York. By the mid-1990s, Fortinos had grown to 17 franchisee stores plus its head office and distribution complex, together employing a total workforce of over 2,700 people.

Now retired, Mr. Fortino maintains an active interest in the business as a consultant to the successful chain of grocery stores. The day-to-day business is run by his nephew, Fortinos senior vice-president and chief operations executive officer Vince Scornaienchi.

Although Fortinos has grown into an enormously successful big business, its continued success is owed to its strict adherence to the basic principles which fueled company growth over the years.

"Our emphasis has always been on fresh foods – we're famous for our quality meats and fresh produce," says John Thiessen, Fortinos director of advertising and public relations, who notes that success also continues to be driven by good pricing and variety.

"We devote a lot of our space to meats, seafood and bakery goods," adds Mr. Thiessen. "That's the trend now in the 1990s," he notes. "But we've always been there – and we'll continue to be there."

• *After years of tremendous growth in the 1980s, Fortinos opened a new head office and distribution centre, located on Glover Road in the east end of Hamilton Mountain.*
                    – Photo by David Gruggen

From Hamilton-area roots, Laidlaw Inc. has grown into the multi-billion-dollar waste management, environmental and passenger services giant that it is today. By the mid-1990s, Burlington-based Laidlaw was a $2.5-billion (U.S.) colossus employing 60,000 people across North America.

Under the capable leadership of president and chief executive officer James Bullock, Laidlaw Inc. refocused on its core North American business operations and today earns 43 per cent of revenue from passenger services, 32 per cent from solid waste management and 25 per cent from hazardous waste management.

"Laidlaw's businesses continue to provide healthy levels of cash flow," notes Mr. Bullock. "Laidlaw will continue to grow and improve profitability," he adds.

The steadily growing giant that is Laidlaw had its first major turning point in 1959. That's when Michael DeGroote acquired Laidlaw Transport Ltd., a small Hagersville trucking business, from its owner, Robert Laidlaw, using a $75,000 down payment borrowed from a bank and a finance company.

Mr. DeGroote began "growing" the company through one acquisition after another. The company would eventually move to Burlington from Hamilton as it grew into one of the largest waste management services and passenger services companies in North America.

"Acquisition was a strategy virtually from the beginning – I intended to make Laidlaw a growth company," recalls Mr. DeGroote, who acquired 500 firms for Laidlaw before selling most of his shares to Canadian Pacific for $500 million in 1991 to begin a new business in Bermuda.

And, Mr. Bullock has continued "growing" the company, taking it to new revenue and profit thresholds.

Traded on the Toronto, Montreal and New York stock exchanges, Laidlaw Inc. is organized into three operating entities.

The Laidlaw Waste Systems entity, headed by president Kenneth Lyons, offers solid waste collection, transportation and disposal, recycling and materials recovery services, energy from waste plant operations, composting, portable toilets and medical waste disposal services.

Laidlaw Waste Systems is the third-largest company of its kind in North America, earning nearly $800 million (U.S.) annually and serving 140 locations in 18 American states and seven Canadian provinces. It has a fleet of 2,600 vehicles, 90 hauling operations and 31 landfill operations. An example of the division's industry leadership is its pioneering role in introducing the Blue Box recycling program in 1981, notes Mr. Lyons, while

• *Laidlaw has been a leader in the recycling industry since 1981, when it founded the 'Blue Box' system of curbside recyclables collection.*

pointing out two more key examples.

"Through our office equipment disassembly service, Laidlaw Waste Systems has developed partnerships, with companies such as Pitney Bowes Canada, to divert more than 95 per cent of used or outdated office equipment from landfills," observes Mr. Lyons.

"Another innovative service, WasteAuditor, helps customers reduce waste volumes, comply with increasingly stringent regulations and manage costs more effectively," he adds. "WasteAuditor tracks waste streams to their points of generation, analyzes their content and provides actionable prescriptions for volume reduction, reuse and recycling."

Noting LWS 1994 income from operators was 87 per cent higher than in 1993, Mr. Lyons stressed his company is providing one-stop service by working closely with sister company Laidlaw Environmental Services, headed by president Kenneth Winger and active in 96 locations in 25 American states, seven Canadian provinces and Mexico.

Laidlaw Environmental Services, the largest company of its kind in North America, offers transportation of

hazardous and non-hazardous waste, recycling and waste recovery services, waste treatment and disposal services, on-site remediation, and household hazardous waste collection services. It boasts a fleet of about 1,000 vehicles and numerous service centres.

And there is the operating entity of Laidlaw Passenger Services headed by president John Grainger and serving more than 600 locations in 43 American states and six Canadian provinces.

A major contributor to the company's bottom line, Burlington-based Laidlaw Passenger Services offers contract school bus operations, municipal mass transit, charter bus operations and healthcare transportation services. Annual net income exceeds $100 million (U.S.) on revenue of $1,086 million (U.S.).

Active in 174 municipalities, LPS takes more than a million children to and from school on a daily basis. Through its health care transportation operation, it transports 1.4 million patients annually.

Noting the company has discontinued European operations and divested itself of non-strategic assets, Mr. Bullock anticipates the decision to concentrate on core North American business interests will ensure the company's continued profitability in the future. "Our focus on our strong core businesses is renewed – and we are set for a period of sustained growth and expansion."

• *Natalie and Stephen Brogan are shown with family and staff members at A-Plus Air Systems and Armstrong Humidifier Service on Rymal Road.*
– Photo by David Gruggen

Stephen and Natalie Brogan readily admit not every couple's marriage could withstand working side by side in a shared business.

But it works for them. And it works for their companies: A-Plus Air Systems and Armstrong Humidifier Service.

"Part of why we're successful is that we work well together," explains Mr. Brogan. "We're married, we're friends and we're partners in both businesses."

Mrs. Brogan describes the move to shared ownership of the firms as "the smartest thing we ever did. It's not for everyone – but it's definitely for us."

This enthusiastic husband-and-wife team married in 1990 and went into business together in 1994 with the start-up of A-Plus Air, a company which specializes in selling builders complete furnace, gas fireplace, humidifier and air conditioning systems to outfit new homes.

For Mr. Brogan it was a chance to run his own company and apply 18 years of experience in the heating and air conditioning business.

And for Mrs. Brogan, it was a chance to apply marketing skills honed from working at syndicated radio and television shows, including Bob Izumi's Real Fishing Show and radio shows Real Radio and Real Outdoor Radio.

"With all these 'real' shows, people started saying I should get a real job," laughs Mrs. Brogan, "and I guess now I've got one." She recently set up a home office to allow her to take care of their one-year-old daughter Nicola.

Mr. Brogan says business the first year generated revenue well above predictions, due in part to a $250,000 contract to install heating and air conditioning systems in the Tabbytown co-operative townhouse project near Highways 20 and 53 for builder John Bruce Robinson and the Ontario government.

The following year, revenue grew well into the seven-digit area following the 1995 purchase of Armstrong Humidifier Service, a 30-year-old business which gave the couple a strong retail presence with a focus on consumer sales of humidifiers and electronic air cleaners.

"It was a real plus being able to get into the consumer market more since A-Plus mainly sells to builders," says Mr. Brogan, "and now we've expanded Armstrong into selling furnaces and air conditioners as well."

The two businesses are located beside each other in separate units in an office plaza at Rymal Road East and Upper Ottawa Street on Hamilton Mountain.

Both companies together employ a team of installation/service specialists to cover the Golden Horseshoe area.

With no shortage of work, 1996 promises to be another very successful year. "We're fortunate to have grown even in slow times," says Mr. Brogan, who cites his wife and staff for the companies' success. "A lot of things are possible with a team of dedicated people," he asserts. "We call it 'if this were my house' attitude," he adds.

"We offer the right price, good quality and licensed people who get the job done right the first time. We've got the right crew in place to really do well as the real estate market recovers."

Nursing the Cootes' Paradise Marsh back to health is a process not unlike a game warden bottle-feeding an injured baby elephant, then releasing it into the animal kingdom and praying for its survival.

Rather than use brute technological strength by draining the area, scientists resolved to work hand-in-hand with Mother Nature for natural and permanent regeneration.

Its ruin took decades. And so, too, may its rehabilitation.

The area is named after Captain Thomas Cootes, a British soldier stationed at Fort Niagara in the 1780s. The legendary and roguish gent took to sitting on the high level to indulge in target practice, blasting away at the ducks as they flocked in from the harbour. A scoundrel by today's standards, Cootes was once the namesake of the Valley Town of Dundas.

Diaries of the explorers describe the area as a Shangri-la. Archaeological digs from a dozen sites show that natives used it as a sanctuary as well as hunting and fishing camp from 1500 B.C. to 1200 A.D. Anthropological studies on artifacts retrieved from the soil are the first evidence of corn cultivation in this part of North America.

As far back as 1819, work crews dredged the Desjardins Canal for a commercial passageway to the "back country" of Dundas. Boats plied the waters, loaded with a cargo of cattle, lumber and grain. Then, at the turn of the century, the land was largely stripped of trees. In the mid-1900s, the water course decomposed in a slippery slope of decay; a deterioration hastened by sediments and sewage from the Spencer Creek watershed. That spawned the major culprit – carp, a grotesque scavenger with a swishy tail that stirs up mud.

Native to central Asia, carp entered the Great Lakes back in the 1880s. Lacking natural enemies and parasites, they flourished. Though estimates vary, by 1993 they numbered some 200,000; their ranks peaking in May, just after the annual spring mating ritual. Adults weigh 15 to 20 kilograms, or 35 to 40

pounds, the size of a strapping toddler. They rout and forage for food, using their snouts much like a pig, sucking mouthfuls of mud and straining out plants and insects. In this shallow bed, they cloud the water and blot out the sunlight.

Free-floating, submergent leaf plants such as the water lily, water milfoil and smart weed, were devastated by that carnage. With them went a diversity essential to the ecosystem, as well as oxygenation of the water, destruction of carcinogens, and a sanctum for young fish.

Scientists radio-tagged 48 fish to track their migration habits through the Desjardins Canal. With this micro-implantation of radio transmitters, "we found the carp actually range a lot more than we thought," says John Hall, director of fish and wildlife restoration for Cootes' Paradise and Hamilton Harbour.

Since Cootes' freezes during the winter, the fish retreat to the protective depths of the harbour. The challenge, then, was to block their return in the spring, and regenerate the marsh bottom by planting a bed of ecologically compatible plants.

Thus in the winter of '95, crews erected a mammoth steel carp barrier across the Desjardins Canal by Highway 403. Similar to a blind, it will allow carp to move one way via louvres, thus blocking their re-entry. Desirable species will be trapped in a grate, separated by hand and released into Cootes' Paradise, their spawning habitat. To prevent an infestation of zebra mussels, the barricade will be cleaned twice annually.

Pike, a natural predator of small carp, have been nurtured in Hendrie Valley. Bulldozers have enlarged spaces for the adults to lay eggs. And nesting platforms have also been erected for osprey, a hawk-like bird of prey.

ABOVE: *The early photographer gets the sunrise as another beautiful day dawns over Lake Ontario.*
– Photo by Dennis McGreal

The success of Stirling Print-All & Creative Services Inc is built on a young man's dream of running his own business. In the mid-1960s, Bob Stirling was a restless teenager, eager for the finer things in life and prepared to work a variety of part-time and full-time jobs to support himself.

At age 18, Mr Stirling was working in the advertising department of Hamilton hardware distributor Wood Alexander. It was there that his hands first came into contact with printer's ink. He learned how to run a press – and he became immersed in the printing business.

Mr. Stirling pursued his growing interest in printing, joining an instant print franchise where he rose to branch manager and then regional manager while still in his early 20s. By then he was eager to start his own business, where he would have the freedom to better employ his creativity and growing depth of knowledge of the printing industry.

In 1974, he took out a second mortgage on his home and opened Stirling Print-All in a little shop on King Street East, employing a press operator and an assistant, Mary – now his wife.

Demand for Stirling's printing services grew and by 1978, the burgeoning firm relocated to its present location, down the street at West Avenue, boasting 19,000 square feet of space.

Today, Stirling's husband-and-wife team has expanded to include Mr. Stirling's brother Bill, sales manager, and approximately 40 employees.

Mrs. Stirling is now company director overseeing payroll and employee benefits at this modern, bustling firm.

In a business where IMAGE is everything, Stirling is fostering its own multi-faceted image.

"There's a slow transition occurring in the public's perception of the printing business," says Mr. Stirling.

"A growing number of people now understand printing has changed and we're more than a print shop," he adds.

"In order to get the print jobs, we had to offer creative services," recalls Mr. Stirling, whose firm produces everything from letterheads and business cards to catalogues, reports and flyers.

"And now, we can best be described as a print shop and full-service pre-press facility using computer and digital output services," he explains.

Mr. Stirling says that his company can receive a customer's advertising prototype via computer, massage the information and provide imaging – and then send the finished digital image back via computer to the customer "anywhere in the world."

The only actual paper involved in this

• Bob Stirling is president of Stirling Print-All and Creative Services. He founded the company, which today has about 40 employees, in 1974.
– Photo by David Gruggen

process, he points out, is the end user's computer print-out of the digital image of the advertisement. It's a largely paperless service employing the best of human creativity and modern technology.

As the company's full title denotes, beyond printing, Stirling's in-house staff offers creative services, taking a concept-to-completion approach that has been built on 25 years of experience.

"Some customers will tell us they don't have any idea of what they're looking for," says Mr. Stirling. "So we put them through an interrogation," he adds with a chuckle. The 'interrogation' (actually a pleasant interview) is necessary to get at the heart of what the customer really has in mind all along, adds Mr. Stirling, who suggests that "most people know what they want – they just don't always

feel they can easily explain it."

Once Stirling's Print-All's expert 'interrogators' have arrived at a concept likely to please the customer, the staff then takes this concept through a full creative process, from design work to finished product, skillfully working in relevant text and slogans in the process.

Everything from computer-assisted graphic design work to film preparation, printing and binding services are offered along with pick-up and delivery in Stirling's full start-to-finish service.

Although Stirling is not an advertising house, much of the company's creative work complements that of advertising firms. Many of these firms are also major customers of the versatile print and creative services firm which provides output services to ad agencies.

"The creative side is the fastest-growing part of our business," notes Mr. Stirling. "Over the years, we've developed a good sense of what our customers want – and we have the skilled people in place to bring these ideas to fruition and make our customers happy."

Mediacom Inc., Canada's largest outdoor advertising company, has deep roots in Hamilton. Famous for its many billboards throughout major centres, Toronto-based Mediacom's corporate roots go back as far as 1904, when it was then known as the E.L. Ruddy Company Ltd.

In 1913, E.L. Ruddy opened a branch office in Hamilton employing one person. By the late 1950s, E.L. Ruddy Co. employed 100 Hamiltonians.

The firm had also invested a further $250,000 in a plant expansion on King Street West, Hamilton, to create advertising to serve the Golden Horseshoe area from Niagara Falls around the Lake to Oakville. This coverage area also stretched as far west as London and as far north as Owen Sound.

Several name changes occurred over the years and by the early 1970s, the company was widely known as Claude Neon Limited and was famous for its electric neon signs and billboards.

In 1979, the name Mediacom was adopted by the company.

Today the diversified firm actively produces numerous billboards, Superboards (oversized billboards), backlighted posters, mall posters and airport and bus shelter advertising for major centres across Canada.

Mediacom owns a large production centre in Winnipeg and two production centres in Mississauga which produce work for Canada, the United States and international markets. The company is a wholly owned subsidiary of Gannet Co. Inc., one of North America's largest communications companies.

Although it has reached an impressive size, Mediacom continues to value its Hamilton roots and the sprawling market that it serves from its Unsworth Drive, Hamilton, home base offices employing 16 people.

"Hamilton is the hub of the marketplace we service from the home base," asserts Trish McIntosh, vice-president and general manager of Mediacom.

In addition to Hamilton, that market includes "Niagara region, London, Kitchener, Brantford, Cambridge, Burlington and Oakville," she adds.

Mediacom's impact on Hamilton-Wentworth region alone includes about 300 billboards and 20 super billboards, 75 mall posters, 17 back light panels and 603 bus shelter advertisements.

A member of the Hamilton & District Chamber of Commerce, Mediacom remains very active in the community, supporting such worthy causes as Big Brothers, Big Sisters, the Advertising and Sales Club and its ACE Awards,

Crime Stoppers, Opera Hamilton and the Hamilton Public Library.

In addition to its impressive role in Hamilton, Mediacom employs more than 500 people and operates 14 sales offices in six provinces. The firm is also the national sales organization for 'The Poster Network' – a group of 25 outdoor companies across Canada.

• In a moving display, this dedicated group of employees easily shows that Mediacom is 'outstanding in a crowd.'
– Photos by David Gruggen

Rich in academic history, Hillfield-Strathallan College is firmly focused on the future. Indeed, while its origins are turn-of-the-century, it's the next century that has captured the private school's attention.

"With the 21st century looming in the very near future, Hillfield-Strathallan College is looking to the next generation's needs for the global information economy," notes Headmaster William Boyer, whose school serves 1,000 students.

"We pride ourselves on our ability to prepare our students for the world as it will be," adds Mr. Boyer, whose school is a recognized leader in innovative education. "Hillfield-Strathallan College was among the first schools to declare technological literacy to be on a par with the traditional literacies, and to build this into its program," he asserts.

"Technology will be a significant aid towards achieving individual empowerment," Mr. Boyer points out.

"We have brought the various pieces together into a College local area network, and this may allow us to develop in a host of ways through multimedia and distance-program sharing. In other words, the students will use the tools in real situations to address important issues."

This approach of treating technology as literacy is yet another advancement for

• Headmaster William Boyer poses with students at Hillfield-Strathallan College. The private school, with a history dating to 1901, today has an enrolment of 1,000 students.
— Photo by David Gruggen

---

a school with a long history of innovative excellence in education.

Founded in 1901 by the late John Collinson with the support of Lord and Lady Aberdeen as the Highfield School for Boys, the school was destroyed by fire in 1918 but was re-established as Hillcrest School by the late Reverend C.A. Heaven, who served as vice-principal.

When the school outgrew its premises, it relocated to Main Street West in 1923 and was renamed Hillfield School, with the late Arthur Killip as headmaster. The school's name was modified again, to Hillfield College, in 1959.

Meanwhile, Strathallan School was founded in 1923 by Janet Virtue and Eileen Fitzgerald with Colonel the Honourable Justice Colin Gibson as chairman. In 1948, a newly formed Board of Directors decided to continue the instruction to Grade 13 and in 1961, the renamed Strathallan College agreed to co-ordinate with Hillfield College.

In 1962, the two schools amalgamated

under a single Board of Governors as Hillfield-Strathallan College on the 50-acre site it occupies today on Fennell Avenue West on Hamilton Mountain. John Page was headmaster and Mrs. R.S. Bruce was headmistress.

When they both retired in the late 1960s, the Board of Governors appointed Barry Wansbrough as headmaster to administer the integrated college as a single co-educational academic institution, including Montessori School, Primary School, Junior School and Senior School offering grades 9 through OAC.

Hillfield-Strathallan reviewed its education through the 1980s and consolidated its position on the constructivist and active side of the learning spectrum.

In 1994, the college opened its Advanced Resource Centre to realize the information and design technology aspects of the program. ARC includes a computer area, children's museum and extension of the old library, plus junior and senior information and design technology studios.

On Mr. Wansbrough's retirement in 1995, Mr. Boyer took the helm. He continues to guide the students into new areas of education while adhering to the college mission statement: "To enable our students to think and to act both for themselves and for the betterment of others."

• *Staffed by a professional and enthusiastic team, Family Fitness Centres offers world-class facilities equipped with the latest in exercise equipment.*
– Photo by David Gruggen

Strong – and determined to grow stronger. That description can be applied equally well to thousands of members at International Family Fitness Centres – and to the business itself, a dynamic and growing chain of health and fitness clubs in the greater Hamilton area.

With great pride, Gene Kay and partner Mike Watson stand at the heart of one of their newest clubs and observe the many men and women exercising in the company's sprawling, 30,000-square-foot health club at South Hamilton Square at Upper James and Rymal Road.

Strolling between rows of gleaming treadmills and lifecycles, Mr. Watson chats with a few of the many thousand members who train regularly at Family Fitness Centres. It's where he feels most at home – rubbing elbows with clientele ranging from their late teens to early 70s.

"I can remember back in 1981 when Gene and I opened our first club on the East Mountain . . . even then I knew this was our future," recalls Mr. Watson. "But today, with our three co-ed clubs and the two new One Club for Women locations, things are really booming," adds the two-time National bodybuilding champion, who is no stranger to earning success through long hours and determination.

A true hands-on marketer, Mr. Watson knows that to realize dividends at the end of the day, the fitness clubs must continue taking a personal approach to working with their members.

The two entrepreneurs have developed their fitness organization into one of the most exciting and recognized industry leaders in the nation. Their corporate strategy was defined and tailored to meet the evolving demands and expectations

of today's health-conscious society.

After becoming famous as Champions Fitness, they continued to pioneer the fitness industry as International Family Fitness Centres. With a 'roll-the-sleeves-up' attitude, they have become one of the biggest success stories in the community.

Voted three consecutive times as best health club in the region by Hamilton Spectator readers, the company continues to maintain high standards of excellence.

Dedicated Hamiltonians, the partners believe in giving back to the community. They're strong supporters of the Ontario Special Olympics and a number of local fund-raising causes.

With a new corporate identity in 1992, International Family Fitness expanded into the domain of exclusive clubs for women. Established operators of The One Club – Women's Fitness location at Lloyd D. Jackson Square in downtown Hamilton, the company recently added the largest exclusively women's location in Canada: a 15,000-square-foot facility at Lime Ridge Mall.

The company remains committed to maintaining state-of-the-art facilities while continuing to aggressively pursue further expansion opportunities.

"The family concept is something we feel very strongly about – it's the primary reason for the name change from Champions," says Mr. Kay.

"Our clubs are designed to offer world-class facilities and services at affordable family rates," he explains.

Utilizing local labor and creative talent, Family Fitness has developed and constructed impressive new clubs combining bold, high energy colour schemes with highly functional interior designs.

The clubs are spacious, reasonably priced and staffed by a professional and enthusiastic team who work with all members to ensure they receive the maximum enjoyment and benefit from their membership experience.

Gone are the days of gruelling two-hour workout sessions. With today's array of technologically advanced exercise equipment, even people with extremely busy lifestyles can attain effective, lasting results in less than 30 minutes in an enjoyable Family Fitness atmosphere.

"People's lifestyles have changed and we knew we had to change with the times," notes Mr. Kay. "Health and fitness are now critical parts of everyone's daily life. Corporations now understand that a fit employee is a positive and productive addition to their company," he adds.

"Many large companies strongly support and encourage employees to exercise at our clubs because they now recognize that positive action leads to positive thinking which ultimately improves a person's self-esteem and over overall capacity to be successful."

Keeping fit is a lifestyle approach to wellness and since being healthy means different things to different people, the company has provided a versatile world-class fitness environment.

"The success of our company was founded on the support of our members and the strength of our co-workers – many of our members have remained loyal to our company since 1981," says Mr. Watson.

As Mr. Watson explains: "It's really encouraging to walk through one of our clubs and see a retiree, at the age of 67, keeping physically fit with a positive attitude and a smile – that's the type of personal reward that makes us realize we're on the right track."

• *Members get an aerobic workout at the newest Family Fitness Centres facility, also shown on opposite page. The sprawling 30,000-square-foot facility is located in South Hamilton Square.*
– Photo by David Gruggen

One stress on the marsh is a sporadic overflow from sewage treatment plants, resulting in a "nutrient loading." Compare it to burning the grass by over-fertilizing your lawn. Plumes of sediment appear after a steady rain, discolouring the water and contaminating the base.

Sanitation crews have worked to rectify the source of the discharge, teaming up with conservation authorities, construction crews, agricultural ministries and area municipalities to control spring and storm run-offs. The RAP plan calls for elimination, or at least a reduction, of soluble phosphorus by its diversion to the Woodward Avenue facility, the installation of sewage overflow tanks, along with upgraded technology at the Burlington Skyway sewage treatment plant.

This unsightly and menacing suspension of particles can also be interrupted by floating dams or log booms, seeded with wetland plants. Since sporadic high water levels in the marsh literally drown the tiny shoots, scientists propagated flats of vegetation, mostly cattails, at a makeshift aquatic nursery operated by the Royal Botanical Gardens (RBG).

"You can't re-plant a whole marsh, but you can inoculate the marsh in different areas, and hope that they will regenerate out from the parent stocks themselves," says Mr. Hall. The six Hamilton-Halton boards of education aided the cause with more than 200 classrooms generating 5,600 plants from seed.

It hasn't been an easy task, this physical transition from the aquatic nursery to the marsh bed. Rather, it has been fraught with challenge and catastrophe, those two meddlers who make success, in the end, all the more sweet. Mother Nature muddied the waters with unseasonably high moisture levels. Then, the man-made fabric in a $200,000 flexible polymer Aquadam burst.

The Aquadam was designed for a multitude of purposes – to seal off a wide swath of Cootes' Paradise by Rat Island, over a three-year period; to artificially simulate a low water cycle with a "draw-down"; to house the 35-hectare mudflat for plantings; and to assist in the germination of dormant seeds. It eventually split and spilled its watery contents back into the marsh.

And when these black, buoyant polypropylene cloth and polyethylene inner tubes collapsed, so too did the hopes of a team of scientists, who trundled back to the drawing boards.

It is intended to be resurrected in another incarnation, with

THE ENVIRONMENT

FACING PAGE: An imposing sight, Webster's Falls is part of the rugged Spencer Gorge Wilderness Area.

RIGHT: Tews Falls is a spectacular sight located in the Dundas Spencer Gorge Wilderness Area. At 41 metres, it's about nine metres shy of the height of Niagara Falls.
— **Photo by Bob Chambers**

possibly smaller sections and a synthetic that is impregnable by hazardous ultra-violet light. "It's proving to be a very difficult task," Mr. Hall explains. "It's a good technique," he adds, "but it is a vulnerable technology."

To compound frustrations, vulnerable sprouts planted close to the shore have been devoured by the herds of deer lurking in the bushes. One night, 250 arrowhead tubers disappeared; their ravaged shoots testament to the four-legged, hoofed Artful Dodgers. Other sprigs have been gobbled by flocks of Canada geese and by broods of mute swans. Muskrats have chewed through cages and have swum destructively through any remaining vestiges of aquatic plant.

Despite heart-wrenching setbacks, there was a silver lining. Breaking new ground in the harvest of marsh vegetation, the plant propagation project has led to a commercial venture of supplying stock to restoration work around the world. Among their clients are The Body Shop, with its experimental green-house using wetland plants to treat sewage.

Much to the chagrin of all involved, there is no miraculous happy ending yet – no sudden waving of a magic wand by a fairy godmother, no crystal-clear marsh sprouting a full regalia of cattails, no schools of pike darting into the depths.

No, today, the project is still in its infancy, spreading its roots. Plans are constantly being rewritten and revised, like the first rough draft of a script.

But it's hoped that someday soon, over the course of this 20-year effort, Cootes' will be the kind of wildlife sanctuary studied and documented by environmental biologists from around the world; our made-in-Hamilton counterpart to the Wye Marsh, with its trumpeter swans and boardwalks.

Because it will be restored, come hell or high water.

W.L. Griffin Printing Ltd. has printed many fine books – including the one that you're reading right now.

"We've done a number of books, including this one on Hamilton's 150th birthday, and Pardon My Lunch Bucket, celebrating the city's 125th birthday," notes John Miller, president and co-owner of W.L. Griffin.

Speaking of anniversaries, as the city celebrated its Sesquicentennial in 1996, W.L. Griffin raised a glass to mark its own 50-year milestone at its 20,000-square-foot plant and offices location on Linden Street in the Gage and Barton Street East area of the city.

Founded in 1946 by Wilfred Lorne Griffin, the company began with eight employees using old letter press technology. Although technology has improved greatly since then, the company has, from its inception, remained true to its original role of performing commercial printing services on behalf of corporate clients.

"Our services are aimed at large customers, not the average consumer – we're not in the instant printing business," notes Mr. Miller, who joined partner Ron Sullivan in acquiring W.L. Griffin. The two men were former employees of the company when they purchased it from the founder back in 1984.

W.L. Griffin's 18-employee workforce performs binding work in addition to the high-quality, glossy colour reproduction found throughout this book and others.

Clients provide the text and Griffin converts it into print, incorporating the text with pictures to form an eye-catching, professional product.

The company produces impressive-looking brochures, catalogues, company annual reports, posters, high-quality flyers and books, in 5,000- to 50,000-copy runs on behalf of corporate clients.

Mr. Miller notes that W.L. Griffin will sometimes produce as many as 100,000 brochures for a customer. The sheer volume of documents produced often requires loading on pallets followed by truck transport to the clients. "We can handle large volumes fairly easily."

Indeed, W.L. Griffin installed a new printing press in 1995, giving it a total of four presses. The company's new four-colour, 40-inch press runs at 9,000 sheets of paper per hour, while the other three run at 6,000 to 7,000 sheets per hour.

After enduring the past recession, the company experienced a growth rate of 10 per cent during the mid-1990s as it continued to serve a long list of corporate clients, including such well-known names as Stanley Tools Co., Canadian Tire Acceptance Co., and Izumi Real Outdoors, the magazine division of television's Izumi Outdoors.

Although constantly busy, W.L. Griffin finds time to devote to local charities such as the Canadian Cancer Society, the Heart Fund, Big Brothers and local hospitals. Mr. Miller is on the board of St. Peter's Hospital. Such involvement often means keeping track of many projects and interests simultaneously – a skill Mr. Miller has honed over the years.

"We always have lots on the go," he says. "It's not unusual for us to have as many as 50 projects in the works."

G ould Outdoor Advertising is declaring its commitment to Hamilton on a billboard. In fact, that commitment is on many billboards across the city.

"We really like the Hamilton market," says Deidre Cole, account executive for Gould, a Toronto-based national company which specializes in billboard advertising on behalf of its clients.

"Hamilton is an under-utilized centre for billboard advertising compared to Kitchener and other centres which have become crowded or have a lot of their available space already tied up," notes Ms Cole, whose company entered the Hamilton market in the spring of 1995.

"This is a growing market for Gould – and we're just going to build, build, build," she adds with a laugh.

She's only half-joking.

From virtually no presence only a year ago, Gould had 130 billboards erected at various sites in the Hamilton-Burlington area in Hamilton's Sesquicentennial year.

According to Ms Cole, Gould checks out

• From virtually no presence in 1995, Gould Outdoor Advertising is showing signs of great growth with over 100 billboards in the area, including some promoting the city's 150th birthday.
– Photo by David Gruggen

high-traffic sites with good visibility for billboard signage. "Then our leasing department approaches the land owner or building owner," she says. "Negotiations start and this hopefully leads to a lease agreement allowing us to place a billboard somewhere at that location. Then we acquire the permits and the billboard goes up."

Given the number of Gould billboards popping up, the negotiations are normally successful. "And there are still a ton of good locations left to lease," asserts Ms Cole.

With a dozen local employees, Gould has scouted out and secured prime locations for billboards in Westdale, Hamilton's East Mountain, downtown Hamilton, Stoney Creek and various sites in Burlington.

Gould's many clients include Union Gas, CIBC Student Centre, Crystal Clean cleaning service, the Ontario Lung Association, Appleby Mall, Y95 and a seemingly endless list of major companies and organizations.

As part of its commitment to the area, Gould also puts up billboards at no charge for charities eager to get their message out to passing motorists and pedestrians.

And Gould is also careful not to overdo it, avoiding a clutter of signs with the strategic placement of no more than a few billboards at prime locations. "That's all part of maximizing the value of visibility and exposure," explains Ms Cole. "The key is to have a small number of billboards in a location so that each captures attention.

"Our intention is cover all the major traffic arteries in this market without crowding too many billboards in any one area," she says. "The site remains uncluttered and the advertiser's message receives good exposure and good visibility. Everyone wins with this approach – and that's the approach we're bringing to the Hamilton market."

Here's a toast to John Howard – a man who has poured his love of fine wine into a growing business. The owner-proprietor of Vineland Estates Winery has expanded the business to include a full kitchen serving an indoor and outdoor patio restaurant complete with a panoramic view of his rolling vineyards, the forests beyond and Lake Ontario.

In this idyllic setting, you can dine on lamb, Chateaubriand or even vegetarian dishes, accompanied by award-winning wines made on-site from grapes grown on this 78-acre property.

Just a short drive away another familiar, impressive vista awaits Mr. Howard: His palatial private residence.

With turrets looming into view, this man's home truly is his castle, a 14-room retreat – dubbed Castle Howard – partly decorated by artist-skater Toller Cranston.

Yet such regal trappings are a world away from Mr. Howard's past life in the 1970s as a high steelworker perched hundreds of feet up in the air on the beams of office towers.

Mr. Howard later became a salesman for Xerox before founding Canon dealership Office Equipment Hamilton. He became a millionaire when OE Canada bought out his dealership and wealth further increased when Canon North America bought out OE Canada in 1992. It was then that Mr. Howard cancelled his plans to take a year off and instead purchased Vineland Estates, which had just been listed for sale.

While another man might be quick to claim full credit for the success of Vineland Estates, Mr. Howard downplays his own accomplishments while paying homage to the winery's founder, Hermann Weis of Germany's Mosel Valley.

Mr. Howard has even erected a plaque commemorating the founder's pioneering work in introducing transplanted vinifera plants to the Niagara region and in advancing winemaking in Canada.

"I didn't create this," Mr. Howard points out. "I'm just a steward who has the responsibility of continuing the high standards set by the Weis family," he says. "The Weis family created this and people remember the artist, not the owner of the painting."

But Mr. Howard has added more than a few finishing touches to this living work of art. He's invested millions of dollars in restoring a carriage house and other buildings on the property, originally a mixed farm dating back to the 1840s. His new kitchen facilities are staffed by skilled chefs and he's invested heavily in winemaking facilities and grape production.

Then there's his investment in people. When Thorold resident Stephen Kealey drove miles out of his way to warn of a fire at the carriage house, Mr. Howard offered him a university scholarship. Mr. Howard

• John Howard, left, is pictured at Vineland Estates with Hermann Weis, an exporter and grower of premium Riesling vines – and the man who established the vineyard in 1979.

now bestows scholarships on staff members showing a strong work ethic and great customer service. Funding is derived from another charitable practice: his annual hosting of the Vine Dining event which raises funds for local theatre and other causes.

Beyond these investments in Vineland Estates, staff and charitable causes, Mr. Howard has also made his mark in promoting and marketing the winery's products to international markets.

While relying on the skilled staff he acquired to continue producing excellent wines, Mr. Howard has proven highly adept at charting a successful strategic plan for Vineland Estates. And it's a plan which places a strong emphasis on export sales.

By 1996, Vineland Estates was producing 20,000 cases (240,000 bottles) of Rieslings and other fine wines annually from its own vineyards. About 80 per cent is exported, primarily to markets in the United States, England and Pacific Rim nations or sold on-site. The rest is sold through conventional distribution in Ontario.

"Niagara wines have achieved international standards and winning numerous awards for quality," explains Mr. Howard, "and I've never seen any reason to be reticent about exporting our excellent products to world markets."

With retail sales up 900 per cent and a doubling of restaurant sales, Mr. Howard began developing other lands into vineyard via a syndicate involving the Weis family and other partners.

While pursuing the next stage of his growing wine business, Mr. Howard can take pride in the contribution of lasting value he's made to Vineland Estates. It's something fans of this winery have come to appreciate – as they savour crisp wines and great food in a setting of unrivalled beauty.

In an old brick and stone building at Stuart and McNab streets, you'll find one of Greater Hamilton's most community-spirited husband and wife business teams.

Marie Robbins owns and operates a family of florist shops from her location on McNab Street North, in the historic, 1829 building which originally housed Dorion Vinegar Works.

Husband Doug Robbins runs a mergers and acquisitions company from his Stuart Street office in this single-storey building the couple renovated extensively after acquiring it in 1992.

Although each runs their business separately, an interior doorway connects the two offices, allowing either business executive to share the fax machines, copiers, computers or staff – exchange ideas with each other – or just drop by for a cup of coffee.

Set between the heart of downtown Hamilton and the harbourfront, the location is appropriate for a couple who has helped revitalize the commercial core in the city's James Street North area.

Mr. Robbins was founding chair and Mrs. Robbins was later treasurer of the Jamesville Business Improvement Area. The couple led the BIA in engineering a successful renaissance of the James Street North commercial district in the 1980s.

"We've always been very involved in the community," notes Mrs. Robbins, who also chaired the Wentworth Libraries board for 12 years. The former teacher for the Wentworth County Board of Education continues to get involved in educational programs at all levels.

Mrs. Robbins, president of F.B. Smith/McKay Florists, is also past secretary of the Hamilton District Florist Association and past president of Zonta. She's an active member of the Mum Show Committee, Stoney Creek Battlefield Park Committee, Hamilton Rotary Club and Hamilton and District Chamber of Commerce.

Founded in 1919, Frank B. Smith Florists was acquired by Mrs. Robbins in 1975. In 1978, she acquired McKay and Company Florist, founded in 1906. She then merged the firms with other acquired florist shops under the business banner F.B. Smith/McKay Florists.

The company, which holds the Flowers by Sears franchise for Hamilton-Wentworth and Burlington, employs 30 people and is rated by FTD as one of North America's top 200 florists.

In addition to the company's head office, F.B. Smith/McKay Florists also owns customer service outlets at Lloyd D. Jackson Square, Eastgate Square, Mostly Roses in Brantford and Stoney Creek

• Marie Robbins is the president of Smith/McKay Florists while husband Doug Robbins heads Robbinex Inc.
– *Photo by Joe Bucci*

Flower Shop at historic Squire's Hall in olde Stoney Creek. Squire's Hall is the meeting place of The Artisans, a group of Stoney Creek-area artists who display and sell work in Marie's Stoney Creek store.

"We're going to continue growing," says a confident Mrs. Robbins, adding that "we always have an eye open for any opportunity that would be a good fit with the business."

Mr. Robbins heads Robbinex Inc., active in a unique sector of the business brokerage field involving confidential merger and acquisition transactions, each worth $250,000 to $5 million.

He notes that since 1975, the Robbinex team has completed approximately 500 transactions, "investing hundreds of hours in each case to bring together a qualified buyer and sincere seller."

As a founding member of M&A Source, Robbinex is in the world's largest, computerized merger and acquisition network linking over 100 business intermediaries across North America.

Mr. Robbins is also president of the Ontario Business Brokers Association, an active chamber member, member and past director of the downtown Rotary Club.

He is also a past member of Mohawk College's Business Advisory Board and was a part-time faculty member at the college for 12 years. In addition, he is a familiar speaker at seminars and workshops addressing issues of concern to the owners of privately owned businesses.

ABOVE: *McKeil Marine's tug LAC COMO, an 800-horsepower twin screw ship berthing tug, sailing in Hamilton Harbour.*
— Photo by David Gruggen

FACING PAGE: *The tug JERRY NEWBERRY is shown towing a barge carrying two furnaces sailing along the piers at Port Colborne en route to Algoma in Sault Ste. Marie.*

B oats have been Evans McKeil's life since he was a youngster in Pugwash, Nova Scotia.

In the 1930s, Mr. McKeil watched boats head out to sea from this fishing port of 600 souls. His uncles sailed cargo-laden schooners across the Bay of Fundy to St. John, N.B. And following World War II, a teenaged Mr. McKeil helped his father, lumber mill owner William McKeil, build a few boats.

So it's not surprising that this transplanted blue-noser is chairman of Hamilton-based McKeil Marine Limited, operating the largest tugboat and barge fleet on the Great Lakes.

During the Hamilton and Scourge 1812 warships project, the 40-year-old marine services, towing, salvage and spill control firm provided surface services.

McKeil Marine is also known for its donated tugboat, used as a children's climbing toy at Pier Four Park. And the Hillyard Street company still runs the 101-year-old iron tugboat the 'Argue Martin,' Canada's oldest working tug.

In 1948, a languishing Maritime economy convinced Mr. McKeil's parents to head for prosperous Hamilton – and he followed them a year later.

After a brief stint as a gas station attendant, Mr. McKeil joined the former McNamara Marine Co. in 1950 as a deckhand on tugs and dredges. In the

fall of 1955 came a fateful suggestion from a Newfoundland skipper familiar with the McKeil family background.

"He said I should work for myself and build my own boats," recalls Mr. McKeil, 66, in an interview at company offices lined with pictures of McKeil boats, ship's wheels and memorabilia.

"So I rented a barn in Ancaster and with my father's help, built a 35-foot-long workboat – the MicMac," he adds.

The all-wood MicMac was launched from Hamilton Harbour Commissioners' docks at the foot of James Street North in the spring of 1956. This launch was the founding of McKeil Marine.

Powered by a six-cylinder Chevy car engine, the MicMac was put to work by Mr. McKeil transporting work crews building the St. Lawrence Seaway system.

McKeil Marine now does everything from ferrying crews at Newfoundland's Hibernia project to assisting ships docking at Hamilton Harbour.

Although he later sold the MicMac to a friend, Mr. McKeil continued to build up a fleet of purchased used boats which, by the late 1950s, numbered 10 tugs plus barges.

In the early 1960s, Mr. McKeil was joined by his brother Doug McKeil, a partner in Clare Moore Refrigeration Service and a master mechanic.

Doug McKeil fixed up many of the

steel boats the firm bought from the Royal Canadian Navy and other sources.

"My brother's ability to make used boats mechanically fit allowed the company to grow with less capital outlay," notes Mr. McKeil.

The family firm employs Mr. McKeil's his wife Florence as secretary-treasurer, son Blair as president and son Garth as a captain and engineer.

By the late 1980s, McKeil Marine had grown to about 85 employees, 25 tugboats and 35 barges, "and was too big to handle alone, so I turned it over to my son Blair, who was mostly responsible for its rapid growth," recalls Mr. McKeil.

Blair McKeil, president since 1992, says he prefers driving Harley-Davidson motorcycles to spending time on boats. His outgoing nature has helped bring out the best in the firm's dedicated workforce, including crews who spend months away from home on tug boats. He has also made it possible for the company to acquire bigger and better boats.

"A lot of the work overlaps," says the 36-year-old, who co-owns the company with his father. "Personnel matters are handled our vice-president, Dave Bush, or by Garth McKeil," he adds.

Blair McKeil attributes the company's success to its hardworking employees. "We're all in the same boat together – and we're all paddling in the same direction."

A ll great cities, all historic cities, are founded on water, according to the Honourable David Crombie, Chair of the Waterfront Regeneration Trust (WRT) and head of the joint federal-provincial Royal Commission on the Future of Toronto's Waterfront.

"Remember this," says the former MP, "everything is connected to everything else. Secondly, human beings are a part of nature and not separate from it." And thus, "it follows that we are responsible for the actions that we take and the things that we do. We're responsible to ourselves, to other people, to other generations and to other species."

F ashion magazines, those purveyors of nouvelle couture, are wont to show before-and-after photos: the first in drizzly black and white; the second a transformation in radiant blushing colour.

The same could be done to portray RAP – our Remedial Action Plan and a makeover destined to go beyond skin deep and mere cosmetics; peeling away as it will the generations of abuse and decline, and revealing the complexion of a lost youth.

Some contend that the waterfront will never be returned to its pristine state; that because of its locale and its industrial heritage, it will forever be listed as one of the prime environmental sores on the body of the Great Lakes.

Others predict slow and steady progress that will not only change the course of the bay, but will put us on the map as a major centre of environmental excellence.

Remember those words, a "centre of environmental excellence." Already, it is estimated that 12 to 14 per cent of our workforce specialize in the environmental field.

At the head of the list of priorities is water restoration. And that is the single-most important reason why we will be

• A group of youngsters in sailboats is led into the bay in preparation for another afternoon of sailing classes.
– Photo by Dennis McGreal

turning the tide on this 6.4-kilometre by 5.6-kilometre mass that constitutes Hamilton Harbour.

Back in the 1800s, or so it is said, the locals speared pike and bass from the teeming pools of fish, in the basin of Hamilton Harbour; part of a haul that accounted for about 15 per cent of the Lake Ontario catch. One area hotel featured a speciality on the menu; soup made from turtles snagged on the shoreline.

And then came "progress," with sewage from suburbia spilling down the banks and spewing into the harbour.

So pervasive was the discharge that, in the 1930s, unsanitary conditions led to postings of closures along the beaches.

Commercial fishing vessels abandoned the contaminated basin. At one point, Lake Ontario was flagged as the most chemically polluted body of water in the world.

And we bade farewell to an era. Or so we thought.

They call them "stakeholders," these people with a consuming passion for the harbour. The bureaucratic term identifies citizens from all walks of life. Some have related fields of expertise like scientists, engineers or academics. Some come with management skills in business and commerce.

Others have a personal stake in the health of the waterfront, perhaps recreational groups or residents. Still others are regulatory bodies such as the Hamilton Harbour Commission and the various municipalities which border the watershed.

Among the RAP team, you'll find no less than three provincial ministries; Environment, Agriculture and Food, as well as Natural Resources.

Other contributors include the Royal Botanical Gardens, Environment Canada, Fisheries and Oceans Canada. Together in 1988, they finalized a report – Environmental Conditions and Problem Definition in Hamilton Harbour – a weighty tome, the most recent edition of which numbers some 250 pages. That was followed by RAP Stage 2, Goals, Options and Recommendations, a 300-plus page document, packed with charts. In all there were 50 action steps.

RAP has been co-ordinated and executed by BAIT, the acronym for the Bay Area Implementation Team.

The Bay Area Restoration Council (BARC) promotes and assesses the actions. Think of it as one group administering the theory and the other monitoring the impact.

Those problems, as the size and titles indicate, were legion; with water contamination by metals (such as zinc, iron, nickel and lead), and organic compounds (PCBs, PAHs, mirex and DDT, among others); most emanating from industry and municipal sewers; as well as chemically laden effluent swept downstream from farm lands and atmospheric fallout.

As a recourse, enfranchised stakeholders responded by asking for the immediate implementation of Ontario's Municipal-Industrial Strategy for Abatement. A manifesto of the '90s regime, it cited offenders and solutions. And, the most obvious of the solutions was the power to target polluters who indiscriminately discharge contaminants into sewers. But like pollution itself, culpability runs far below the surface of the problem.

It's easy to point a finger at an unscrupulous fly-by-nighter who dumps a barrel of toxic chemicals in an abandoned field. But what about the householder who sprays herbicides on yard weeds, or the handyman who tosses a can of paint stripper in

the garbage? That's why RAP urged expanded public education; vigourous household hazardous waste collection; and a reassessment of pesticides used in public greenspaces. It was tantamount to a new order for the corporate sector and the citizenry.

As custodians of our own backyard, watchdogs will monitor, report and review handling procedures for harbour spills; devise alternatives to chlorination of sewage discharge (which can create potentially harmful compounds when reacting with other chemicals) and initiate the removal or treatment of contaminated sediments.

• Rowers take advantage of some ideal conditions for an early evening training session on Hamilton Bay.
– Photo by Dennis McGreal

Like Cootes' Paradise, the harbour's cloudy, oxygen-deficient water robs plants of sunlight, and thus decreases food supplies for fish and wildlife. Excessive nutrients in the system, particularly phosphorus and nitrogen, foster "algal bloom," the spread of algae on the water surface. And when it decays, it compounds the cycle by blocking those nourishing rays.

Among the remedial measures are ploughing or tillage practices that reduce soil erosion in farm communities; stricter controls for builders of new subdivisions; as well as promoting water-conserving fixtures in homes, and re-adjusting water rates to reflect the true costs of treatment.

And then there is the dilemma of heavy rainfalls which compounds bacterial contamination. Storm runoff from lawns and streets floods into the sewage system. Treatment plants can't cope with the sudden excess. So, it overflows directly into the harbour.

Among other steps recommended was the installation of retention basins to hold back the untreated water until it can be properly handled.

Wade through the research and you will detect the quagmire of crisis and complexities in this, nature's domino theory, where one piece topples another.

For example, scientists now suspect that the carcinogens found in harbour sediments might play a role in liver tumors among white suckers and skin tumors in brown bullheads.

Eradicate trace contaminants and restore the oxygen supply, and you're left with other stresses; especially the loss of spawning and feeding sanctuaries, any number of which have been bulldozed under by infilling.

So the plan is to revitalize vegetation in Cootes' Paradise and the mouth of Grindstone Creek, construct artificial reefs; control the carp; and create nesting spots for waterfowl as top priorities.

If it sounds all so technical and research-intensive, it is. But you only have to stroll along the bayfront to see the results. It doesn't take a Ph.D. to meander along the boardwalk, or scoot across the lake in a sailboat to observe a slow-motion miracle.

It has cost an estimated $600 million in the last 15 years to rehabilitate the harbour. Another $800 million will be spent before the job is complete. (Some $15 million alone has been earmarked for the removal of 20,000 cubic metres of toxic sediment at Randle Reef, west of Stelco's Hilton Works; with the federal government pledging one-third of the tab.)

But much of the investments will be borne by municipalities, and applied to stormwater management and upgrading of sewage treatment plants.

Brock Dickinson, former executive director of BARC, is now the United Nations Secretary General in charge of executing plans from the Brazil conference on environmental cleanup.

RAP is "probably one of the best examples, anywhere in the world, of local partnerships for action," he says. "This was a process that involved all levels of government; it involved local industry and local citizens, and it produced very real change."

Typical of the synergy is a yellow drain storm sewer program – an educational project where school children paint fish symbols alongside drain covers to remind residents not to pour their household chemicals or auto waste down the system. Another example is the stewardship outreach where landowners, particularly those backing on to Spencer Creek, are encouraged to take remedial action on property that leads to the watershed.

And finally, the last word goes to Mark Sproule-Jones, a Professor of Political Science at McMaster University. He is also Principal Investigator of ECOWISE, a $2.1 million McMaster-based investigation of the Harbour.

Mr. Sproule-Jones is the current president of BARC and a leading proponent of environmental restoration. "The success of the Hamilton Harbour," he says, "is because the citizens led the way and dragged the governments after them."

Despite a few faltering steps, sidelong shuffles and some foot dragging, RAP has inspired us to dance to a different tune.

In the analogy of the before-and-after picture, this cosmetic surgery could be the start of something beautiful.

• As part of the Hamilton Harbour Remedial Action Plan, a total of $2.2 million has been invested in the redevelopment of Pier 4 Park. Included in the 2.8-hectare park is an interactive water play area for children and a lookout pier, with a sun shelter and benches, from which to view the surrounding marinas, parkland and vistas of the bay.
*— **Photo by Dennis McGreal***

• A true success story, QSI Windows & Doors continues to experience tremendous growth in the Hamilton area. Company president Terry Bobiak, centre, is
pictured with his brothers Michael and John at the QSI showroom.
— **Photo by David Gruggen**

I t's a long way from a basement workshop to 7,000 square feet of showroom and warehouse facilities, and a fleet of five trucks. But that's the story behind QSI Windows & Doors.

QSI stands for Quality Sales and Installations. And, over the past two decades, the family company has grown steadily through word-of-mouth-recom- mendations and a reputation that has lived up to its moniker.

With the success of its impressive 5,000 square foot showroom at its Nebo Road site on Hamilton Mountain – a spacious storefront that covers a range of products from windows and doors to a full display of three- and four-season sunrooms – QSI is planning to open a full-scale display showroom to serve its expanding customer base in neighbouring Burlington in the very near future.

The reason for the company's growth is twofold. The first is the product itself.

Through those 20 years, QSI Windows & Doors has, without question, consis- tently delivered the most technologically advanced product on the market.

QSI's replacement windows and doors feature cutting-edge innovations which are teamed with decorator styles, some of which evoke the halcyon days of the Victorian era.

Another area where QSI continues to experience tremendous growth is in the sales and installation of pre-fabricated all-season sunrooms.

While far from a necessity, a sunroom brings an attractive extension to the home and allows the homeowner an opportunity to enjoy the outdoors year-round.

The second reason for the success of QSI lies in the nature of the family firm, and the hands-on approach it takes when doing business.

Terry Bobiak is president of QSI, brothers Michael and John are in sales, and John also manages the installations. The rest of the staff are treated as a part of the clan; from the administration office to the team that installs the purchase; a crew that are employees of the company and not a casual, sub-contract force com- monly used in the industry.

A Hamilton success story with a window on the future, Terry Bobiak says that the prospects for growth are exciting, especially considering how far the firm has come from its humble origins.

"You can't stand still," he adds. "You have to move forward."

With their paint fumes and solvents, few people would consider an auto body shop to be environmentally friendly.

But Kelly Auto Body Ltd. leads the industry in reducing pollutants and waste.

In fact, this auto body shop on the corner of Upper Wellington and Hester streets has won regional and provincial awards for its environmental measures.

"We're the first auto body shop ever to have won an environmental award," notes Larry Kelly Jr., business general manager and a frequent speaker on improving the environment.

Mr. Kelly says his firm uses high-volume, low-pressure spray guns which affix paint to a vehicle more effectively, reducing the volume of paint and fumes by 25 per cent.

To clean the spray guns, the company puts them in a wash of recycled solvents – a departure from a former industry practice of cleaning by spraying solvents from guns into the air.

Paint is also recycled, along with 520 gallons of solvents annually for an overall waste reduction of 80 per cent – and a savings in solvent purchases alone of $2,000 a year.

An emphasis on protecting the environment, running a very clean shop and using the latest computer equipment truly sets Kelly Auto Body apart.

The company was founded in May 1977, when Mr. Kelly's parents, Larry and Jean Kelly, purchased and then renamed the former Whitmore auto body shop to provide a source of income for themselves and their five children.

"We saw an opportunity and since we had a family and wanted to provide opportunities for them as well, we bought the business," recalls Mrs. Kelly.

"Although we didn't know that much about body work at the time, we knew how to manage a business and we hired the right licensed people to do the body work," she explains.

Larry Kelly Sr. is Kelly Auto Body owner-president, overseeing all operations while Mrs. Kelly is company co-owner and vice-president.

And it remains a family firm with full-time involvement by the couple's four sons, including licensed body person Stephen, paint shop manager Christopher and marketing director Seamus.

As the business grew, it added a second paint shop location further south on Upper Wellington, opposite the Day & Campbell concrete company.

Today, the steadily growing firm employs a total of 16 people, including licensed mechanics for general repairs, painters and auto body persons.

"The business has really changed over the years – it's become much more computerized," notes Mrs. Kelly.

Indeed, Kelly Auto Body now uses a computer imaging system which can transmit damage photos to an insurance company's office, zoom in on the damage and provide essential information, saving the adjuster a trip out to the shop.

"That also saves the customer a lot of time," Mrs. Kelly points out, "because we can get the okay to do the repairs and the customer can get his or her car back that much quicker."

In 1996, Kelly Auto Body celebrated nearly 20 years in business by offering detailing work – including pin-striping, decals and other details – along with interior shampooing services.

"These are things the customers were asking for," says Mrs. Kelly. "And in all the services we provide, we always strive to give the customer what they want."

• Founded by Larry and Jean Kelly, Kelly Auto Body is a true family affair with the couple's four sons, Larry Jr., Stephen, Christopher and Seamus, shown above, all playing an active role in the running of the business.
– *Photo by Joe Bucci*

• *Representing the Royal Insurance claims, administration, underwriting and marketing departments are, from left to right: Caroline Turcotte, Mike Conlon, Debbie McNamara, Sophie Kumfert, Drew Zehr and Rena Lampkin.*
                                                    – Photo by David Gruggen

The city of Hamilton has long been a highly valued market for Royal Insurance, one of Canada's oldest and most trusted insurance companies.

In 1996, Hamilton celebrated its 150th anniversary as a city, one year after Royal Insurance marked a similar milestone as a company with special events at its offices around the world.

The company was founded in England in March 1845, responding to a need for fairer prices, better value and improved service. Royal took as its motto the Latin *Tutum tu sistam* (We hold you safe), a commitment that continues to this day.

In his own hand-written notes, the company's first general manager, Percy Dove, urged appointed insurance agents to: "with confidence state that the Directors are determined in every case of legitimate loss to enable the company to distinguish itself by its promptness in the settlement of claims."

As Royal's reputation grew, so did its business. By October of the first year it had insured properties in India, South America, the West Indies, Gibraltar, Singapore – and in New Brunswick.

Six years later came expansion to the New World. Mr. Dove set sail in 1851 for North America, there to establish Royal Insurance in the United States and Canada. Agents were appointed in New York, Boston and Cincinnati. In Canada the bustling cities of Montreal, Toronto and Quebec City acquired Royal agents.

Keeping pace with Canada's growing industrialization, the company established agents in Hamilton in 1860, together with St. John, N.B., St. John's, Nfld., Victoria, B.C. and several smaller centres.

The acquisition of other companies quickened the pace of the parent company's progress. The National, the Brighton & Sussex Union Fire, the Midland Counties and the Queen Insurance were all bought, making Royal the largest fire insurer in the world.

Later, in 1919, Royal acquired the London and Liverpool and Globe in what was then the largest merger in British insurance history. Here in Canada, Royal Insurance continued its steady expansion.

By the early 1930s, it had 10 active companies and over 3,000 independent insurance brokers in cities, town and rural centres across the country.

In 1955 came Royal's recognition of Hamilton's growing importance with the opening of an office on James Street South. Within a decade this grew to full branch office status and, by the time the company's branch moved to the Stelco Tower at Lloyd D. Jackson Square in 1975, the staff had expanded to 35.

Three years of continued growth saw the company move to its present location in Phase Two of Jackson Square, where it commands annual sales of $45 million, directly employs 135 people and has an annual payroll in excess of $3.5 million. Hamilton is also served by the company's Personal Lines' Regional Centre for Ontario, based in Etobicoke, supervised by Regional Manager Grace Webster.

The manager of the Hamilton Regional Centre is Debbie Green, who stresses that Royal Insurance's corporate philosophy is a reflection of the principles which have proved so successful over the years.

"We have earned a reputation for reliability and for fairness in dealing with our customers," she explains. "These are priceless assets for any company."

Throughout the post-war era, Royal has continued to grow, matching this country's economic base. The company today serves every province and territory through a network of 1,700 independent insurance brokers. There is a staff of 2,200 in 17 regional and district offices plus representatives in urban and rural centres from coast to coast.

With its 1994 purchase of Sun Alliance's Canadian operations, Royal Insurance's annual sales rose to over $600 million, its assets to well over $2 billion.

The company is maintaining its industry leadership in many ways.

It has recently introduced advanced new customer service techniques that employ modern technology.

The Claims Response Call Centre uses a Canada-wide 1-800 telephone number to link Royal customers to claims service assistance 24 hours a day. Many of the company's insurance brokers have direct computer linkage to Royal, and a special Broker Call Centre provides them with immediate access to trained staff for a wide range of business needs.

"To be able to focus clearly on its future, a company must be able to draw strength from its past performance," says

President & Chief Executive Officer Bob Gunn. "Our reputation has been built on the professionalism of our people. They are the key to our success, and these are the reasons we view the next 150 years with confidence," he explains.

In Hamilton, Royal Insurance continues to value the local market and the area's rich potential.

From its modern Jackson Square offices, the company looks forward to meeting local insurance needs while playing an important role in Hamilton's continuing growth and prosperity.

• Maria Battista is one of the many representatives working in the Claims Response Unit at Royal Insurance's Hamilton regional offices.
— Photo by David Gruggen

Unveiled back in 1993, Pier 4 and the neighbouring Bayfront Park stand as a lesson in salvaging lands for a public playground. Once known disparagingly as the Lax property, an abandoned dumping ground for unwanted fill and toxic chemicals, the reclaimed stretch of pristine and gently rolling terrain now compares to any popular bayshore, be it Kingston, Ontario or Vancouver, B.C. This, surely, is the phoenix rising from the ashes.

Today at Pier 4 Park, members of a Scout troop dip their canoes into the bay at the boat launch ramp. Couples rollerblade and stroll along the paved walkways that snake their way around the waterfront. Some sit on the benches that line the beach, wiggling their toes in the sand and watching ducks bob for bits of bread. Fishermen bait their hooks and rhythmically cast into the sunset – a ritual punctuated only by the quiet plop of the sinker as it hits the surface. In a nearby enclave, children splash in the waves. Not since the 1930s have Hamiltonians witnessed swimming in this bay.

Along the shoreline lie the specially designed "reefs" which shelter species such as large-mouth bass and northern pike. During the past few years, hundreds of mature walleye have been released in these waters – some measuring up to 60 centimetres, and tipping the scales at 2.3 kilograms.

Shipped in temperature-controlled and oxygenated holding tanks from the Bay of Quinte, they have been intro-duced into the homogenous habitat of our harbour.

As it turned out, it was a study in a public body and private citizens blending their talents for mutual goals. Because together they transported this fragile cargo in a communal convoy all the way from Belleville, Ontario; this motley group of biologists and anglers hovering like mothers around newborns. All under the watchful gaze of the attending specialists – in a delivery monitored by the provincial Ministry of Natural Resources and the federal fisheries department.

Today, this expanse is another realm – minutes yet millennia removed from the skyline of apartment complexes and office towers. For the West Harbourfront Study steering committee, it is but a single step towards "A new century, a new waterfront."

The $500-million plan calls for the redevelopment of a 40-hectare area from Bay to Queen, and Barton to the bayfront. Along with demolishing derelict buildings on industrial sites, and relocating the CN rail marshalling yards to Aldershot, it proposes a village atmosphere, not unlike Niagara-On-The-Lake – with restaurants and boutiques, gardens, a show-stopping

10,000-seat amphitheatre; as well as an Imax theatre, aquarium or museum; much of it backed by private-sector funds.

Due east, a few lengths from the Leander Boat Club and Royal Hamilton Yacht Club, a crowd gathered around Sheila Copps; federal Environment Minister, Deputy Prime Minister, and the second most powerful person in all of Canada; Hamilton born-and-bred; hometown proud. Sporting a wetsuit, with flippers, snorkel and goggles, she waded in to join the corps of scuba divers who picked up debris on the bottom of the bay.

Mayor Robert Morrow, who welcomed her on behalf of the city, mentioned he took a plunge in these same waters nine years previous; prior to the most recent clean-up effort.

While it was not free from impurities, as a rabble of Greenpeace protesters was quick to point out, it was safe for swimming with an E. coli bacteria count of 60, well below the advisable 100. And, on the scale of the last half-century, that's progress.

"Most of you know what was here before. To do this you have to be able to dream," she told the gathering.

"Hamiltonians know how to dream, and this is just the beginning," she added.

"We're going to make this a place where the whole of Canada can come and see what can be done when you start to rebuild your environment."

If ever necessity was a mother of invention, it is here. Once an industrial heartland, our skies punctuated by the black clouds belched from smokestacks, our shores littered with dead fish, our polluted bay cordoned off to pedestrians – it was as if our shame was writ large in the soiled sand. What a difference a decade makes.

Now we are a bellwether of environmental excellence.

As the Honourable David Crombie put it: "Hamilton has done it; The emerald necklace from Cootes' Paradise, to the Royal Botanical Gardens to Pier 4 – to all the work in the harbour, and to the work that can be done in the Windemere Basin. You are creating something that I tell people in other places: Go to Hamilton. See what they've done."

Like the creature of popular legend, our own bird of paradise has spread its wings.

ABOVE: *The setting sun brings a special warmth to the Hamilton waterfront as another lazy day draws to a close.*
– Photo by Dennis McGreal

FACING PAGE: *Canoeing is among the many activities the entire family can enjoy at Christie Conservation Area.*

An addendum to the Honourable David Crombie's Royal Commission on the Waterfront Regeneration Trust concerned the volatile issue of the Red Hill Valley and the north-south transportation corridor; a political hot potato if ever there was one.

The Red Hill Valley, which snakes through the eastern end of the city, blankets a 647-hectare tract of gently sloping land. A link in the Niagara Escarpment and thus a part of the UNESCO designation as a World Biosphere Reserve, this greenbelt shelters "significant remnants" of the once-pervasive Carolinian Forest.

It is also home to deer, ring-tailed pheasants, dozens of species of breeding birds and butterflies, reptiles, amphibians, and vegetation. Five kilometres of the Bruce Trail cross the Red Hill Valley – not to mention hiking paths on both sides of the creek and along its tributaries.

The rock formations by Albion Falls date back 400 million years. Archaeological evidence indicates that the Valley was home to indigenous people 5,000 years ago.

And in the 1700s it was the among the first settlements of the United Empire Loyalists – with relics of a church, tavern and industries excavated from its banks attesting to that fact.

Despite the efforts of groups such as Friends of the Valley, Save the Valley, the Hamilton Region Conservation Authority, the Hamilton Naturalists' Club, the Conserver Society and the Bruce Trail Association, urban encroachment threatened its future. Not the least of these threats was a paved route from the mountain to the Queen Elizabeth Way; an issue that had dogged the region for 35 years. The Red Hill access was to be linked with an east-west artery, already under construction, and leading into Highway 403 at Ancaster.

Swept into Queen's Park in 1990, the NDP promptly scrapped a six-lane, north-south expressway approved by the previous Liberal government. But after a prolonged and vocal hullabaloo raised by the freeway proponents, Premier Bob Rae acted on the advice of Mr. Crombie and offered a compromise of a four-lane road through the greenspace. The package deal contained a commitment for an environmental rehabilitation of the valley. Among those measures was an enhancement of stream flow and water quality, sediment control and habitat regeneration.

It proposed that the Red Hill Valley should become a permanent natural area by a conservation easement; that ownership should be transferred from the city to the province for the sum of $1; and that the Ontario government fund restoration work in Red Hill to the tune of $24 million over five years – in the process creating 240 person-years of employment.

An initial $3 million would fund a 7.2-kilometre path from Red Hill Marsh to the Bruce Trail and lay the foundation for the World Biosphere Interpretive Centre. Co-ordinated by the Hamilton Region Conservation Authority, the plan would have showcased the local initiatives in environmental technology and serve as a focal point for outdoor education.

The Windemere Basin, a 47-hectare pool at the mouth of the Red Hill Creek, traces its origins to a 1950s East End industrialization which triggered the filling of wetlands, and to the development of the East Port facilities abutting the Q.E.W.

Tying the historical steel mills with this waterfront restoration and incorporating Hamilton's Beach Strip and Van Wagner's Pond would offer the natural extension to a Lake Ontario Greenway, according to Mr. Crombie's report.

That changed with the provincial election of 1995, when Mike Harris and the Conservative Party steamrolled to victory in Ontario. Part of their platform had been a commitment to build the Red Hill Creek Expressway; a promise waylaid due to deficit-cutting measures.

Today the fate of the Red Hill still remains very much up in the air – in an environmental no man's land.

And, perhaps it will take the next 35 years to iron out a compromise between Carolinian forests and concrete.

Chapter **2**

• *The Children's Hospital at Chedoke-McMaster is an integral part of Chedoke-McMaster Hospitals' services. Chedoke-McMaster Hospitals, also shown on the preceding pages, is one of Hamilton's largest employers with more than 3,800 staff members.*
– Photos by Dennis McGreal

C hedoke-McMaster Hospitals is a teaching hospital whose goal is to set the standard by which other teaching hospitals will measure the excellence of their patient care, the success of their education, research and management initiatives and the quality of working life for their staff.

The hospital offers six major programs to the community: Children's Health, Women's Health, Specialty Adult Health, Specialized Rehabilitation, Health Services for the Elderly and General Adult Services. These programs are supported by a full range of diagnostic and therapeutic services.

The hospital, which was formed in 1979 by the merger of Chedoke Hospital (opened in 1906) and McMaster University Medical Centre (opened in 1972), has a 24-hour Emergency Unit at its McMaster site and an Urgent Care Unit, operating 10 hours a day, at its Chedoke site.

All hospital departments and programs are amalgamated under one corporate director for both sites.

The hospital is one of Hamilton's major employers, with more than 3,800 staff. An additional 1,000 medical staff are associated with Chedoke-McMaster.

Being a teaching hospital means Chedoke-McMaster is not only a place where patients are cared for, but it is also where important health care research is conducted, and where students in a variety of health disciplines come to learn their professions.

Research and teaching is carried out at both the McMaster University Medical Centre (MUMC) site and the Chedoke Hospital site. Because the MUMC site is shared with the Faculty of Health Sciences of McMaster University, it has more research labs than any other hospital site in the city.

Following are just some of the areas of key research activity, carried out in collaboration with the Faculty of Health Sciences:

• **Brain and Behaviour**

Research shows that the brain is involved in, and controls, many aspects of illness. This gives the hospital the opportunity to help a variety of patients including those with seizure disorders, psychiatric illness and digestive disorders.

• **Thromboembolism**

Getting a better understanding of blood clotting disorders is the focus here. Staff is developing new, non-invasive diagnostic tests for high risk populations as well as studying the reasons for clotting problems in certain populations.

• **Immunology/Inflammation**

This research is directed at finding better ways to diagnose, prevent and treat chronic chronic inflammatory diseases, such as lupus, which often involve the respiratory tract and joints.

• **Children at risk for emotional/behavioural problems**

The Centre for Studies of Children at Risk looks at the prevalence and causes of mental illness in children and the effectiveness of various interventions.

• **Management research**

The impact of hospital restructuring on the quality of working life is a major research project launched in 1995. The study hones in on how hospital staff feel about their work, and what effect changes in the workplace might have on their well-being.

Conveniently everywhere, Big V Drug Stores really are an amazing part of your life. Today, there are 16 Big V Drug Stores in the Hamilton-Wentworth and Burlington area.

Together, these Big V stores employ about 500 people. The stores offer – and deliver – a wide array of merchandise from pharmaceuticals to food items, stationery, periodicals, and gift items.

Rick Brown, Director of Operations for Big V's Hamilton area, takes pride in the extensive community role the local stores have played during more than 20 years in the Hamilton area market.

"We sponsor a lot of children's teams in hockey, baseball, soccer, and each store sponsors an average of two teams," notes Mr. Brown, whose regional headquarters are located in Hamilton at Sherman Avenue South at Main.

"In fact," he adds, "a lot of what we become involved in is of benefit to children, whether it's sponsoring teams or providing those huge inflated mazes kids get to crawl through at Festival of Friends or at local schools."

Another attraction is Big V's mascot, The Crusader, whose floating, sometimes helium-filled presence is always an attention-getter. The Crusader was a 'float' in the 1995 Hamilton Santa Clause Parade.

Big V Drug Stores began in 1962 when a group of independent pharmacists in the Windsor area united to form a buying group. In 1973, with a number of established Big V stores in Windsor and Essex Country, the company entered the Hamilton market.

By the mid-1970s, Big V had expanded again to include operations in the Sarnia area along with four London pharmacies. The head office and warehouse were moved from Windsor to London in 1977 to keep up with ongoing expansion in Southern Ontario. In the early 1980s, Big V added stores in Burlington, St. Catharines, Chatham, St. Thomas and the Kitchener-Guelph market area.

In 1985, the company began operations in Dundas, Mississauga and Mt. Forest. The following year, Big V opened stores in Cambridge, Welland and Owen Sound.

Expansion continued into the late 1980s as London-based Canada Apothecary Shops joined Big V, which also opened numerous other stores across the province.

In the early 1990s, Big V also added stores in Brantford and other Ontario centres, taking its total number of stores to more than 100.

During 1994 to 1995, Big V opened five more stores in Brantford and one in Paris, along with stores at Windsor, Belle River, Lasalle, Wallaceburg, Brockville, Kingston, Jackson's Point, Gananoque and Trenton. And in 1996, the total number of stores was 135 – and growing.

While Big V continues to expand, it has never lost sight of its commitment to Hamilton. "We're also involved as a sponsor of community causes and events, including the Hamilton International Air Show, Hamilton Sesquicentennial events and the Hamilton Tiger-Cats," says Mr. Brown, adding Big V not only sponsors the 'Cats, its stores also sell game tickets.

"Big V is really into the community. We're tied to Hamilton in a lot of the things we do," he concludes.

• *Pharmacist/manager Susan Nuttall is shown at McAuley Big V, one of the 16 Big V stores in the Hamilton area.*
– Photo by David Gruggen

ROYALCREST LIFECARE GROUP INC.

The stress of moving to a nursing home can become traumatic if it also forces the separation of spouses. Yet many elderly couples are indeed separated when one requires more intensive care than the other.

While one senior citizen moves to a nursing home, the other remains in a retirement home miles away.

This separation can prove extremely difficult to accept at a time in life when the aged may be struggling with losses of independence, self-reliance and control over personal finances.

Fortunately, Royalcrest Lifecare Group Inc. offers a solution to the separation dilemma. The Hamilton-based company offers what it calls 'Lifecare' facilities, offering both a nursing home and a retirement home in the same complex.

"These residences allow seniors to receive the services required without moving out of the facility," says company president Al Martino.

"They move internally as their level of care dictates," he explains.

His brother, John Martino, company vice-president and chief financial officer, points to additional benefits of such multi-use facilities.

"This allows spouses with different care levels to continue to live together in the same facility," observes John Martino, whose company is located on Main Street East in a former Victorian residence that has been converted into the executive corporate offices of Royalcrest Lifecare Group.

"The management of these facilities is under one corporate structure and allows the company to take advantage of savings in costs and purchasing," he adds.

Donna Spasic, vice-president operations, administers the leadership and control that is required to ensure that the residents we accommodate in Royalcrest Lifecare Group will receive the service and independence that is expected by our clients," states John Martino.

Carol Lechner, development and marketing manager for Royalcrest Lifecare Group, notes this continuum of care has "really been the key to the company's success over the years.

"Royalcrest Lifecare pioneered the concept of providing the 'continuum of care,' from independent living to complete quality nursing care, within one facility," adds Mrs. Lechner, who works with architects in design of the facilities' buildings, provides interior decorating skills and appropriately furnishes the suites with furniture best-suited to com-

• Al Martino, left, is the president of Hamilton-based Royalcrest Lifecare Group Inc., while his brother John Martino is company vice-president and chief financial officer.
– Photo by David Gruggen

fort needs of an aging clientele.

Also driving the company's success is its emphasis on service and the thoughtful consideration it shows its elderly clients.

"Every person regardless of age is entitled to be treated with dignity," asserts Al Martino, noting that this respectful attitude exists at all of Royalcrest Lifecare

Group's long-term care facilities. Each home also prides itself on its integrity, compassion and commitment to value.

The Martino brothers founded their company in 1981 with a retirement home on Victoria Street in downtown Hamilton. This original site still houses that first retirement home, Victoria Manor I, along with a second complex, Victoria Manor II.

Today, Royalcrest Lifecare Group has grown to become the largest privately held nursing and retirement home operation in the province. All told, it operates in 10 Ontario municipalities, offering a total of 3,000 nursing and retirement suites in 17 facilities, including St. Olga's and Townsview, Cathmar and Hillview in Hamilton, Stoney Creek Lifecare Centre and Brantwood in Burlington.

Al Martino also cites the facilities' experienced and skilled staff for his company's success.

"To guarantee residents receive the attention they deserve, we have staffed each facility with professionals capable of delivering services and operating a long-term care facility to its peak efficiency."

ealth sciences education, research and service are the lifeblood of the Faculty of Health Sciences at McMaster University. Founded in 1974, two years after the construction of the Health Sciences Centre on campus, the Faculty prepares health professionals and health scientists through its partnerships with teaching hospitals and affiliated health and research institutions.

More than 1,400 faculty members and about 600 staff members teach, study, practice and work within the Faculty.

McMaster has been educating health professionals since the School of Nursing opened in 1946. Twenty years later, the university began its undergraduate program in medicine.

Today, more than 2,800 students are enrolled in the undergraduate and graduate programs offered by the Schools of Nursing, Medicine and Rehabilitation Science, and the departments of anesthesia, biochemistry, biomedical sciences, clinical epidemiology and biostatics, family medicine, medicine, obstetrics and gynecology, pathology, pediatrics, psychiatry, radiology and surgery.

A hallmark of all of the Faculty's education programs is the "McMaster approach" that stresses life-long, self-directed learning based on problem-based, small group tutorials. Considered a revolutionary way to teach health sciences when it was first introduced, this approach has since been adopted wholly or in part by health sciences faculties in universities worldwide.

Research by members of the Faculty of Health Sciences ranges from basic science to clinical research at the bedside and in the community.

The Faculty's strengths include research in asthma and lung diseases, brain disorders, health economics and policy analysis, gerontology and clinical epidemiology, pediatrics, molecular virology and immunology, cardiovascular disease, intestinal diseases and vaccine development. Based on these research strengths, McMaster ranks consistently among the top 20 universities, with health sciences faculties worldwide.

The Faculty ranks in the top third of Canadian health sciences centres in peer-reviewed funding and receives more than $49 million worth of research funding from external sources alone, including the Medical Research Council of Canada, the Heart and Stroke Foundation, the Rockefeller Foundation, the National Cancer Institute and the U.S. National Institutes of Health.

The Faculty of Health Sciences integrates its education, research and services across the Hamilton region through a variety of partnerships. Locally, these partnerships link Faculty members with teaching hospitals and affiliated institutions from Chedoke-McMaster Hospitals, Hamilton Psychiatric Hospital, Hamilton Regional Cancer Centre, St. Peter's Hospital, St. Joseph's Hospital and Hamilton Civic Hospitals to the district Health Council and regional health and social service agencies.

The links enable the partners to co-operate in identifying community health-care goals and making decisions to avoid duplication of health care services. Globally, the Faculty of Health Sciences takes part in professional exchange programs, co-ordinates faculty and student involvement in international health projects and supports education programs in developing countries, notably through the Aga Khan project with its partner institution in Pakistan, the Aga Khan University.

• *The Faculty of Health Sciences at McMaster University, founded in 1974, prepares health professionals and health scientists through its partnerships with teaching hospitals and affiliated health and research institutions.*
– Photo by Dennis McGreal

W ith a history dating to 1848, Hamilton Civic Hospitals is renowned as a significant and important health care resource to the people of Hamilton-Wentworth. Its mission is focused on caring for people with dignity, respect and compassion and on achieving excellence in research and education as a university-affiliated teaching hospital.

Hamilton Civic Hospitals is an independent corporation that operates the Hamilton General Division at 237 Barton Street East and Henderson General Division at 711 Concession Street. It also operates the Hamilton Civic Hospitals Research Centre, Hamilton Men's Detoxification Centre and Hamilton-Wentworth Central Ambulance Communications Centre.

Hamilton Civic Hospitals is well known for its expertise in cancer care, cardiac disease, community hospital services, orthopedic joint reconstruction, multiple injuries (major trauma), burns, neurosciences (brain trauma), blood vessel disease and women's health.

Hamilton Civic Hospitals is very active as a teaching hospital affiliated with McMaster University's Faculty of Health Science, Mohawk College and Michener Institute of Applied Health Science. Clinicians, technologists and technicians benefit from valuable hands-on training and experience with clinical placements at Hamilton Civic Hospitals. Its medical and professional staff provide clinical and academic leadership to an estimated 3,500 students each year.

In co-operation with McMaster University's Faculty of Health Sciences, Hamilton Civic Hospitals also provides support for the Stonechurch Family Health Centre and North Hamilton Community Health Centre.

These two Health Centres are the Family Practice Unit extensions of the Hamilton Civic Hospitals. Stonechurch Family Health Centre at 549 Stonechurch Road East caters to the health

• Hamilton Civic Hospitals, with a history dating to 1848, is an independent corporation operating Hamilton General Division on Barton Street in the lower city and Henderson General Division on Concession Street on the Mountain.
– Photo by Dennis McGreal

needs of Hamilton Mountain communities. The North Hamilton Community Health Centre at 554 John Street North provides programs and services for the North End communities.

Hamilton Civic Hospitals is internationally known for its research endeavours. Hundreds of staff members are involved in research initiatives that span every health care discipline.

The Hamilton Civic Hospitals Research Centre at the Henderson General site has become an international centre of excellence for research into heart disease and blood clotting.

Hamilton Civic Hospitals plays an integral role in many regional health delivery services. It provides diagnostic expertise to all the Hamilton hospitals through the Hamilton Health Services Laboratory Program.

It plays an active role in the Regional Breast Screening program. In association with the Hamilton-Wentworth Health Department, Hamilton Civic Hospitals provides services for the region's sexually transmitted diseases clinic.

Hamilton Civic Hospitals operates the Chief Gordon V. Torrence Regional Forensic Pathology Unit providing expert opinions on criminal cases across the entire Niagara Peninsula. Although Hamilton Civic Hospitals is funded primarily by the Ontario Ministry of Health, the Hospital depends on the Hamilton Civic Hospitals Foundation and its generous donors to provide the funds that support education, research and the purchase of equipment at Hamilton Civic Hospitals.

"It's a labour of love. Some people play golf – I go to work." This insightful assertion from Irv Miller explains Miller's Shoe Store's enduring legacy as a Hamilton institution.

At an age when many business people look forward to a retirement on the greens, Mr. Miller, 64, still eagerly rises each morning to spend 12-hour days at his landmark downtown shoe store.

"It's the people I most enjoy," Mr. Miller says of his continued zest for working alongside his son Brian in this thriving family business, which offers customers one of the largest selections of footwear in Ontario.

"And we're eternally grateful for mother and dad starting the business and making it a little easier for each generation to carry on," adds Mr. Miller, the store's owner and president.

Founded in 1926 by Barney and Bella Miller, Miller's Shoe Store was initially a two-person business occupying just a fraction of the space it currently utilizes at its James Street North location between Wilson and Cannon streets.

As the business struggled through the Great Depression of the 1930s, the Millers raised their son Irv in two floors of space above their little shop.

"We had a lot of space although it wasn't well-heated," recalls Mr. Miller, whose boyhood chums were also the offspring of neighbouring business people who lived above their stores.

"I started working in the store when I was 14 and it wasn't until I was 15 that I realized other people had lawns in front of their homes."

Born into the family business, with downtown Hamilton as his neighbourhood, Mr. Miller says it was "a foregone conclusion that I would join the business – and I've never regretted it."

Mr. Miller subsequently took over the store which by the mid-1990s employed seven people and occupied around 18,000 square feet of space on four levels.

"The business has changed over the years," notes Mr. Miller, whose store celebrated its 70th anniversary in 1996.

"We've gone from being a neighbourhood store to being a destination store that attracts people from Kitchener, Niagara and other parts of Southern Ontario," he explains.

Some things haven't changed. Miller's Shoe Store definitely remains service-oriented. "We still get a great deal of satisfaction from properly fitting people with the shoe that's right for them," says Mr. Miller, adding the process involves taking precise measurements of the foot and can also result in the customer trying on numerous pairs of shoes.

• Miller's Shoe Store is operated by Irv Miller and son Brian. The store is located on James Street North.
– Photo by Joe Bucci

"No one is ever rushed," he stresses. "It doesn't matter how many pairs of shoes are tried on or how long it takes, the important thing is that when people leave our store they're wearing comfortable footwear they're pleased with. That's our greatest source of satisfaction."

Miller Shoe Store's wide selection of footwear includes sizes ranging from a Lady's Size 4 to a Men's Size 16. The store also receives many referrals from area doctors whose patients suffer from arthritis or other ailments requiring special orthopedic footwear.

Mr. Miller is also pleased that he'll one day leave his store in good hands.

"My son Brian is as dedicated as I am," he says. "Our customers can look forward to many more years of good service after he takes over the store."

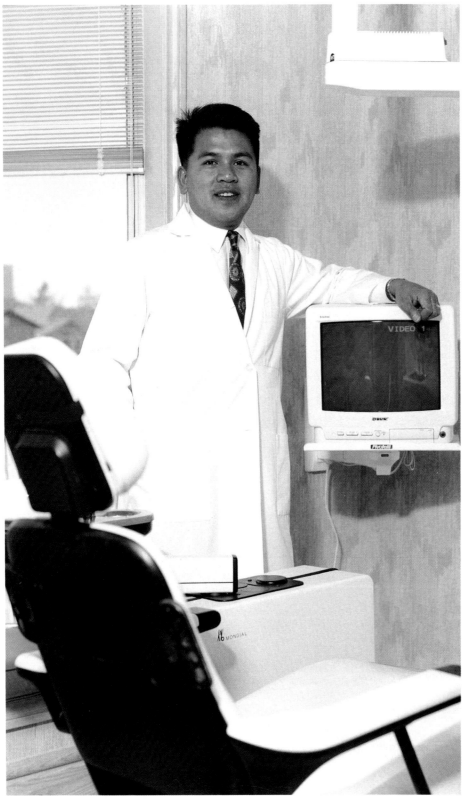

• *Hard work and dedication have paid off for Dr. Roland Estrabillo, who made Hamilton his home after immigrating to Canada from The Philippines in 1980.*
– Photo by Joe Bucci

When it's time to visit the dentist, most people can think of someplace that they'd rather be. But Dr. Roland Estrabillo is a dentist who takes pride in making such visits more pleasant by cutting in half the time required for many dental procedures.

"We're working faster," notes Dr. Estrabillo, who attributes his time-saving techniques to the best practices he's picked up from other dentists and from a lifetime of continuous learning.

Born and raised in The Philippines, Dr. Estrabillo immigrated to Canada in 1980 at age 20 and made Hamilton his home town. After graduating in 1987 from the University of Toronto with a degree in dentistry, Dr. Estrabillo set up practice on Upper Wentworth Street in a strip mall opposite Lime Ridge Mall.

Building up his practice from scratch, Dr. Estrabillo went from an empty appointment book to 6,000 to 7,000 active patients by the mid-1990s.

By the early 1990s, he had outgrown his strip mall location and relocated to renovated offices at his former home, also on Upper Wentworth Street.

By 1996 he was contemplating yet another move to larger quarters to accommodate his growing practice. Fuelling this impressive growth are referrals from satisfied patients who appreciate the extra care Dr. Estrabillo takes to make their visit pleasant – and brief.

"We have a system," explains Dr. Estrabillo. "I've learned from other doctors and I've taken courses regularly throughout my career. I copied a lot of the other dentists' better techniques and added some of my own and put it all together to share with others."

That sharing takes place during seminars Dr. Estrabillo hosts to pass on to other dentists some of the efficient, time-saving techniques he's picked up during a cumulative, shared-learning experience spanning his full career.

Although general family dentistry still accounted for 75 per cent of his practice in the mid-1990s, Dr. Estrabillo was concentrating more on full-mouth reconstructive dentistry as a growing, and satisfying, part of his work.

"After the orthodontist and periodontist have treated the patient, I perform the bridge work, teeth implants, crowns, veneers and cosmetic improvements to their teeth," he explains.

"Normally a crown takes an hour. Now we can cut that to just half-an-hour, so the patient is more comfortable."

Dr. Estrabillo notes this full-mouth reconstruction, comprehensive dentistry can improve chewing efficiency, improve the functioning of the jaw, save teeth and

• Dr. Roland Estrabillo is shown with members of his staff at his offices on Upper Wentworth Street.
– Photo by Joe Bucci

"actually make people look younger with whiter, rearranged, straighter teeth which support the mouth better."

Through referrals from satisfied full-mouth reconstructive dentistry patients, Dr. Estrabillo's work has drawn patients from Seattle, Washington, Texas, California and the Philippines.

"That's an exiting part of this process – we can help people even from a consider-able distance," says Dr. Estrabillo, who has provided basic dental care at no charge to residents of nursing homes in an effort to give back to the community by helping people who might otherwise never seek out dental services.

And Dr. Estrabillo is quick to attribute the success of his busy practice to his staff of 12, including a fellow dentist, a hygienist and support staff.

"My staff is the best in the world," he asserts. "Without them, I could not have achieved anything that I have achieved. They play a very big role in our success. They run my office and they take very good care of our patients."

Dr. Estrabillo also credits his wife Maria, who operates her own laboratory from his office, for "being the technician who does the laboratory work for crowns bridges and veneers. Maria helps us provide customized care to every patient."

And Dr. Estrabillo is grateful for the input, advice and support he has received from "my mentors," fellow dentists and friends from all walks of life who have helped him overcome problems and achieve new levels of success in a demanding, time-consuming career.

"Success is never something you achieve all by yourself," he says.

"It's when you learn from others and share your own experiences that you improve in the process. And everyone benefits from this type of sharing."

For many of our senior citizens, getting old means an isolated life in an institution removed from family, friends and the outside world.

Happily, that life of isolation can't be found at St. Joseph's Villa, an award-winning home for the aged that actually strengthens ties to family, friends and the outside community.

It is here that you will find facilities for both able-bodied and frail seniors, along with many community programs at Governor's Road and Overfield Street in Dundas, the original site of the House of Providence, which was founded in 1879.

"We're providing a continuum of care with seniors' housing and a health-care facility at the same site," notes Paul O'Krafka, executive director of St. Joseph's Villa, the largest facility of its kind in Ontario and winner of regional and provincial awards for innovative care-related programs.

"And we're focusing on the spiritual needs of our clients," adds Mr. O'Krafka, whose facility offers an inter-denominational chapel where daily Catholic mass and services of other religions regularly take place.

St. Joseph's Villa is a private, non-profit charitable organization owned by the Sisters of St. Joseph. The facility operates using charitable dollars raised by the St. Joseph's Villa Foundation and through the extensive service provided by more than 400 volunteers and Guild members.

Together with St. Joseph's Hospital in Hamilton, the facility is a member of St. Joseph's Health Care System, and is linked to the Father Sean O'Sullivan Research Centre conducting research related to aging.

The 18-acre St. Joseph's Villa site contains a main health care facility housing 370 long-term residents who cannot manage independent lifestyles and may need specialized nursing care and programs which compensate for mental or physical frailties.

The location also accommodates 110 respite care, short-stay seniors and 179 day visitors who participate in the activities of the SJV Adult Day Program

before returning to their homes in the Hamilton-Wentworth community. The central location is also nearby off-site shopping and transit services.

In March 1996, St. Joseph's Villa lands also became home to St. Joseph's Estates, a seniors life equity facility that houses 93 residents who can manage an independent lifestyle but want to be near the swimming pool, bowling, therapy, friends and social amenities offered by the Villa.

A second 54-suite life equity building is currently under construction, with completion planned for the winter of

"As well, with people simply moving from one residence to another, close friends can stay in touch and continue to share in social, recreational and outreach activities," he explains.

Board Chairman Jim Forbes notes the respite care program can actually bring families closer together by easing the burden of caring for an elderly relative.

When the family members need a vacation, they can bring their elderly relative over to St. Joseph's Villa," he explains, adding the relative can also have a vacation and enjoy the amenities while

• Paul O'Krafka, executive director of St. Joseph's Villa, is shown with (standing from left) Linda Young, manager of food services and Sister Beatrice Schnarr, a member of the board. Seated are Sister Benigna Zister, Eileen Simpson and Tom Bacon, members of the executive of the villa's residents' council.
— Photo by Joe Bucci

1996/97 to house an additional 100 seniors. This innovative facility enriches the lives of seniors through outreach programs on the Villa campus which give seniors contact with children, pets, entertainment and education courses.

Mr. O'Krafka points to many advantages in having different housing for seniors requiring various levels of care – but all located at the same 18-acre site.

"It means that if the health of a wife of husband deteriorates, the frail partner can move to the health care centre and be a two-minute walk from the healthier partner," says Mr. O'Krafka.

the family gets a much-needed break.

The day-visitors program allows seniors living off-site to visit friends and enjoy the meals, pool, therapy and other features of St. Joseph's Villa. It also allows working couples a place to take seniors who can't be left on their own during the work day.

The degree of care offered depends solely on the amount of care needed.

"We're building on the strengths of each resident," asserts Mr. Forbes.

"We focus on their abilities rather than their losses and frailties – and our staff are phenomenal at achieving this."

From its establishment in 1890, St. Joseph's Hospital in Hamilton has grown to become a 500-bed, active treatment general hospital, complemented by a chronic care unit, with a staff of over 2,600 full- and part-time employees.

The Hospital's Strategic Plan establishes Kidney and Urinary Diseases; Chest and Lung Diseases; Musculoskeletal Diseases; Maternal Child – Obstetrics/Neonatology; and General Medicine as Centres of Excellence. Laboratory Medicine is a Diagnostic Centre of Excellence and Values and Catholic Identity is a Centre of Excellence.

St. Joseph's Hospital is a major and active participant in the St. Joseph's Health Care system and is also a major component of the McMaster University Faculty of Health Sciences System, and a major teaching hospital within the rationalized Hamilton Health Care System.

In conjunction with its primary role of caring for the sick, St. Joseph's Hospital has stressed the importance of teaching and research programs. It participates in the clinical training at both the undergraduate and graduate level.

Some recent developments at St. Joseph's Hospital include:
• the opening of the Regional Dialysis Centre in 1967, with a new and expanded Centre opened in 1985;
• the first kidney transplant in Hamilton in 1970, the opening of the Renal Transplant Unit in 1972;
• the first live kidney transplant in 1974;
• the opening of the Firestone Regional Chest and Allergy Unit in 1979;
• the opening of the Self-Care Dialysis Centre in 1981;
• the opening of the Rheumatic Diseases Unit in 1986;
• the opening of the Hamilton Women's Detox Centre in 1987;
• the opening of the St. Joseph's Hospital Spinal Centre in 1988.

In 1991, St. Joseph's Hospital opened the St. Joseph's Community Health Centre to serve the people of Stoney Creek and East Hamilton. Programs and services offered at the Centre were those identified by the community as high priority needs.

The Centre has a free-standing Urgent Care Service with supporting laboratory and X-Ray facilities. There are no beds, and programs are conducted on an outpatient basis.

These programs include a Geriatric Day Hospital, Communication disorders, East Regional Mental Health Services, Bereavement/Grief Counselling, Consumer Health Information, Lifeline, Chiropody, Diabetes and Parent/Child Program. Through an affiliation with McMaster University, the St. Joseph's Community Health Centre provides a wide range of educational training opportunities, in a community setting, to the next generation of health care professionals.

Medical research which "really counts" – directly affecting patient care and care for family members – is the focus of the Father Sean O'Sullivan Research Centre at St. Joseph's Hospital in Hamilton.

The Centre draws together investigators from many fields providing them with specialized support services as well as an invigorating environment for discovery. The Centre also formalizes the Hospital's long-standing commitment to research and to the well-being of the community it serves.

The Father Sean O'Sullivan Research Centre encompasses people, programs and activities throughout the Hospital and the St. Joseph's Community Health Centre in east Hamilton and is affiliated with the Faculty of Health Sciences at McMaster University. The initial emphasis of the Centre will be on four areas of research for which St. Joseph's has already received international recognition. Those areas are:
• chest and lung diseases;
• kidney and urinary diseases;
• musculoskeletal diseases;
• optimal drug therapy.

The Research Centre at St. Joseph's is named after a well-known Hamiltonian, Father Sean O'Sullivan. He was a successful politician, a committed and visionary priest and a courageous patient. Father Sean was a great friend of St. Joseph's and his spirit lives on in the Hospital and Research Centre.

• Established in 1890, St. Joseph's Hospital has grown to become a 500-bed, active treatment general hospital with a staff of more than 2,600 full- and part-time employees.
– *Photo by Dennis McGreal*

I used to think that having a mental illness was the kiss of death. Like my mother, I inherited a manic depressive disorder that has played havoc with my marital, professional and social life. After having suffered from this scourge for over 20 years, I was referred to the Mood Disorders Program at HPH. It was a little risky on my part; HPH is referred to as the "loony bin" where I come from.

At HPH, they were extremely vigilant and monitored my progress continually. I am truly grateful for the care and consideration I received during my three-month stay. I am currently an outpatient and haven't had to be hospitalized for several years. There is no other service like it!"

— Susan Voss, author
Add Courage And Stir

• A progressive teaching and research hospital, Hamilton Psychiatric Hospital celebrated its 120th birthday in 1996.
– Photo by Dennis McGreal

In 1996, Hamilton Psychiatric Hospital celebrated its 120th birthday. Its foundation of respect for patients as people first is still rock-solid, but the hospital is pleased to say that today its treatment methods and approach vastly differ.

The HPH doesn't believe that a psychiatric hospital should conjure up images from a gothic horror novel. Think instead of a modern, dynamic teaching hospital where patients are busy in programming, where volunteers push tuck carts and students come to learn. No one "lives" there anymore. The hospital doesn't want them to! It tries to help about 4,000 people every year to maintain successful functioning in the community.

Staff at Hamilton Psychiatric Hospital provide acute treatment and care for patients with a prolonged major mental illness (ie. schizophrenia and mood disorders); promote stabilization following acute recurrences, and design and implement treatment programs for complex behavioural and/or psychiatric problems for people with an acquired brain injury, complex multiple psychiatric diagnoses and seniors.

In the community – HPH serves Hamilton-Wentworth, Brant, Haldimand, Niagara and Halton – the hospital pilots psychiatric treatment and rehabilitation programs, provides consultations to community agencies, assigns staff to community treatment programs and provides advocacy and education to both clinical service providers and to the general public.

A progressive teaching and research hospital, HPH is affiliated with McMaster University, Mohawk College and the World Health Organization.

So when you think of your neighbourhood, picture the therapist at the local seniors' clinic, the support group that meets in your local church, the presentation being made to your child's class . . . those are just some of the services HPH performs to assist people with a mental illness to lead the lives they desire in their communities. Now that's an accurate picture.

DR. ROBERT PYE

It's 5 a.m. Sunday. A junior hockey player lies on the ice moaning in agony, his right hand gingerly touching a broken jaw that just stopped a puck.

The injured youth is rushed to the emergency ward of a local hospital where a nurse makes a fast telephone call.

Moments later, the youth is greeted by Dr. Robert Pye, who quickly sets about performing emergency surgery to the young man's broken jaw.

When the job is complete, the youth still can't manage a smile as yet, but he will – thanks to the efforts of Dr. Pye, one of less than a dozen oral and maxillofacial surgeons in greater Hamilton.

Elsewhere in the city, another grateful former patient glances in the bathroom mirror at a normal-looking jaw which was once grotesquely deformed – until Dr. Pye performed surgery.

"When someone comes to you with trauma or a jaw deformity and you make their jaw right, they can be so grateful and happy," reflects Dr. Pye. "I find that can be very gratifying."

But what of being awoken at 5 a.m. to treat a hockey injury?

"That's where the job offers variety," replies Dr. Pye. "Emergency surgery can't wait. It has to be done right away and it changes your day completely. It adds a touch of excitement."

Dr. Pye spends a day plus one to two evenings a week at Joseph Brant Hospital in Burlington. The remainder of his week is divided into half-days spent in each of two offices: one on Hamilton Mountain at Upper Wentworth Street, the other in Burlington at Brant and Ghent streets.

His work is also divided, between emergency surgery and elective surgery, including the removal of wisdom teeth and correction of deformities. "I enjoy it," asserts Dr. Pye. "Every day is different. Every day is a challenge."

More challenging cases can involve multiple problems, such as an enlarged overgrowth of upper jaw along with under developed lower jaw, which must be corrected in a co-ordinated manner to provide a sense of balance to the face "and bring it within the range of normal."

Other difficult cases can involve multiple injuries from a car accident, requiring Dr. Pye to work as part of a surgical team correcting a combination of injuries.

Prior to establishing his practice in the 1970s, Dr. Pye spent five years at the University of Toronto, where he earned a dental degree. After interning for a year, he went on to complete three years of graduate work in oral and maxillofacial surgery and anaesthesia.

"I simply found this specialized work to be more interesting and satisfying than regular dentistry," Dr. Pye recalls of his decision to specialize in a form of surgery which can generate some astonishing improvements in both the functionality and appearance of the jaw.

His patients still go to a regular dentist for fillings and routine dentistry. But for surgery to the jaw joints, dental implants, tooth extractions or other such problems with a dental background, they make an appointment to see Dr. Pye.

"It really is possible to provide a dramatic improvement with the right surgical procedures," says Dr. Pye. "When patients attain such pleasing results, my efforts are completely gratified."

• Dr. Robert Pye is one of less than a dozen oral and maxillofacial surgeons in the greater Hamilton area.
– *Photo by David Gruggen*

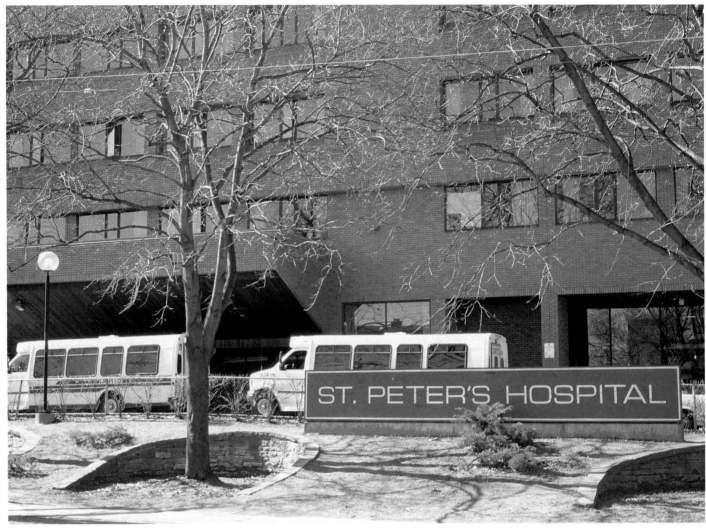

A s its motto states, St. Peter's Hospital is "leading the way for seniors." The 284-bed chronic care hospital provides a comprehensive range of health care services to people 65 and older in Hamilton-Wentworth.

The hospital is a progressive health care organization which began in 1890, when Reverend Thomas Geoghegan started a home to care for people suffering from terminal illnesses.

His compassion has been a driving force guiding the hospital throughout its 105-year history.

St. Peter's Hospital is an accredited teaching hospital affiliated with McMaster University and Mohawk College of Applied Arts and Technology. Each year, more than 200 students gain valuable hands-on experience through hospital placements in medicine, occupational therapy, physiotherapy, nursing, chiropody and more.

St. Peter's 10 inpatient specialty programs include Stroke Rehabilitation, two Post-Stroke Management programs, Musculo-Skeletal, Neurological, Palliative Care, Major Systems and three Behavioural Health programs. The programs are specifically designed to meet the needs of each patient's clinical diagnosis and to maintain or improve their quality of life.

The Community Services program provides a range of services to seniors living in the community.

It includes a Chiropody Clinic for the diagnosis and treatment of foot disorders; a Falls Clinic, which provides an assessment and prevention service for seniors who are at risk of falling; and a Seating Clinic for those people who are in need of seating and mobility devices such as a wheelchair.

The health care industry is changing rapidly and St. Peter's Hospital has kept up with the changes by introducing new initiatives and projects including:

Research Department: The hospital's commitment to providing the most up-to-date care is evident with the creation of a Research department in 1994. Research projects into issues such as rehabilitation and quality of life are ongoing.

Easy Street Environment: The state-of-the-art rehabilitation centre celebrated its fifth anniversary in 1995. Since it opened, more than 37,000 seniors have travelled Easy Street on their way to increased mobility, independence and self-confidence.

Long-term goals for St. Peter's include redeveloping the hospital's aging south wing and continuing to develop linkages and partnerships with the community.

These new projects and initiatives, in addition to the hospital's long-standing commitment to providing seniors with the highest quality of care available, will ensure St. Peter's Hospital effectively meets the challenges facing the health care industry today and in the future.

• *Mohawk College has earned a reputation for providing quality training and education in the health care field.*
– Photo by Dennis McGreal

Mohawk College has been educating professionals in the health care field for many years. Since the establishment of the Faculty of Health Sciences in 1971, changes in the educational delivery and location of several facets of the health care area have occurred.

In 1975, Chedoke Campus officially opened as the Health Science Education Centre of Mohawk College. Also that year, the implementation of Newstart Nursing – a program offered to nurses from other countries or provinces, and designed to meet the requirements for registration in Ontario – opened the door of opportunity for many registered nurses returning to the field.

The following year saw continued growth and expansion as renovations were under way to the existing nurses residence of the Chedoke campus to accommodate Physiotherapy and Radiography departments and mark the introduction of the Chedoke Health Sciences Centre.

Today, with increasing financial constraints facing the Health Care system and education, it is becoming increasingly difficult to meet the demands of the growing health care field.

However, Mohawk College has always maintained a solid commitment to this vital area.

Mohawk ensures that despite continuing challenges, it will continue to offer the quality training and education that the public has experienced and come to expect over the years.

Its mission will always be to deliver selected educational and training programs, courses and services in an innovative lifelong learning environment designed to contribute to the economic stability and quality of life of the communities it serves.

At Mohawk College, they are acting on the needs of today, and prepared for the challenges of tomorrow.

• Donald Dunn, right, and his brother, Ed, are the two driving forces behind Ford Dunn Insurance Brokers.
— **Photo by Joe Bucci**

Deep ties to Hamilton and to sports have made Ford Dunn Insurance Brokers a familiar name locally – and across Canada.

The Hamilton firm is well-known in amateur sports, locally, provincially and nationally as the exclusive brokers for All Sport Insurance Marketing Ltd., a company that provides insurance to amateur sports groups across the nation.

"Our name comes up in various parts of the country through our connection with amateur sports coverage," notes company vice-president Ed Dunn, who has a personal sports connection.

Mr. Dunn, who entered his 50s in the mid-1990s, can look back with fondness to his days as a former player with the Hamilton Hurricanes football club of the Ontario Junior Football Conference. He was also a Canadian Football League official throughout the '80s and served for years as president of the St. Joseph's Golf Tournament, a hospital fundraiser.

Older brother and company president Donald Dunn, who was in his mid-60s in the mid-1990s, played football for a fore-runner of the CFL Hamilton Tiger-Cats. He's also a past president of the Catholic Youth Organization in Hamilton. And on more than one occasion, he and his family have led Ivor Wynne Stadium crowds in singing the Canadian National Anthem.

The Dunn brothers are proud, life-long Hamiltonians with a long history of contributing to community causes, including the annual Christmas Tree of Hope.

Their company also enjoys a lengthy history, with origins dating back more than 60 years.

The company was founded in the early 1930s by Wilfrid Ford as Ford Insurance Agency, providing an array of not only insurance but also real estate appraisals and other services for several decades.

In 1965, the company was purchased by Donald Dunn, who remains president.

And in 1981, the name was changed to Ford Dunn Insurance Brokers to recognize the contribution of the current and former owners and to comply with legislation requiring insurance brokers to use the word 'broker' in their company name.

With the name change came years of steady growth as the firm proved adept at shopping the market for the best insurance packages available from 10 different insurance companies.

"We've become one of the larger insurance brokers in the area," notes Ed Dunn, "and we pay special attention to meeting our clients' needs at reasonable cost."

In addition to individual clients, Ford Dunn also provides insurance to many large clients, including hospitals and the Hamilton-Wentworth Roman Catholic Separate School Board.

In the past 20 years, the firm's work-force has more than tripled to 16 employees working out of Ford Dunn's James Street South offices at the Professional Arts Building.

As Ford Dunn looks forward to future years of growth, the company isn't forgetting its history of service.

"We act as an intermediary between the insurer and the consumer to get our clients the insurance package that's right for them," notes Ed Dunn.

"And consumer referrals are now a major part of our business."

DR. HARRY HOTZ

Tiny tots love Dr. Hotz. If ever there were a shred of doubt about that statement, it happily vanished when pediatrician Dr. Harry Hotz received an unusual gift marking his recent move into semi-retirement.

It was a set of photo albums stuffed with pictures and testimonials from some of the thousands of children he has cared for over a lifetime of making ill tots well.

"Dr. Hotz: Thank you for all the years of being there when I was sick," reads a carefully printed note below a photograph of a smiling young boy.

"To Dr. Hotz, a doctor who showed how much he cared by always being there for his children. A heartfelt thank you from the Hogan family," reads another note, this one above a picture of a healthy and happy family.

One youngster captured a thought on many patients' minds with this comment: "Dr. Hotz: Thank you for making going to the doctor a happy time."

And below the photograph of a pretty, teenage girl was the neatly written message: "Dr. Hotz, thank you for taking care of me all these 16 years."

Such remarks are typical throughout the photo albums presented to him by his nursing staff. "They did this behind my back – but it was nice of them to do this – it's all very flattering," says Dr. Hotz, 75, sporting his trademark bow tie and wry sense of humour.

"And it's especially gratifying for a septuagenarian such as myself. I've been practicing for so long, I think I've just about got it right," he adds, displaying a flash of the self-depreciating humour that endeared him to children and parents alike during more than 40 years – and counting – of practice in Hamilton.

"I don't deliver them – I just look after them after they're already here."

Dr. Hotz graduated with a medical degree from the University of Toronto in 1944. After residencies at the Hamilton General Hospital, a stint as Captain in the Royal Canadian Army Medical Corps and further residencies at the University of Chicago and the Children's Hospital in Honolulu, Hawaii, he opened his pediatric practice in Hamilton in Main Street East offices in 1950.

Dr. Hotz also married a registered nurse and raised six children of his own. And he has five grandchildren.

But Dr. Hotz's full family is much larger than that. It consists of thousands of children over three generations who happily placed themselves in his care.

"We still have about 3,000 patients," notes Dr. Hotz, who continues to visit his old office at least one day a week to check up on little ones. He also makes

• *Sporting his trademark bow tie, 75-year-old Dr. Harry Hotz still visits his old office at least one day a week. He also makes house calls and hospital visits.*
– Photo by David Gruggen

house calls and hospital visits.

In the late 1980s, when many people his age would be focused on retirement, Dr. Hotz travelled to China and Russia to learn different pediatric techniques.

Dr. Hotz has been a president of Temple Anshe Shalom. And he's to be named Chairman of the Section of Pediatrics of the Hamilton Academy of Medicine for 1996-97.

Lynn Trafford Willenbrecht is a registered nurse who was a patient of Dr. Hotz's and says that she is "proud to be a member of your alumni."

"I only hope that you will be around to look after my grandchildren," Mrs. Willenbrecht writes in a framed letter commemorating the doctor's move into semi-retirement, "because Tiny Totz do love Dr. Hotz – and so do their parents."

Gennum Corporation has experienced remarkable growth by focusing on a select market for the tiny integrated circuitry and miniature amplifier components that go into hearing instruments.

In fact, Gennum is today the world's leading manufacturer of integrated audio amplifiers for hearing instruments.

And keeping this emphasis on the small, the Burlington-based firm also uses its integrated circuitry know-how to manufacture and market miniature video broadcast switching components which are in use around the globe, including Barcelona, Spain, where they were used in the 1992 Olympic Summer Games' master video switching system to route video signals.

• *Dr. Douglas Barber is the president and chief executive officer of Gennum Corporation. He is also a part-time professor at McMaster University.*

Dr. Douglas Barber, Gennum president and chief executive officer, credits his company's niche marketing approach for helping it achieve success with small products for the specialized markets that larger high-tech companies have bypassed. "We have found areas we know we can succeed in," adds Dr. Barber. "And our focus is still very much on producing circuitry for hearing instruments."

Dr. Barber sees new signs of growth ahead in a market which is embracing the Canadian technology company's addition

of hybrid circuits – including integrated circuits and external components – to offer a more complete hearing instruments systems part in a single package.

"Now we're applying a value-added approach that will make the hearing instruments niche a lot bigger," notes Dr. Barber, who is also a part-time professor in engineering physics at McMaster University, the author of dozens of scientific papers and the holder of several patents on semiconductor devices.

In a sense, the same value-added approach is also being taken to Gennum's second-biggest source of business, its video switching and transmission component products, where it is participating in its customers' conversion of broadcast studios from analog to digital systems.

"The shift from analog to digital will in time mean the replacing of the existing market with one that is digital," predicts Dr. Barber, whose company is poised to add to its two-thirds share of a video switching and transmission equipment market that has warmly welcomed Gennum's video mixers, buffers, sync separators and the GENLINX chip set, which aids digital video signal processing.

It's a remarkable success story for a company which began as a spin-off venture when Westinghouse Canada Inc. decided to get out of the microelectronics business. Dr. Barber joined partners Dr. Wally Pieczonka and Bob Simpson in purchasing the solid-state electronics division of Westinghouse Canada in 1973, bringing with them 22 former Westinghouse employees. The bold 1973 purchase has clearly paid off.

The company – which began as Linear Technology Inc. before renaming itself Gennum Corporation in 1987 to avoid confusion with a like-named firm – celebrated its 20th anniversary in 1993 as the dominant player in its markets, with revenue of $27.5 million.

Gennum surpassed this record revenue in 1994 when it achieved new revenue of $33.2 million and profits of $5.1 million, up from $4.2 million the previous year.

The company went public in 1982 and trades on the Toronto Stock Exchange under the symbol GND.

Operations are currently housed in two modern plants located in Burlington.

Gennum today employs more than 250 people who are highly skilled and experienced, the majority of whom are also shareholders in the company.

Gennum's quality systems achieved the Geneva-based International Organization for Standardization's ISO 9002 and ISO 9001 registrations in the 1990s, increasing the acceptability of its products and follow-up services in discriminating markets around the world.

Despite global profitability and a majority of sales made outside of Canada, Gennum is in no danger of outgrowing its Burlington location.

"We're comfortable here, we belong here, and this is where we intend to stay," notes Dr. Barber, who enjoys the area's quality of life and a dedicated local workforce while freely tapping into international markets. "We are a company that plays very carefully in what I call segmented markets," he adds.

"Whether you call them segmented or niches, we pick markets that have distinctive needs and we operate in the global market. We want to be playing in the total world market and we want to be a significant player in it. The areas that we have

• Products above are a typical cross-section of Gennum proprietary devices. Those in the foreground are principally for hearing instruments. The standard packages in the rear of the picture are for video and broadcast applications.

chosen are all in communications and information. I believe that area is going to continue to grow for quite some time."

Gennum devotes almost a quarter of its sales revenue to research and development. This commitment supports the company's innovative adaptation of existing technologies and the development of new products and processes.

Customer satisfaction is also a priority. It's a devotion that generates numerous one-to-one personal customer relations, a

devotion that finds staffers burning the midnight oil in Burlington to discuss business with customers in a distant time zone preparing for lunch.

And with all its success in integrated circuitry for hearing instruments and in video switching components, Gennum continues to explore new products and markets. Indeed, Gennum Corporation looks to the future with confidence as it prepares to meet tomorrow's challenges and opportunities.

A major part of Hamilton's history, Royal Bank continues to play a vital role in the city's present and future. In fact, Royal Bank has been serving the banking needs of Hamilton-area residents for generations. The Hamilton main branch is one of the bank's oldest branches in Ontario, with origins dating back to 1885.

During Hamilton's 1996 Sesqui year, Royal Bank celebrated its own milestone of 127 years in business. The bank's roots date back to the establishment of the Merchant Bank in Halifax in 1864.

In 1869, the company gained a charter as the Merchant Bank of Canada and by 1901 was renamed The Royal Bank of Canada with branches from coast to coast.

In 1987, Royal Bank acquired a majority interest in RBC-Dominion Securities and in 1993, merged with Royal Trust. Today, Royal Bank Financial Group is Canada's largest financial institution, offering a full range of financial services and products to approximately 10 million customers through one of the world's largest delivery networks.

Royal Bank operates in 35 countries, providing such services as corporate finance,

• Customer service and a commitment to the community are top priorities for Royal Bank and its employees. Royal Bank Financial Group has over 400 employees in Hamilton and many are actively involved in the community.
– Photo by David Gruggen

---

treasury products, residential mortgages, investment services, credit cards and loans.

In Hamilton alone, Royal Bank Financial Group has 20 facilities, including 16 Royal Bank branches, two Royal Trust branches, a business banking centre and an RBC-Dominion Securities office.

Royal Bank Financial Group employs more than 400 people in Hamilton, many of them actively involved in the community.

Terry Teeple, Royal Bank's Hamilton area manager, chaired the city's 1995 United Way campaign. Mr. Teeple and the employees are also involved year after year in the annual Chedoke-McMaster Children's Hospital fund-raising campaign.

Indeed, Royal Bank's commitment to the Hamilton community runs deep. In addition

to their key role in supporting local charities, a number of Royal Bank Financial Group employees, including Mr. Teeple, have been actively involved in the city of Hamilton's Sesquicentennial celebration.

And Joyce Morrison, manager of personal banking at the Locke and Main branch, organized the city's time capsule.

In 1992, Royal Bank employees issued a challenge to all banks in the Hamilton area to help the Hamilton Red Cross. Since then, bank employees in Hamilton participate annually in the Bank Challenge blood drive. The bank is also a strong supporter of Chedoke-McMaster Children's Hospital.

The company and its employees are also actively involved in a number of education organizations, including the Skills Canada competition, the Industry Education Council and a student exchange program.

Whether it's supporting local charities, participating in blood drives, organizing community events – or investing in the dreams of businesses and local citizens, Royal Bank Financial Group continues to play an enduring, supportive role in the Hamilton community.

Downtown Hamilton will always be home to Moore & Davis Limited. One of Canada's oldest insurance broker firms, it was founded August 26, 1858 on James Street N. at King Street by James Gage Davis and William Pitt Moore, a descendant of United Empire Loyalists.

Originally established as a real estate and insurance business, Moore & Davis would later evolve into today's highly successful general and life insurance brokerage.

But in the late 1850s, the young partnership was busy making its presence known in a downtown core of mud streets and horse-drawn carriages. Their office was in the very heart of a bustling city of fresh opportunities where hard work and $2,000 could buy a house with stables.

The little office was heated with wood stoves while the partners relied on oil lamps for light as they worked their way late into the evenings, dealing with the policies and concerns of a growing clientele.

In 1862, Moore & Davis moved a few doors down James Street to second-floor offices in the Lister Building at James and King William streets. Gas street lamps illuminated the city core at night. It would be another 16 years before the first telephone switchboard in the British Empire was

• Moore & Davis moved to a second floor office in the Lister Building in 1862 and stayed there for 114 years.

established just a few blocks south on James Street. After the partnership dissolved in 1882, the Moore family continued to own and operate Moore & Davis, with son William Ghent Moore joining as a partner.

Fred Moore, grandson of the founder, joined the firm in 1895 and remained active in the business into his 80s. His brother, Art Moore, also a partner, achieved fame as a halfback for the Hamilton Tigers, the rugby team which later merged with the Wild Cats to form the Hamilton Tiger-Cats Football Club. Football lore cites Art's spectacular running plays during Hamilton's 11-5 championship win over Montreal in 1906.

In 1976, after 114 years in the Lister Building, Moore & Davis moved south on James to a second-floor office in the Canada Permanent Building. By this time, the company was being operated by Ghent Moore and his brother, Kenneth.

Ghent Moore's son, David, was also working in the office, learning a business which brokers insurance through such insurers as Royal Insurance Co., (since

1882); Dominion Canada General Insurance Co. (founded by Canada's first Prime Minister Sir John A. MacDonald in 1887); Pilot Insurance Co.; Commercial Union Assurance; and Halifax Insurance Co. (since 1809 – Canada's oldest insurance firm).

Today, David Moore heads Moore & Davis, now located in eighth-floor offices on Hughson Street South. The firm has been solely involved in providing general and life insurance since 1981 when legislation required insurance brokers to specialize in that single profession.

Joined by his wife Janis, secretary-treasurer and a licensed broker, Mr. Moore is proud to continue operating from the heart of Hamilton. Children Krista and Mathew have also worked in the office, and Mathew intends to join the firm full-time one day.

With a computerized operation, allowing brokers to work from home, Moore & Davis has come a long way since 1858. But one thing hasn't changed – the firm continues to build on a tradition of serving generations of clients, such as Wm. Groves Limited and Ontario Auto Collision-CARSTAR.

"The downtown has survived some tough times," says Mr. Moore, "but it has always been possible to find success here and we're committed to staying in the core of this city."

• PasWord Communications Inc. has come a long way since its humble beginnings in 1961. Today, president Paul Lloyd oversees an operation that employs a total of 130 people at its offices in Hamilton and Toronto.
– Photo by David Gruggen

The personal touch seems harder to find these days. Even getting a telephone answered is often a task that's given over to a machine rather than a real live person.

PasWord Communications Inc. has been watching this trend over the years and has found a way to marry the efficiency of a machine to answer customers' phones with that personal touch that's so important to business communications.

Hamilton-based PasWord allows customers to choose between the latest voicemail technology to answer their phones and a live telereceptionist who is trained to sound just like a customer's own staff receptionist. Or they can choose service options which combine the two.

The company was founded in 1961 at the Professional Arts Building on James Street South, in a tiny, nine-foot-by-nine-foot room that is today used as a janitorial closet. Such were the humble beginnings of a highly successful company which today employs 130 people at its offices in Hamilton and Toronto.

Company president Paul Lloyd recalls the original office looked like something right out of a Lily Tomlin sketch with its cumbersome switchboard and jumble of heavy cords and plugs. This very small business was then known as Professional Answering Service, a name customers quickly shortened to PAS. The company provided off-site telephone answering, paging and message-taking services for firms and professionals spending a lot of time away from the phone.

But advancements in both technology and services provided by the company convinced Mr. Lloyd to change the company name in 1981 to PasWord Communications to reflect its expanded role as a provider of numerous telecommunication services.

"The whole business has evolved dramatically," says Mr. Lloyd. "We still answer phones on a computer and offer a full range of voice mail services but we're also benefitting from a consumer preference for live operators who can provide services more effectively than a machine."

A prime example of this, he observes, is the explosion of 1-800 services PasWord offers. These range from taking credit card orders over the phone to helping callers locate a client's nearest retail outlet. "And the calls could be from 30 to 3,000 miles away," adds Mr. Lloyd.

At the same time, the company continues to offer the industry staple: telephone answering and paging for busy people on the go.

But PasWord has gone a step beyond all of this by also offering remote receptionist services, giving clients the services of a PasWord telereceptionist who sounds just like a client's staff receptionist when taking calls, relaying messages, setting meetings and dispensing information.

"In some ways, things have come full circle. There's a backlash from people who are tired of listening to long automated voice menus," he says. "They want a live attendant to answer the phone. Our aim is to combine the technology with the skills of our people to give our customers the best of both worlds."

• Frank Silvestri
is the founder
and chaiman
of Silvestri
Investments.
He's flanked by
his son Paul, left,
and his son-in-
law Giulio Trulli.
*– Photo by
Joe Bucci*

Sometimes land parcels will lay dormant for 20 years before being developed, notes company founder and chairman Frank Silvestri.

Mr. Silvestri recalls just such a 20-year wait for a subdivision he developed in Burlington. "The rezoning alone, from industrial to residential, took seven years," he recollects, noting this housing development project, in a 100-acre land parcel in the Mainway and Walkers Line area, established Silvestri Investments as one of the biggest developers in the area.

By the mid 1990s, the development was under way with roadways. Plans called for the building of 230 apartment units, 180 single-family homes and eight acres of commercial development.

Among Silvestri Investments' many Hamilton developments is a subdivision on Upper Gage Avenue, north of Highway 53, which by the mid-1990s was starting a second building phase.

The successful company has also built subdivisions and developed lands in Ancaster, Fort Erie, Welland, Grimsby, Niagara Falls, Stoney Creek, Guelph, Kitchener and Waterloo.

Silvestri Investments has also built in Montreal, Florida and Houston, Texas.

"We started building in Houston 11 years ago," Mr. Silvestri recalls. "At a time when Houston was depressed and a lot of Americans were leaving the area, here you had a group of Canadians coming into Houston to invest."

From 1985 through 1991, Silvestri Investments bought up depressed Houston-area properties and remodelled and improved them. The firm sold its renovated office towers and rented out six luxury apartment buildings, each with 120 units. Impressed with the amount of investment and employment brought to his city, in 1993, the mayor proclaimed 'Frank Silvestri Day' in Houston.

Mr. Silvestri has also contributed to a number of worthy causes, including the Hamilton senior citizens' club Associazione Nazionale Combattenti E Reduci Sezione di Hamilton, Canada.

In 1994, the Italian government, in co-operation with Canada's federal government, proclaimed Mr. Silvestri a Cavaliere, the Italian equivalent of a knighthood. And this knight has built a stunning modern-day castle, home to himself and his wife Lea.

Set on 171 acres of greenery, the all-brick-and-stone, two-storey, 220-by-80-foot home is located off Highway 53.

Mr. Silvestri is ably assisted by his sons in running his company.

His eldest son Paul is president, son Danny is vice-president and son-in-law Giulio Trulli is also vice-president.

Secretaries Marie Memmolo and Angela Bartolomea also assist the firm, which subcontracts out most work.

The company intends to continue its patient strategy of acquiring lands for future development, building when the time is right, says Mr. Silvestri. "We'll continue developing land and building homes," he adds. "That is our future."

Chapter 3

McMaster University

The work of McMaster University professor Bertram N. Brockhouse dealt with what has been called "the definitive dance of the atoms" in the lattices of solids and liquids.

His fascination was a study of infinitesimal crystalline structures, ricocheting neutrons into the atomic nuclei of molecules. What he did was develop a way to view those atoms. That invention led to a Nobel Prize, the most prestigious tribute in the scientific world.

Were journalists schooled in the gyrations of atoms, it would still be presumptuous to condense the life's work of this nuclear physicist into a single sentence, especially in a subject beyond the scope of a layman's text. But what Dr. Brockhouse devised was a "microscope" to extract relevant observations about the dynamics of atoms, a discovery that led to our comprehension of materials – including high temperature superconductors. It was, for all the world, a textbook case of mind over matter – and science on the cutting edge.

Through research conducted in the 1950s and '60s with neutrons produced by fission in nuclear reactors, Dr. Brockhouse invented the triple-axis spectrometer. And that resulted in the discovery of the inner configuration of molecules.

With hindsight, "neutron scattering" proved revolutionary – if only because it allowed scientists to examine, in the most minute detail, the atomic structure of matter. It provided the building blocks with which to dismantle and re-construct the physical world. Thus, 40 years later, Dr. Brockhouse shared the 1994 physics prize of $1.25 million (Canadian) with Clifford Shull, the American professor of the Massachusetts Institute of Technology in Cambridge Mass., for individual contributions to a study of condensed atomic matter.

According to the Royal Swedish Academy of Sciences, the body which administers the award, "Clifford G. Shull has helped answer the question of where atoms are, and Bertram N. Brockhouse the question of what atoms do."

The 76-year-old Dr. Brockhouse, with his intense concentration and propensity to sing Gilbert and Sullivan tunes while conducting nuclear fission experiments, had taught at McMaster since 1961. A former chair of the University's physics department, he retired in 1984. Along with a host of other awards, in 1982 he became an officer of the Order of Canada, which recognizes an outstanding contribution to the fabric of our country.

Canada's 14th Nobel laureate since the 1923 award to insulin pioneer Sir Frederick Banting, Dr. Brockhouse accepted the diploma and the gold medal at a ceremony which was held in Stockholm's Concert House.

ABOVE: *Nobel Laureate Bertram N. Brockhouse is an Honourary Patron of Hamilton's Sesqui celebrations.*

RIGHT: *University Hall is one of McMaster University's six original buildings. The university's first charter rests in a copper tube buried in the building's cornerstone.*
— Photo by Dennis McGreal

I n many ways they're the builders' builder. Bono General Construction Ltd. builds the roads, sewers and holding tanks essential to any new housing development.

Before developers begin their newest subdivision, they call on Bono to build the necessary roads, sewers and other infrastructure for their land parcel.

And before the first basement is dug, the developers travel Bono-built roads in quiet admiration of a low-key company they've come to rely on to perform the crucial early building work needed for their subdivision to proceed.

Company founder Carmelo Bono left Italy for Canada in 1953 and quickly establishing himself in Hamilton, the nation's industrial heartland.

Mr. Bono worked for a number of employers the next few years, including construction contractor Cope & Sons and Stanley Steel, until a layoff convinced him it was time to act on a long-held dream of starting his own business.

Starting out as a one-man operation in 1958, Mr. Bono gradually built his business and within 10 years was already involved in installing roads, sewers and

• Bono General Construction founder Carmelo Bono is pictured above with his son Sam, who is OBN president and construction manager.
                        – Photo by Joe Bucci

tanks in subdivisions, establishing a reputation for dependable, high-quality workmanship. Bono also built several 12-foot diameter sewers in the Highway 53 and Nebo Road area in the late 1970s.

Bono also built 12-by-18-foot sanitary storm sewers at Upper Wentworth Street and Stone Church Road.

"We clear the land, put in sewers and services to the property line of the houses, and we have everything ready for the builder, who then comes in and does the rest," says Mr. Bono, whose company has also been a dedicated recycler of concrete, asphalt and stone since the late 1980s.

Today, much of the company's road work is performed by its OBN (a variation of Bono) division, headed by Mr. Bono's son Sam, who is OBN president and construction manager.

Bono General Construction is where you can find Mr. Bono's daughters Grace

Barrow, assistant office manager; and Carla Bono, office worker, along with his nephew, Joe Muraca, the office manager. They're among key members of the team pulling together at this family firm.

Although it occasionally subcontracts out speciality jobs, much of Bono's work is performed by its own workforce of up to 150 employees.

Company crews can often be seen performing paving, watermains and sewer installation work using Bono equipment, sometimes modified for particularly large projects. "We've done a lot of complicated and difficult jobs," recalls Mr. Bono, whose company built the $8-million, 110-metre diameter underground storage tank located beneath three acres of land at Greenhill Avenue in Hamilton's east end.

In Hamilton's 1996 Sesquicentennial year, Bono General Construction was busy performing many millions of dollars worth of construction work on a number of the city's main routes, including Sherman and Gage avenues.

"We'll expand more in the future," Mr. Bono confidently predicts, "and we're looking forward to getting involved in many more successful Hamilton projects."

MARKEY FAMILY FUNERAL HOMES LTD.

"We strive to serve with excellence those in our community who have suffered a loss." This mission statement is taken to heart by Lynne Lee, general manager of Markey Family Funeral Homes Ltd. which includes Cresmount and Markey-Dermody funeral homes.

"Experience is the key in fulfilling this mission statement," says Mrs. Lee. "Combined, our staff has over 150 years experience in service to Hamilton."

The handicapped-accessible funeral homes provide a Christmas memorial service for people who used the services of the homes during the year.

Mrs. Lee notes that the funeral home staff members have also taken pains to ensure the homes provide a "warm, friendly appearance, both inside and out, so that the families will feel as comfortable as if they were in their own homes."

Funeral director Paul Sakalauskas observes that many of the staff members are also life-long Hamilton residents who play an active role in supporting many community groups, service clubs and associations.

"The commitment to providing quality care and service is what our reputation is built on," explains Mr. Sakalauskas, whose views are shared by funeral director Jan Nichols, Markey-Dermody manager Rod Sturrock and Cresmount manager Bob VanLouwe. "The personal touch we offer is always most appreciated," he concludes.

That personal touch has been expanded in recent years to include both homes offering space for post-funeral receptions. These are places the bereaved can meet for fellowship and support without having to concern themselves with preparation or clean-up.

• Markey Family Funeral Homes includes Markey-Dermody funeral home, pictured above, and the Cresmount location, shown below.
– Photos by David Gruggen

And there is bereavement counselling at no added charge to the families.

"For the most part, people believe that once a funeral is over, the process of mourning has ended," notes Mrs. Lee.

"However, the grieving process may be a long and difficult one," she cautions.

"Recognizing this, Cresmount and Markey-Dermody funeral homes offer every family – at no additional cost – the services of a full-time bereavement counsellor," says Mrs. Lee. "It might mean chatting with a family at the funeral home or a telephone call. It may be as intense as ongoing home or office visits over many weeks or months."

"Our bereavement counsellor can also suggest other avenues of support in the Hamilton community," she adds, noting that the Cresmount Family Centre hosts monthly 'Living with Loss' presentations in an effort to provide support in a group setting.

The funeral homes also provide educational services concerning the subjects of death and funerals. Presentations are made to schools, agencies, organizations and church groups. Also available are tours of the funeral homes which feature extensive resource libraries dealing with grief and bereavement.

"Ultimately," asserts Mrs. Lee, "we strive to be attentive to the families we serve in offering quality, caring service."

• East Hamilton Radio, an East End landmark at the corner of Barton Street
and Kenilworth Avenue, has been serving the city for the past 65 years.
– Photo by Peter Haentjens

When East Hamilton Radio began in 1931, the founders probably had a dream that it would one day grow to be a successful family owned home entertainment business. Little did they know!

During the passing decades, the face of Hamilton has changed enormously, as has the vast variety of electronics products for homes and automobiles. In keeping with those changes, East Hamilton Radio, conveniently located at the corner of Barton Street and Kenilworth Avenue, has grown to become the city's premier source of home entertainment products.

There are many good reasons for East Hamilton Radio's success, but chief among them are the introduction of the latest innovations, the expertise of the sales staff, the service provided to customers, and low prices.

These traditions have succeeded in keeping East Hamilton Radio in business for 65 years, but the credit for making the company as big and well-known as it is belongs to President Ron Taillon.

When he came to work for the company in 1980, he introduced his own approach to doing business: In his first year, business grew by 470 per cent. After the first five years, business had grown 1,500 per cent. Four years later, in 1989, he bought the company and premises.

Mr. Taillon points out that his business philosophy is a simple one. "I tell my staff, 'The customer is your boss.' They always have to demonstrate their willingness to satisfy the customer."

East Hamilton Radio offers its customers everything from complete stereo systems to digital receivers, amps, speakers and CD players. The store also stocks TVs, VCRs, camcorders and satellite dishes and receivers.

The range of products on the shelves is impressive: The best in brand-name audio and video – Sony, NAD, Pioneer, Pioneer Elite Series, Panasonic, Technics, Denon, Rockford Fosgate, Carver, Sharp, ADCOM, Fisher, Sanyo, Monster Cable, Polk Audio, Signet and Paradigm.

But home entertainment isn't the only area of expertise – the store's technicians are renowned for their award-winning car audio installations.

East Hamilton Radio also has a large selection of the finest in audio receivers, amplifiers and speakers for cars and trucks – and an expert installation staff.

A car audio system installed by one of the store's technicians was named among the Top Twenty Best Car Audio Systems in the world for 1995 by the American magazine Mobile Sound Competition. East Hamilton Radio is also one of only 18 Pioneer I.C.E. (In Car Excitement)

dealers of premium car audio products in Canada. That means that the store is able to sell top-of-the-line Pioneer items not available at other stores.

Because East Hamilton Radio is a family business, Mr. Taillon says he thinks of his staff as family too, because they spend so much time together working with him, his wife Maggie and son David.

"I'm grateful that we've been able to attract and develop the best staff in the industry. But you also have to show staff that you care for them," he says. "And because this is a 'people' business, when you have contented staff you'll have contented customers."

Ron Taillon the businessman is proud of his store's Hamilton location, and says that the area is a more diversified and prosperous marketplace than its old reputation suggests.

Proof of this can be found not only in the corporations which come to Hamilton for raw materials, services and finished goods, but the number of customers who come to his store from as far away as Toronto, London and Niagara Falls.

Mr. Taillon's approach to life – hard work, a square deal and optimism – is a reflection of Hamilton's attitude through the good times and the bad. "I hope the city's profile will evolve to get the credit it really deserves," he says.

• Flek Fire Systems president and general manager Tom Cole, right, is pictured with his wife Heather and staff members at the company office on Lancing Drive in Hamilton.
– Photo by David Gruggen

F ire! The word alone can cause business executives to cringe when they think of expensive equipment getting damaged in a sudden blaze.

Indeed, an after-hours fire can build slowly, causing horrific damage before alarms can be responded to.

But Flek Fire Systems is bringing peace of mind to a growing number of commercial and industrial customers, from McDonald's to Procter & Gamble.

Tom Cole, president and general manager of Flek, says his Hamilton-based company has built a solid business inspecting, installing and testing fire suppression systems for grateful clients.

"There's a growing demand for the services we provide," notes Mr. Cole, whose Hamilton Mountain company experienced a tenfold increase in business in the five years following 1990.

Mr. Cole notes that Flek's main source of revenue, accounting for about 60 per cent of its business, is the installation, inspection and testing of kitchen exhaust systems. Contained in kitchen grill hoods, they react to the extreme heat of a fire,

releasing an extinguishing agent which puts out flames quickly and efficiently.

The next largest part of the company's business lies in the sale, servicing, testing and recharging of fire extinguishers.

Yet another key part of the business is a system that has proven especially effective protecting sensitive computer equipment from heat and smoke damage.

On detecting fire, the system sounds an alarm, giving anyone present enough time to leave the room. An extinguishing agent is released in a gaseous cloud, quickly consuming the oxygen in the room and suppressing the flames.

Mr. Cole notes his company has developed a solid business relationship with McDonald's Restaurants of Canada Ltd.

"We've installed our systems in the

vast majority of McDonald's outlets in Ontario and we even installed one in an outlet in Newfoundland. McDonald's outlets in Walmart stores are also giving us a new source of income."

Mr. Cole is a former Stelco employee who worked part-time for a fire protection firm during the Stelco strike of 1980.

This sparked an interest in the business and he began taking an evening fire protection course at Mohawk College in the early 1980s. While enrolled at the college, Mr. Cole met Jack Kelf, who had founded Flek in 1980 as a one-man operation from his Burlington home. The company name is Kelf spelled backwards.

Mr. Cole bought the company in 1985 and has since expanded it into a 2,400-square-foot location on Lancing Drive, employing a staff of seven.

"We would like to expand into other fire protection services such as alarms and sprinkler systems," says Mr. Cole.

"And our goal," he explains, "is to continue being a leader in all of the fire protection services we provide to our industrial and commercial customers."

ABOVE: *Education comes first, but there's still plenty of fun to be had on campus, as this colourful group of students shows.*

FACING PAGE: *A familiar sight on campus, students relaxing and enjoying the outdoors during a break from their studies.*

While it's the first Nobel Prize for McMaster, Dr. Brockhouse is by no means the only celebrity among the grads and faculty, past or present. Among the distinguished roster of alumni and professors is astronaut Roberta Bondar, the first Canadian female to orbit the earth.

Circling the globe at a blistering pace of eight kilometres a second, Dr. Bondar performed a series of experiments aboard the space shuttle Discovery. She touched down with much more than a log of statistics and figures.

Awed by the vision of Earth looming in the distance, the payload specialist (a NASA term for an on-board scientist) carried with her the message of preserving the planet.

Former Ontario Lieutenant Governor Lincoln Alexander came from the halls of McMaster, as did scores of doctors, scientists, professors and business people. Mac's medical school has been the model for medical schools throughout the world.

McMaster earned top marks as the most innovative university in the country, according to a 1994 survey by Maclean's magazine. In its fourth annual ranking of post-secondary institutions the publication conducted "hundreds of phone calls, dozens of meetings and then used a consulting statistician to compile the data. Considered the nation's most "comprehensive" and "accessible" survey – especially in a once impenetrable fraternity – Maclean's formulated several dozen questions that calculated 20 indicators of quality in half a dozen areas, from student body to class size and from finances to faculty.

The magazine interviewed 1,040 public leaders, the country's decision makers: from corporate CEOs to academic administrators and high school guidance counsellors from coast to coast.

Deciphering the results is a complicated process, requiring almost a degree in itself. But not only did Mac take the honours for innovation in what's called the "reputation" category, its fourth in as many years, it also took third in that section for producing the finest crop of "Leaders of Tomorrow" – those graduates most likely to succeed. McMaster also placed fifth in the section on universities with medical schools and a broad range of PhD programs.

(It's worth noting that McMaster University had the highest grades for most faculty members holding PhDs; and was among the top medical/doctoral universities with a major commitment to PhD programs and research).

In keeping with McMaster's reputation for innovation, and producing "Leaders of Tomorrow," nowhere is that map of the future more tangible than in the two undergrad "theme schools," International Justice and Human Rights, and New Materials and Their Impact on Society. Opened in September of 1993, the theme schools demonstrated Mac's pledge to innovation, self-directed learning and interdisciplinary studies.

• From left Dino Mendoza, Doug Ing, and Tak Chan of Comtronic Computer are shown on-site with a client during another successful network installation.
– Photo by David Gruggen

Computer clones had only been in existence for a few years when a young Tak Chan caught the edge of a new wave that would wash across the western world.

"The Personal Computers industry is a young industry that did not really exist before 1980," notes Mr. Chan. "And PC clones have only existed since around 1984," he explains.

In April of 1987, Mr. Chan formed a partnership with some friends to seize the business opportunities inherent in a variation of computer technology then in its infancy. The result was Comtronic Computer Centre, a versatile business which began as a computer wholesaler.

It now provides consultant services and software packages, assembles customized IBM-compatible computers to specific needs and offers complete systems and network solutions to corporate customers. And the company boldly began business by opening three outlets simultaneously.

"It was a gamble," acknowledges Mr. Chan, adding that he has benefitted from business experience and from having the good fortune of investing in an industry which has experienced steady growth even during recessions.

The first three outlets – in Toronto, Markham and London – were joined in 1988 by a fourth outlet at Upper Gage and Fennell avenues in Hamilton.

By the mid-1990s, Mr. Chan's one-man outlet had grown to include eight employees, sales had quadrupled and the customer base was expanding rapidly from customer referrals.

"We are very fortunate," Mr. Chan says, "to have survived the recession and to have grown the way we have."

"The whole company has also found many opportunities and has grown substantially," notes Mr. Chan, adding, "we started out as a wholesaler but we've become a service company as well."

Indeed, Comtronic Computer Centre prides itself in custom-fitting computers to each customer's needs. The company will also install computers on-site and provide tutorial lessons on request.

By the mid-1990s, Comtronic Computer Centre had grown to a total of eight outlets across Canada, including outlets located in Atlantic Canada, Quebec and British Columbia.

"Our company is growing slowly but steadily by adapting to changing customer needs," explains Mr. Chan.

"Our goal," he adds, "is to continue to help our company grow by expanding the services we offer our customers."

• *Tak Chan, Doug Ing and Dino Mendoza are partners in Comtronic Computer Centre, which has outlets in Toronto, Markham, London and Hamilton.*
         – Photo by David Gruggen

• Win, lose or draw, there's always tremendous support for McMaster University's sports teams. In 1995, four of the Marauder varsity teams finished in the top 10 in the country and 18 of the university's athletes were named all-Canadian. Below, the crowd cheers on the Marauder football team while, at left, a Mac football player studies the game from the sidelines while waiting to take his turn on the field.

W ith upwards of 15,000 students, a budget of $350 million and some $76 million generated annually in national and international research grants, Mac is one of the largest employers in Hamilton-Wentworth.

In July of '95, Dr. Peter George took over as president and vice-chancellor. A former professor and dean of social sciences, the Dundas resident sought a leave of absence from McMaster in 1991 to head the Council of Ontario Universities.

His return signals a new era, one that starts with shaping a new vision for McMaster, a navigational guide which will chart the course into the 21st century. Mac has been touted as a headquarters for a United Nations research and training centre specializing in water, environment and health issues. It would be the first of its kind in North America and one of only five around the world. The UN's other centres are natural resources in Ghana, new technologies in The Netherlands; economic research in Finland and software technology in Macau. The project is contingent on government funding approval.

Mac's International Network on Water, Environment and Health would feed seven satellite centres in post-secondary schools across the province, such as Carleton and Waterloo. Relevant data would be transferred to developing countries.

Another "feather in the cap" of both the university and the community, in the words of David Ludwin, professor and associate dean of research in health sciences, was a recent $10 million award from the federal government to develop a national network of centres of excellence in health research.

Designed to streamline costs, make Canada's health care system more efficient and still maintain quality, the project will be led by Dr. George Browman, professor and chair of clinical epidemiology and biostatistics in Mac's faculty of health sciences. With private sector partnerships, the results could be a model marketed to other countries.

One of the areas to examine will be diagnostic, rehabilitative and therapeutic services, where up to three-quarters of health care dollars are spent with questionable success.

• *'Man Releasing Eagles' is a popular landmark on campus.*

• *Judy Marsales and members of her real estate team regularly hold bi-weekly meetings of the company's two offices at the Royal Hamilton Yacht Club.*
– Photo by Joe Bucci

In January 1988, with a sales force of six people, Judy Marsales Real Estate Ltd. had its modest beginnings in half of a Westdale Village storefront operation near McMaster University.

Within the same year, the growing company took over the remaining half of the building, which it continues to operate with its numbers expanded to more than 20 people. The company's distinctive navy and white signs with their bold metallic gold 'M' monogram are today a familiar sight throughout the Hamilton-area real estate market.

The group's success is due in part to the friendly neighbourhood environment of its location, where members of the public feel free to drop by and chat informally as they stroll through the village.

As a natural extension of the west-end location, a Dundas branch office was opened in July of 1995. Close ties are maintained between the two groups, which share regular meetings chaired by

Judy Marsales, business broker-owner and a highly successful salesperson in her own right. Ms Marsales continues to provide hands-on direct leadership to her sales team through intense, one-on-one sales training and weekly sales meetings where, with seemingly limitless enthusiasm, she inspires her representatives.

With an emphasis on the group approach, there exists an open working atmosphere among the salespeople as well as a strong sense of loyalty to the firm.

The main objective of this group is to live up to its motto to "do the best job possible in assisting the general public with its real estate needs," and emphasize business ethics and consumer rights.

Ms Marsales achieved immediate success when she entered the business in 1980. Feeling the need to run her own show, she set up her own firm on a modest budget and has overseen its steady progress ever since.

Needing yet another challenge, in 1991

Ms Marsales became the first female president of the Metropolitan Hamilton Real Estate Board after having served on a number of board committees. She and her company continue to be outspoken advocates for the advancement of professionalism in the real estate industry.

In 1996, Ms Marsales became president of the Hamilton and District Chamber of Commerce during the city's Sesquicentennial year. It's a job she approaches with enthusiasm.

As an ardent booster of Hamilton, Ms Marsales hopes to apply the same team approach used in her company to solve some of the city's problems and to encourage both business and culture.

In addition to her own community involvement, she encourages her sales staff in their many volunteer and community commitments which include Meals on Wheels, Heart & Stroke Foundation, Hamilton Entertainment and Convention Facilities Inc. and Opera Hamilton.

ANGUS EMPLOYMENT LTD.

A t Angus Employment Ltd., success is measured on the strength of a time-honoured maxim: "Treat all persons with the same respect and courtesy with which one expects to be treated and you can never go wrong," says John Stewart, company president.

"This is especially true when you're in the recruitment business," he adds, "because you are dealing with one of the most fundamental human needs – to make a decent living from the strengths, abilities and skills one possesses."

Mr. Stewart is proud of his "golden rule," which he and the Angus recruitment specialists live by. They must be doing something right: In 1996 Angus Employment marked its 30th anniversary in the employment business – and the prospects look better than ever.

"We succeed because we put people first," explains Mr. Stewart. "In our agency, the priority is in fitting the right person to the right job in the right company. We're not satisfied until our clients are – and that includes both the employers and the job-seeking candidates."

Mr. Stewart elaborates: "We are a matchmaker, if you will. It's not an exact science, but you can achieve great satisfaction by connecting employers and candidates if you just take the time to learn what their respective needs are."

The process begins when Mr. Stewart, or a member of his team of professionals, takes a job order from an employer.

Mr. Stewart takes the time to develop an in-depth company profile and to understand the personal and professional dynamics of that employer. Only then can he begin to screen prospective candidates, confident in the knowledge that he understands exactly what type of person the employer requires.

"Quite often, the initial interviewing process between employer and applicant is reduced to a check list of superficial attributes as each tries to impress the other," notes Mr. Stewart. "It's what I call the 'Dance of the Peacocks.' It is superficial and achieves nothing," he says.

"You can't make an informed choice on a candidate based on a resume and a brief interview," he explains. "I see it every day. Often some very bright, capable people don't market themselves well on paper, or become tongue-tied in the pressure of a first interview.

"Yet, they may be the most reliable, hard-working individuals you could ever hope to come across," he adds. "We take the time to develop a relationship with all our applicants so that when an employer calls us for a referral we know exactly whom we're marketing."

Mr. Stewart is an experienced 'match-

maker' who is usually successful. But in those rare cases when the match doesn't work out, Angus offers a replacement guarantee: If an employee leaves or is terminated, Angus will replace the individual at no charge. It's no wonder that Angus is the longest-established employment agency in Hamilton.

Over the years, clients have come to rely on Angus' ethics and unimpeachable professionalism. Mr. Stewart and his team are skilled at filling positions from temporary contract positions to full-time, permanent placements at all levels.

Whenever companies have a position to fill, they call on Angus.

• John Stewart is the president of Angus Employment Ltd., a firm that has been successfully fitting 'the right person to the right job in the right company' for more than 30 years.
– Photo by David Gruggen

Chapter 4

Sports & Recreation

Oskee Wee Wee
Oskee Wa Wa
Holy Mackinaw!
Tiger-Cats
Eat 'em raw

It was said they had exhausted their nine lives – these Tiger-Cats of ours: That our famous roar had dulled to a whimper in the face of mounting debts and dwindling crowds. The Canadian Football League bosses went so far as to decree euthanasia – a shot to put us out of our misery.

In December of 1994, the Grinches that would steal Christmas issued an ultimatum; either pack those stands and stock the coffers or we'll close down the game.

They knew not the grit of Steeltown, nor our long love affair with the black and gold; a club that sprang from the 1869 campaign and clawed its way into our hearts. No, this city boasts a rich tradition of gridiron glory and raw guts.

And never was it more evident than after this threat to revoke the franchise. In one of the worst recessions to hit this country, Tabbie fans dug deep into their pockets and went the distance in a last-quarter drive to notch a record 15,000 season tickets sold and more than $1 million in corporate donations.

"I'm overwhelmed," said a relieved Roger Yachetti, chairman of the board, and the man who quarterbacked the club to victory in a community-based ownership group and limited partnership that was headed by investor David Macdonald.

No one summed it up better than Mayor Robert Morrow. "This," he said, "was a great success story. People were just amazed. We weren't. Because we know we have done it in so many ways over the years."

It's a story typifying the esprit de corps of the Ambitious City.

❑ ❑ ❑ ❑

But the cheerleading wasn't confined to corporate pledges and charitable donations – or to crowds jostling for season's seats at the front ticket office, streaming through the Balsam Avenue North gates and snapping up T-shirts at the Roarrr store.

The hand that moved the city reached all the way into the heart of Los Angeles, stirring a comedian and movie star who still nurtured a warm spot for his boyhood heroes.

A s much a fan as the late John Candy was to the Toronto Argonauts, so Martin Short is to the Tiger-Cats – minus, of course, the ownership investment.

Short is an SCTV alumnus and Hollywood icon; a confrere of legends the likes of that "wild and crazy guy" Steve Martin and "Christmas Vacation" star Chevy Chase.

In 1993 Short became a member of the distinguished Order of Canada.

At the ceremony, among the crowd of dignitaries, he was heard to remark: "Boy, am I out of my league!" But through decades of fame, he still dotes on the Tabbies, a passion that dates back to his Steeltown roots.

He even aired humourous sketches on the beloved 'Cats during his short-lived comedy series and explained the dynamics of the CFL on the David Letterman show. Informed that two clubs had a Rough Rider moniker – albeit one abbreviated to a single word – Letterman quipped: "We don't have two teams called the Packers in this country. You only have eight teams. It's not like you've used up all the names."

But aside from the hilarity, there was still a matter of debts and jilted creditors in Tiger Town.

And when the football club dropped the ball in the financial arena, it was Martin who partially recovered the fumble with a fund-raising dinner and auction. The hometown hero was lured back to Hamilton on April Fool's day in 1995 for a tribute headlined "A Short Affair."

Among the audience were gridiron greats like Angelo Mosca, or "Big Ang" to his fans, Bernie Faloney, Neil Lumsden, Willie Bethea, Dave Marler, Reg Wheeler, Wally Zatylny; and current Tiger-Cats coach Don Sutherin.

When Short, sporting a tux and his trademark tousled hair, bounded down the centre aisle at the Convention Centre, the 1,200 guests raised a montage of Ed Grimley masks, like bleachers of fans bearing placards at a Grey Cup intermission.

Master of Ceremonies singer Ian Thomas – a boyhood chum who once came to fisticuffs with his Grade 4 buddy – related rollicking schoolyard tales. Later in the program, event organizers Marnie and Larry Paikin, longtime family friends, received an autographed Tabby helmet. But the fun had just begun.

ABOVE: *Colourful characters, like this furry fan, add to the ambience during Hamilton Tiger-Cat home games.*

FACING PAGE: *Game action between the Tiger-Cats and the Edmonton Eskimos at Ivor Wynne Stadium.*
– Photos by John Sokolowski

PAGES 92-93: *The Hamilton Reps minor peewee AAA hockey team was one of 16 city rep teams to call the Chedoke Twin Pad Arena home for the 1995-96 season. Opened in April of 1993, the $10-million facility, on the city's west Mountain, boasts two rinks, including an Olympic-size ice surface. Some 5,000 hockey players, from house league to rep, use the facility each week.*
– Photo by Bob Chambers

• Hamilton Mountain Bowl, located on Stone Church Road, boasts 60 10-pin lanes. The 54,000-square-foot facility also features a lounge overlooking the lanes and a video arcade.
– Photo by David Gruggen

T he Brooks family knew very little about bowling when they arrived in Canada. But they certainly threw a strike when they built the successful Hamilton Mountain Bowl.

Phillip Brooks, part-owner and general manager of the busy bowling centre, recalls immigrating to Canada from Jamaica in 1974 – and watching people bowl for the first time. "Coming from Jamaica, I had never seen bowling before," recollects the Oakville resident. "I decided to try bowling – but I wasn't very good at it," he says with a chuckle.

"But bowling seemed to be a good business investment opportunity," adds Mr. Brooks, recalling he was impressed with the large crowds and steady business at a bowling alley in Oakville he had visited shortly after arriving in Canada.

An investment decision was made: Mr. Brooks' father, Clive Brooks, established Burlington Bowl in 1975. "It looked like a good business to be in and it was – and still is," says Phillip Brooks.

Three years later, they sold this busi-ness to build Hamilton Mountain Bowl.

The business is also partly owned by two silent partners, Philip Brooks' brother Cary who operates a thoroughbred race horse business in Florida and Laurie Silvera, a thoroughbred horse trainer.

Located on Stone Church Road East, Hamilton Mountain Bowl features 60 10-pin bowling lanes in its cavernous, 54,000-square-foot premises.

The facility employs approximately 25 people, some of whom have been with the company since its Burlington years. These long-standing employees include manager John Dowell and mechanic Brad Male.

Also featured at Hamilton Mountain Bowl, in a lounge overlooking the lanes, are five dart boards and three pool tables.

You can also find a video arcade in this facility, which provides a wide choice of entertainment pursuits in addition to the mainstay attraction of bowling.

"More than 30 bowling league teams regularly meet here," Mr. Brooks says of the large facility, which also features a restaurant-snack bar. It's a favourite site for birthday parties and special events. Hamilton Mountain Bowl offers a number of birthday and special day package deals for individuals and companies.

Hamilton Mountain Bowl is active in the greater Hamilton community: The company is a major supporter of Big Brothers and many other worthy causes, including Chedoke-McMaster Hospitals and the Canadian Arthritis Society, which is the recipient of funds raised through the company's Bowlathon.

"We strongly believe in giving back to the community," says Mr. Brooks.

It all adds up to a successful approach that's most evident every time throngs of bowlers create the familiar din of crashing pins at Hamilton Mountain Bowl.

• As company president, Ian Leppert is today the driving force behind Leppert Business Systems. Founded by his parents, Peggy and Richard, the company is located at the corner of King and Dundurn streets in the city's west end.
– Photo by David Gruggen

When it comes to buying expensive computer equipment, the lowest price can be much less important than effective service and expertise.

That's the philosophy of Leppert Business Systems Inc., a Hamilton-based firm which adds same-day service calls and consultations to the computers, photo copiers and other office equipment it leases to business clients around the Golden Horseshoe.

"The most rewarding relationships are when we're able to bring the client to a fuller understanding of the technology so he can utilize it more effectively," explains company president Ian Leppert, whose firm employs 25 people at its spacious King West and Dundurn streets headquarters.

"We feel it's our major strength," he adds, noting his firm's technicians will at times cure a computer virus, solve operating problems, perform remote diagnostics or bring about maximum connectivity by connecting a personal computer to a wider, multifaceted network.

"It's an important part of our business, because 85 per cent of all corporate PCs are on a network," asserts Mr. Leppert, who is assisted at the company by his wife Lori,

who handles everything from the keeping of a client data base to running the sales desk and problem solving.

"We research a client's problems and needs and find solutions," Mr. Leppert points out. "We're doing more and more consultative work and it's value-added as part of the lease. The customer receives a real benefit from this, usually within a four-hour response time – even though we're not always the lowest-priced company."

Mr. Leppert notes his firm also offers special leases allowing clients who require the latest technology to easily upgrade to the newest advanced equipment without penalty.

"One way we do this is though our cost-per-copy photo copier leases," he says. "The client will pay so many cents per copy and can upgrade to a better machine costing perhaps half a cent a copy more."

As the constantly evolving office equipment market shifts from analog to digital machines, keeping up with technology can be a challenge. Mr. Leppert says after years of relatively few advancements, some photocopiers are now multi-function machines.

For example, Konica has produced a photocopier which can copy both sides of

a sheet of paper simultaneously. It produces 50 copies a minute and can operate with a high-speed laser printer. The machine also staples, three-hole punches and collates. It can also fax, e-mail and scan a document back to a personal computer.

"The only problem we have with it," deadpans Mr. Leppert, "is trying to decide if we should still call it a photocopier."

Now building a reputation for its networking, consultation, leasing and servicing of advanced office equipment, Leppert's roots actually date back to 1936 with the founding of Herb Blake Office Machines, a typewriter sales and repair firm.

Mr. Blake sold the business in 1975 to Mr. Leppert's parents, Peggy and Richard Leppert, who built up the business over 20 years. Richard Leppert brought the Magna Carta to Hamilton and was active in other community causes, including the Rotary Club and Hamilton and District Chamber of Commerce. He continues to play an active role in sales at the profitable firm.

Ian Leppert notes the family firm has changed dramatically over the years. "We hardly sell any typewriters now. We're focused on offering new technology."

• Lakeport Brewing Corp. has grown steadily since being founded in 1992. The company currently employs more than 130 people and there have been many expansions at the Burlington Street East brewery since it first opened.
– Photo by David Gruggen

This is no small beer. Lakeport Brewing Corp. is a fast-growing Hamilton brewery with international appeal. And it produces enough beer to slake an international thirst.

Popular brands include Dave Nichol's Personal Selection Light, Strong, Regular and Ice; Dave's International Selection Doppelgold and Hollander; Laker Premium Lager, Laker Premium Light, Ice Strong and Dry; Pabst Blue Ribbon; Lone Star; Master Choice Strong and Master Choice Cold Filtered; Lakeport

Pilsener; and Truly Naked, which was launched in the fall of 1995.

Add to this impressive list four brands available in the United States, including Laker Canadian Lager, Laker Ice Canadian Lager, Barrington Red, and Truly Canadian – a beer made with sparkling clear Canadian water and barley from the prairie provinces and featuring an illustration of Canada's first Prime Minister, Sir John A. MacDonald.

It's all something of an enduring tribute to the entrepreneurial drive and

imagination of William Sharpe, who founded Lakeport in March 1992, when he acquired the former Amstel Canada brewery from Heineken Group of Amsterdam.

Since making that fateful acquisition, Mr. Sharpe, a former Carling-O'Keefe and Molson breweries executive, has initiated a number of expansions at his Burlington Street East brewery, taking it from a total of 80 employees to more than 130 in just four years.

"We now have 100 brands and package sizes," notes Mr. Sharpe, whose brewery has built on additions giving it the total potential capacity to produce 7.7 million cases of 24 annually, although current demand levels are for four million cases.

Yet for all its international acclaim, Lakeport is very much a home brewing company, remaining vitally active in the Hamilton community.

Through its Pabst Blue Ribbon brand, Lakeport has also been an enthusiastic supporter of the CFL Hamilton Tiger-Cats throughout the 1990s.

And this mid-sized brewery keeps on growing and growing. "Since we've taken over the brewery, we've increased capacity 300 per cent," notes Mr. Sharpe.

"And we hope to take it to full capacity," adds Mr. Sharpe, whose firm also sells bottled and canned Private Selection beer products at Ralph's Supermarkets in California, Arizona, Illinois and New Mexico, with new state markets opening up due to mergers between Ralph's and other grocery stores.

Lakeport is also working with a United Kingdom brokerage firm to sell its beer in four-packs in British grocery stores.

It's all heady growth for a brewery some industry observers felt was in trouble after Labatt Brewing Co. won its former President's Choice beer contract.

"About 50 per cent of our business was lost overnight," explains Mr. Sharpe, who began offering new brands to rebuild from the loss of PC beer.

"We've recovered from that – and we move fast enough to make the big brewers nervous," he adds.

The brewery is currently filling 1,000 bottles per minute and may soon hit the 1,400-bottle mark – the maximum speed capable by the line.

Russ Hutchings, Lakeport vice-president sales and marketing, notes Dave's Doppelgold is a low-key, Bavarian-style beer and solid performer that has "sales that are five times our expectations."

Mr. Hutchings also observes that Dave's Hollander Dutch-style beer is gaining market share, while Laker Canadian Lager and Laker Ice Canadian are now being sold in Michigan, Pennsylvania and New York. Canadian beer, equally priced to some U.S. brands and in returnable bottles, now accounts for a third of all beer sold in some states.

"We're also selling beer in California – and we hope to be in Florida by the end of summer," adds Mr. Hutchings, also noting that Lakeport is again selling its Norois and Norois Dry brands in Quebec's Metro-Richelieu grocery stores after a lengthy court battle against the Canadian beer giants.

The Lakeport brands have already captured approximately 2 per cent of the

Quebec beer market, Mr. Hutchings says, while adding that much of this growth is driven by Lakeport's dual commitment to high quality and good pricing.

Lakeport's Laker Premium Lager sold for $12.50 a case of 12 in 1996, a savings of approximately $2.50 per case from what national brands were charging.

"Our prices are considerably lower – but we don't compromise on quality," asserts Mr. Sharpe. "People want a great-tasting beer as well as reasonable prices," he adds, "and Lakeport prides itself in delivering – on both counts."

• Lakeport Brewing Corp. has made a case for its beer through commitment to high quality and good pricing. Laker Dry Premium Lager is just one of the many popular Laker brands.
– Photo by David Gruggen

On the auction block were some two dozen pieces of memorabilia signed by the denizens of tinseltown – stars of screen and sports. Among them was a pair of Wayne Gretzky autographed sticks from the game in which he scored his 802nd NHL career goal. Under the hammer of Toronto actor Harvey Atkin – and his resonant staccato prompting – they alone fetched a fancy price of $2,200. A corporate box for a Tiger-Cat game with Martin Short hit a record $4,200.

And we'll remember these words: "Hi. My name is Forrest. Forrest Gump." Not just because of the Academy Award-winning performance. No, a Forrest Gump poster on which Oscar winner Tom Hanks had penned "Save The Tiger-Cats" was picked up for $3,000 by lawyer and club chairman of the board, Roger Yachetti. And, that's not all. Hanks, the Best Actor who parlayed innocence, a poverty of intellect, but a richness of heart into national heroism, matched that amount with a subsequent cheque for $3,000 – in U.S. funds, no less.

When the final gavel hit the podium with a resounding thud, the auction, tallied with an earlier silent version and a sale of commemorative T-Shirts – reaped a windfall $36,000. Teamed with the proceeds from the capacity crowd paying $125 a plate, the evening raised $100,000 for unsecured creditors.

As the clock ticked past midnight, Mayor Bob Morrow sat down to tickle the ivories as Short belted out an impromptu Steeltown ditty, and then a rousing ode to the Tabbies.

Before bidding au revoir, "Marty" as we had come to know him, added a final thought: "One's identity comes from your city. And this city's identity is very much tied with the Tiger-Cats." And it was as if he had never said goodbye.

❏ ❏ ❏ ❏

Now, in the sesquicentennial of our days, we'll host the Grey Cup festivities – having beaten out Baltimore by a whisker.

We've spruced up Ivor Wynne Stadium; primping and preening like a Cat for what is now an international audience. This December 8, we are no longer plagued by the ghosts of Christmas Past. For we are the face of the future – with a hail and hearty, "Oskee Wee Wee. Eat 'em raw."

That's nine lives down, Mr. CFL, and another thousand to go.

There was only one person missing when they christened Copps Coliseum in November of 1985. There was a platform swollen with dignitaries and a room bursting with VIPs. But the name on everyone's lips was the same one that graced everything from the flashing electronic scoreboard to the flourish of letters at centre ice – the double-barreled C for the man who made the dream a reality: Victor Kennedy Copps.

Almost a decade had passed since the annual Around The Bay road race in which Vic collapsed. In this, the culmination of his vision, he remained at his Fairfield Avenue residence – unable to attend the coliseum's debut.

A past master of the ad-libbed one-liner, Vic revelled in the stage. His 1963 inaugural speech "Hats off to the Past, Coats off to the Future," with a theme of rolling up sleeves, and shoulders to the wheel, elicited guffaws of laughter that were music to his ears. On that solemn occasion, he recalled an earlier swearing-in ceremony in which the orchestra struck up the unlikely melody, "Go Feather Your Nests."

Vic was 20 years ahead of his time. In his maiden term he addressed the basic issues that affected the residents; issues like hospital care, job retraining, low-rent housing, elimination of bureaucratic duplication. His mayoralty was a study in the open door policy. In 1965 he described our present society as if he had been whisked through a time machine. He outlined our transportation corridors, right down to the proposed monorail system. To the incredulity of his councillors, he predicted the coming of the computer and the electronic age, and the Third Wave a la Alvin Toffler that would replace industrial society.

One of his pet projects was urban renewal, along with the construction of recreational amenities. To that end he pledged us an arena that would put us "back into big league hockey after an absence of almost 50 years."

With his thinning gray hair, cherubic grin, and mile-wide humanitarian streak, Copps could have been mistaken for an easy mark. But he attacked a dare with a bulldog tenacity that became his trademark.

"Everything was a Mount Everest. It had to be climbed. And he had to do it," recalled Jack Jones, the retired executive assistant to four consecutive mayors. "I remember the mayor of Flint, Michigan, challenged him to a game of ping pong. He accepted. And for weeks we were over at the Y playing ping pong. And he had the experts over there teaching him."

In the early 1970s, Vic opposed the two-tier system. Assured that the matter wouldn't be raised at Queen's Park without some advance notification, off he went to a municipal association meeting at Trent University, sending his driver, Tom Durney, back to Hamilton.

"Jack Jones called me," recalls Durney. "He told me to go to Toronto and pick up the Mayor. I asked him what he was talking about: I dropped him off at Peterborough this morning."

Suspicious that his adversaries had rigged the out-of-town seminar to eliminate his objections, Copps had hailed a cab, sped to the legislature, and chained himself to the gallery, eloquently expressed his stance, and eventually was bodily evicted.

"There was nobody that had more interest in this city, and nobody worked harder, longer hours than Vic Copps," said Durney. "I know because I was there. He had the vision of the (Canadian Football) Hall of Fame (and Museum) . . . He convinced the (Hamilton) Board of Education to put their building downtown. He raised money for Hamilton Place. If he accomplished one, he had another going the next day. He never got discouraged. He could always see the bright side. But most of all he could always see the funny side."

Vic also had a quiet side. He never revealed a secret, never betrayed a confidence. He was the first and foremost guy who cared deeply about others.

Says his widow Geraldine: "He could have papered his room with IOUs. I gather he was 'the touch.' If anyone who needed money came into his office, they always came out with a couple of bucks, no questions asked."

Vic had hoped to qualify for the Boston Marathon. The race was his big ambition, according to Gerry. Not just for himself, but as a recognition for the sports town he so loved. It's only fitting, she adds, that the Victor K. Copps Coliseum, which he fought so long and hard for, should be erected as a testimonial to his legend and his quest for the top of the mountain.

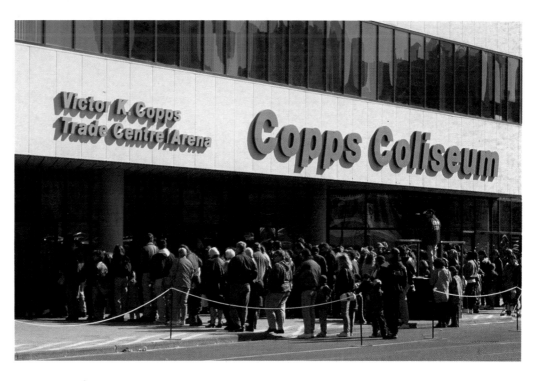

ABOVE: *A crowd files into Copps Coliseum, which bears the name of one of Hamilton's most-beloved mayors.*
– Photo by Dennis McGreal

FACING PAGE: *When the Hamilton Tiger-Cats needed a financial boost, number-one fan Martin Short came home to help as the city rallied to the aid of the ailing CFL club.*
– Photo by Mark Okrainec

• *CHML's Christmas Tree of Hope campaign has raised more than $1.5 million since its inception 20 years ago. The money has been distributed to various charities throughout the Hamilton-Wentworth and Burlington region.*

When Hamilton celebrated its 150th anniversary in 1996, it was fitting that Hometown Radio CHML be designated the 'Official Voice' of Sesquicentennial celebrations.

After all, CHML's radio roots run extremely deep in Hamilton. "We've been around for 69 of those 150 years, and we're very proud to be a part of this great city," asserts CHML Program Director Darryl Hartwick.

Indeed, with its call letters standing for Canada, Hamilton and Maple Leaf, CHML was founded in 1927 by George Lees with just 50 watts of power.

After a decade of struggle, the late broadcasting legend Ken Soble became station manager and revamped the station to put an emphasis on news and views. In 1944, he bought the station and increased its wattage. Today the station uses 50,000 watts to reach its audience.

Highly involved with Sesqui activities is newscaster Bill Sturrup, a 35-year CHML veteran covering major 1996 events, from the CANUSA Games in Flint this year to the Ford World Curling Championships, to the Grey Cup at Hamilton's Ivor Wynne Stadium.

CHML is the proud voice of Tiger-Cat football, with comprehensive play-by-play coverage by Bob Bratina and veteran newscaster Bob Hooper.

The station's Sesquicentennial Editor, Bill Osborne, wrote and produced the familiar 60-second Sesqui Moments airing five times daily, highlighting Hamilton's history and achievements.

These reflections on the city's past have focused on the "Ambitious City's" growth . . . everything from the Gore Park Fountain to Sir Alan Napier McNab and the Hamilton Farmers' Market.

Hamilton's 150th anniversary also marked the 20th year for CHML's Christmas Tree of Hope campaign, which since its inception has raised more than $1.5 million distributed to various charitable organizations throughout Hamilton-Wentworth and Burlington.

The idea was the brainchild of CHML President and General Manager Don Luzzi, who observes "it's really symbolic of what our station represents."

"Putting something back into the community has been an integral part of CHML ever since it signed on in 1927," explains Mr. Luzzi.

"Since 1976, everyone on staff has contributed their time and energy to make this campaign a success," adds Mr. Luzzi, "enabling us to touch thousands of lives in our Hometown community."

The Sesquicentennial year was also the kick-off year of the spirited new Hometown Morning Show hosted by Lisa Brandt and John Hardy, whose other popular show – Moldy, Goldy and Hardy – entered its 16th year in 1996.

"Lisa, Bob Hooper, Al Craig and I enjoy each other's company," says Mr. Hardy, adding "when we're having a good time, it shows."

Such depth of talent – there are others too numerous to mention – helps to keep CHML and its sister FM station Y95 fresh, alive and relevant to listeners in an information-rich era.

Radio buffs can only look back nostalgically to another era, decades ago, when entire families would pull up chairs to their radio (as physically large as a still-to-be-invented TV set) and listen to news, big bands and drama shows.

Yet in many ways, radio still plays a central, immediate role in our lives.

"Radio can still touch the lives of people everywhere," says Mr. Hooper.

"When a snowstorm happens, people instantly go to the radio to find out what's been cancelled or how much more snow to expect or how bad the roads are and what streets to avoid," says the 35-year CHML stalwart. "Radio will never return to its glory days – I don't think those days will ever return," he adds.

"Radio has been through some rough times. But radio will always be there."

900 CHML has always prided itself with its service and commitment to the communities it reaches. A part of Hamilton, Hometown Radio, CHML.

ABOVE: The CHML 900 community cruiser is a familiar site in the city.

LEFT: CHML is the voice of the Tiger-Cats with coverage by Bob Bratina and Bob Hooper.

• Built at a cost of $42.7 million and opened on November 30, 1985, Copps Coliseum remains a world-class, multi-use facility in the heart of downtown Hamilton. Over the years, the coliseum, with a regular seating capacity of 17,500, has hosted everything from concerts to conventions and numerous sporting events including hockey extravaganzas like the Canada Cup and the Memorial Cup. At left, current Philadelphia Flyers superstar Eric Lindros celebrates a goal as an Oshawa General while, above, Wayne Gretzky and Team Canada teammates celebrate after winning another Canada Cup championship on Copps ice.
— **Photos by Dennis McGreal**

• Stretching along the South Service Road, Stoney Creek Furniture's sprawling store is a familiar sight for motorists travelling the Niagara-bound QEW.
— **Photo by David Gruggen**

From virtually any level of Stoney Creek Furniture's multi-level showroom, the customer's eye is greeted by an inviting sea of furniture.

Next comes the hard part: Navigating through choices in this sprawling furniture warehouse to select your absolute favourite from a list of favourites.

"Our store is a little unusual because we're spread out on three levels – and on any level, you can see the whole show-room. It's a bit like being in an amphitheatre," notes Dennis Novosel, president and owner of Stoney Creek Furniture.

Mr. Novosel finds his warehouse also differs from others in another respect.

"We have one of the best selections anywhere of wood furniture – coffee tables, end tables, dining room furniture, cabinets – all types of wood furniture."

"For us, about 60 per cent of our sales volume is in wood products – mainly oak – while for the industry, it's 60 per cent volume in upholstered furniture," points out Mr. Novosel, whose strategy has always been to promote his store as a leader in wood furniture selection.

"We've exhibited wood furniture at home shows, carried some exclusive lines and it's given us a good footing in a larger market territory," notes Mr. Novosel, whose sprawling store stretches along the South Service Road at Lewis Roads between Fruitland Road and Fifty Road in Stoney Creek. The store is also a familiar sight for motorists travelling the Niagara-bound Queen Elizabeth Way.

"We also specialize in medium-priced, traditional and casual-style furniture," adds the owner of the award-winning business, which draws half of its customers from the Hamilton area, the rest from across south-central Ontario's Golden Horseshoe, taking in a number of communities from Oshawa to Fort Erie.

Now one of the largest furniture stores in Ontario – and the winner of a number of small business awards – the success story of Stoney Creek Furniture had modest beginnings.

Mr. Novosel was 19 years old and had just graduated with a Grade 12 diploma from Glendale Secondary School when he founded Stoney Creek Furniture in 1969.

"The business started out out as a one-man operation selling used furniture and appliances," he recalls.

"Although I was fairly young, I still had some experience in business," adds Mr. Novosel, whose father, John Novosel, had owned and operated Hamilton Movers, and Saltfleet Movers for many years. "As a kid, I had helped my dad out with his businesses and looked forward to running my own business some day," he recalls.

It wasn't long before the thriving furniture business was feeling a little cramped at its original 3,000-square-foot location at Barton Street East and Gray's Road in Hamilton, just west of the Stoney Creek border.

That prompted the company's first move, says Mr. Novosel. "About five years later, we sold the first property and moved across the street, where we rented 9,000 square feet of space," he notes.

"Then, 14 years later – in 1987 – we moved to our current location." It offers considerably more space – 86,000 square feet – but the company is still growing.

By the summer of 1996, Stoney Creek Furniture was considering nearly doubling its space with a major expansion at its nine-acre site within a year.

In sharp contrast to its original one-man operation, Stoney Creek Furniture employs approximately 70 people full- and part-time – including 20 sales people and approximately 40 support staff.

With its new expansion, the company is anticipating increasing its staff to approximately 100 people.

STONEY CREEK FURNITURE

• *Stoney Creek Furniture was founded by Dennis Novosel as as a one-man operation in 1969. The award-winning furniture store today employs approximately 70 full- and part-time people, some of whom are pictured here.*
– Photo by David Gruggen

"It helps when you've got a great team of people – and we are planning to add to our workforce as the business grows," asserts Mr. Novosel, whose furniture store celebrated more than a quarter-century in business during 1996.

Since 1975, Stoney Creek Furniture has exclusively sold new furniture and has grown into one of the area's largest new furniture stores. The reasons for this success aren't difficult to find.

"We've always done our very best to offer a good selection, outstanding customer service and fair pricing, and we've given a consistent message over the years for good value," says the company president.

"It's given us a good name and we get a lot of repeat business and referrals."

"In fact, during the recessions we made some of our biggest gains," notes Mr. Novosel. "In a recession, money is scarce so people look for value as well as low prices. We offer both and because of that, we actually grew during the past two recessions. And we're still growing."

Although it's easy for any business to make claims regarding quality and pricing, the evidence strongly supports each of Mr. Novosel's assertions.

Not only did Stoney Creek Furniture grow during the past two recessions, it experienced increases in both showroom traffic and sales – and it won several business achievement awards.

Among the honours for Stoney Creek

Furniture was being named one of the Top 50 fastest-growing companies in Canada, listed by Small Business (now Profit) magazine in February, 1989. It also won the 1989 Outstanding Business Achievement Award, presented by the Hamilton & District Chamber of Commerce; and it won two 1992 ACE Awards for advertising excellence.

Today, Stoney Creek Furniture is busier than ever, with a fleet of seven delivery trucks keeping up with customer demands. "We're looking forward to continued growth," says Mr. Novosel, "because we're offering a large location with a great selection of good quality furniture at good prices – and that's what our customers want."

LEFT: *Runners respond to the starter's gun as another Around The Bay Road Race gets under way in Hamilton. The competition, one of the oldest road races in North America, was first held in 1894.*

BELOW: *The Hess Village Bicycle Race, a popular yearly event, takes participants through the streets of downtown Hamilton.*
– Photos by Dennis McGreal

A free spirit and innovative approach have always been hallmarks of CHCH TV 11, one of Canada's largest independent TV stations.

In 1994, Hamilton's home-grown TV station marked its 40th year on the air – and looked forward to providing programming excellence for the next 40 years.

Founded by Ken Soble in 1954, "Lucky Channel 11" began broadcasting as a privately owned affiliate of the CBC Network. In 1961, under Mr. Soble's leadership, CHCH disaffiliated from the network to become Canada's first independent television station. A short time later, Mr. Soble converted the former Kenmore Theatre on King Street West into TV11's Telecentre and began building up his TV station's presence.

Mr. Soble, who died in 1966, had founded a broadcasting empire with an air of modesty which included his stock phrase: "I don't really have any talent of my own, unless it's a knack for finding good people to run my businesses, and then leaving them alone."

In 1984, CHCH linked its familiar historic headquarters – a stately 1840s Georgian-style mansion – with a modern, high-tech facility allowing the company to bring its operations under one roof.

Since 1993, CHCH has been owned and controlled by WIC Western International Communications Ltd. – an integrated broadcast, communications and entertainment company encompassing the Westcom TV Group, which includes TV11 along with stations in Victoria, Vancouver, Kelowna, Lethbridge, Red Deer, Calgary and Edmonton.

Although Hamilton-area residents proudly call TV11 their own, the station's signal is actually broadcast across Southern Ontario and into rural and remote communities across Canada – including the high Arctic – via the Cancom satellite service. CHCH has a reach of more than 4.2 million viewers, coast to coast to coast. CHCH is also in the middle of the Southern Ontario market, often described as the world's most competitive TV market.

To ensure that the station would be able to compete equitably in the future, in 1996, CHCH made application to the CRTC to expand its coverage area to become an Ontario regional system. CHCH proposed adding rebroadcast transmitters in 10 Ontario Markets: London, Kingston, Peterborough, Ottawa, Muskoka, North Bay, Sudbury, Sault Ste. Marie, Timmins and Thunder Bay.

"The filing of our Ontario expansion applications is by far one of the most important undertakings in the station's history," states CHCH president Jim

• The executive offices of CHCH are located in an 1840s mansion, built of local limestone. Bishop Fuller, the first bishop of the Niagara Diocese, and publishing pioneer William Southam II both once called the mansion home.

Macdonald. "We compete in arguably the most competitive television market in North America where recent takeovers, mergers and ownership transfers have dramatically changed the landscape of the market and the industry," he explains.

"The approval of these applications is essential to CHCH's long-term interests," adds Mr. Macdonald. "First and foremost, however, our commitment is to serve the people of Hamilton and Niagara and our focus will continue here."

CHCH has forged a highly competitive presence in this market, he notes. "We're rebuilding and positioning ourselves in a very customer-focused way. Our cornerstones are firmly in place now and they will enable us to move forward with clear objectives and a clear mission."

With programming being the key cornerstone to a stronger presence, CHCH has focused its news on the Hamilton-Halton-Niagara area, shoring up its regional base while reaching out to a larger audience through aggressive title acquisitions of such shows as Hope & Gloria and NewsRadio.

Described as a mainstream station with a great deal of spirit, CHCH has acquired the critically acclaimed Homicide: Life on the Street, and taken chances on exceptional properties with lower commercial appeal such as My So-Called Life and picked up such live action series as Nancy Drew and The Hardy Boys, both produced by Canada's Nelvana.

In the area of sales and marketing, CHCH is taking an integrated approach toward solving its clients' problems and has branded itself as a dynamic and innovative media partner.

CHCH has launched a number of successful partnership campaigns for the Ontario Jockey Club and Heart and Stroke Foundation and its sponsorships have included the Molson Indy.

The television station has also joined with Bell Mobility, Young Drivers of Canada and Canadian Tire in the Ontario Ministry of Transportation's Road Safety Partnership program.

By the mid-1990s, CHCH had grown to approximately 170 employees, with facilities that included a state-of-the-art broadcast centre; two microwave mobiles, three production studios, two full-size television production mobiles for remote broadcasts, and several editing suites and post-audio facilities.

But, despite all of these modern advances, Ken Soble's philosophy still holds true today at CHCH, where the station strives "to employ people who have both an astute understanding of the fast-paced industry – and an enthusiastic commitment to excellence."

STONEY RIDGE CELLARS

Stoney Ridge Cellars has a problem that most companies would love to have: popularity threatens to increase the winery's sales and size.

But Hamilton-Wentworth's only winery wants to put a cork on its growth and remain at a size that its partners can comfortably handle. "We'll probably grow to 50,000 gallons in 1996 and I'd like to keep it at that manageable level," says Stoney Ridge president Jim Warren.

"If you grow much beyond that, you're into a whole new set of complications and expenses such as hiring a lot of salespeople to sell your product all over the place," explains Mr. Warren, a retired high school teacher who enjoys running the winery in the east Winona area of Stoney Creek, just steps from the Niagara region border.

His partner, Murray Puddicombe, feels much the same way.

"We've been averaging 20 per cent growth annually for the past five years," notes this seventh-generation member of the Puddicombe family, which has owned and operated a farm since 1797 on scenic, fertile acreage spreading out from the base of the Niagara Escarpment.

"But we really don't want to get much above 50,000 gallons," adds Mr. Puddicombe, whose family farm operates as a separate business which is owned by the Puddicombe family. The farm site also houses the winery, a retail store and bakery shop.

Keeping the winery small may not be that easy. By the mid-1990s, employment at the little winery had climbed 40 per cent to 14 full-time and part-time employees from 10 in the early 1990s.

Strong demand for its products has fueled the winery's rapid growth, taking it from 1,000 gallons (500 cases) when it opened in 1985 to 26,000 gallons (13,000 cases) in the early 1990s and to more than 40,000 gallons (20,000 cases) by the mid-1990s, when the winery celebrated its first decade of business.

Suddenly, 50,000 gallons – or 25,000 cases – seemed just around the corner.

By the mid-1990s the winery was planning to add 1,700 square feet of processing space, making room for additional oak barrels in a wine cellar that had reached a capacity of 225 barrels.

And the winery was by then offering 40 different wines – including its mid-priced popular Cabernet-Merlot red and Bench Chardonnay white wines. Special vintages include the Vin Roarrrr offering honouring the CFL Hamilton Tiger-Cats and a Sesquicentennial wine commemorating Hamilton's 150th anniversary.

Also featured are a variety of fruit wines, including raspberry, peach,

• *Jim Warren, left and Murray Puddicombe are partners in Stoney Ridge Cellars, a successful Winona winery offering some 40 different vintages – including a Sesquicentennial wine commemorating the City of Hamilton's 150th birthday.*
– Photo by Joe Bucci

cranberry, black current, iced apple and 'bumbleberry' – a mixture of fruit wines – all under the Puddicombe Farms label.

With the family farm and land farmed under leasing agreement taken into account, Mr. Puddicombe farms a total of 250 acres, with 150 acres in grape production, the rest in other fruits.

Add in the separate business of an on-site retail store – complete with the winery's full selection of wines and souvenir items from sweatshirts to

decorative grape motif candles and corkscrews plus a seasonal baked goods shop – and you've got a popular tourist destination which draws larger crowds every year, including school tours eager to visit the Puddicombe petting farm.

"Our tours are getting a lot more traffic," notes Mr. Puddicombe.

"And a lot more consumer interest is being generated. Our sales keep increasing, we're selling a lot more wine . . . it's not going to be easy to stay small."

• Area track and field fans are treated to world-class competition each year when some of the sport's top athletes compete at the Indoor Games held at Copps Coliseum.
– Photos by Dennis McGreal

• Shaquille O'Neil of the Orlando Magic was among the NBA stars in town when the World Basketball Championships came to Copps Coliseum. Here, an opponent looks on helplessly as Shaq slams another two points home for the American Team.
– Photos by Dennis McGreal

L ike a penetrating blast from his Fox 40 whistle, Ron Foxcroft has a way of getting noticed. The famous whistle is the brainchild of its inventor, Mr. Foxcroft, who markets it through Fox 40 International – one of several successful firms owned and operated by the NCAA basketball referee.

Mr. Foxcroft is also well-known as the president of Fluke Transport, a large locally owned trucking company with the disarmingly unforgettable slogan: If it's on time . . . it's a Fluke.

After years of working as a cost accountant for a number of construction firms, Mr. Foxcroft realized a long-held ambition and went into business on his own. "We really started from zero in 1983," he recalls "I had an idea of getting into business on my own, borrowed some money and took it from there."

Mr. Foxcroft gave vent to his entrepreneurial spirit by borrowing $150,000 to purchase Bob Fluke's small trucking firm with just three trucks and 10 employees.

By the mid-1990s, Fluke Transport had grown into the Hamilton area's largest locally based trucking firm, with more than 100 trucks and 125 employees.

The company includes a less-than-truckload division created from a merger with T.A. Collins company. A related warehouse division, expanded through a merger with Hamilton Terminals, boasts 350,000 square feet of space.

Founded by Mr. Fluke's father, Joe Fluke, the company celebrated its 75th anniversary in 1995, a much larger entity than many would have foreseen. Bob Fluke remains with the company under a

• Ron Foxcroft, left, is shown with wife Marie and other members of his team in front of the Fluke Transport/Fox 40 headquarters in Hamilton's east end.
— Photo by David Gruggen

lifetime contract and the company anticipates continued steady growth.

While many businessmen would have been content to run just one successful business, Mr. Foxcroft enjoys seeking out new challenges. His idea for a 'pealess' whistle came to him after his whistle jammed while he was trying to call a foul during a pre-Olympics game in 1984.

After piling up debts of $300,000 attempting to market the whistle, Mr. Foxcroft walked into a dormitory filled with 400 sleeping referees at the 1987 Pan-American Games and gave them two shrill blasts on his whistle prototype.

That was all the convincing evidence needed. Orders poured in for 20,000 whistles and by the mid-1990s Fox 40 International was selling Fox 40 and Fox 40 Mini whistles in 90 countries.

With further companies, including his Gage North Holdings real estate firm and his overall holding company Foxcroft Capital Corp., Mr. Foxcroft is capably assisted by skilled managers – "we refer to them as team leaders."

And he's helped by the extensive involvement of family members. His wife Marie controls all financial aspects of the various Foxcroft-owned firms while sons Steve and Dave and daughter-in-law Carolyn run Fox 40 International. Even little Ronnie Jr. has got into the act. At

age 2, he was the model in a Fox 40 advertisement published in a national referee magazine in the United States.

"I'm fortunate to have surrounded myself with talented people – and lucky my family is very involved in all aspects of my businesses," notes Mr. Foxcroft.

Despite having the demands of several companies to consider, Mr. Foxcroft has also found time to serve as 1995 president of the Hamilton and District Chamber of Commerce and was the co-chair of the 1995 Canadian Chamber of Commerce Convention held in Hamilton.

He was also the fund-raising manager for the Terry Cooke Regional Chairman Campaign, director of the Hamilton Tiger-Cats Football Club, on the Board of Governors of Hamilton-Wentworth Junior Achievement, and chairman of the 1994 World Championship of Basketball Hamilton Organizing Committee. He's currently co-chair of Grey Cup '96.

He's also served as Honourary Corporate Chair of the Lung Association of Hamilton-Wentworth, chairman of the Business Advisory Council at Mohawk College and was a member of the Business Advisory Council for McMaster University and Sheridan College.

And, he gives eight speeches a month on entrepreneurialism to local schools and he regularly assists – at no cost – fellow inventors in getting their products to market. With so much of his time devoted to his businesses, basketball refereeing, community projects and charitable work, surely something has to give?

"There is a cost to all of this," he says, candidly. "My golf game is suffering."

• Frank Mercanti is the owner and president of Mercanti Auto Body, a respected Hamilton business that he founded in 1952 as a two-man shop.
— Photo by Joe Bucci

Mercanti Auto Body is definitely a family business. President Frank Mercanti operates his business on John Street North at Cannon Street along with five of his six sons.

In the mid-1990s he had opened a second auto body and repair shop further down John Street – known as John North Collision Inc. – and was busy planning for future outlets to be run by his sons.

It all began in 1952 when a 19-year-old Mr. Mercanti was working at an auto body shop at the rear of a car sales lot, both owned by the late Frank Richter. When Mr. Richter decided to sell the little two-bay auto body shop, Mr. Mercanti and his brother, the late Ralph Mercanti, went in together and bought the shop.

After a year together, the brothers changed location and opened separate shops. Frank went on his own, opening a shop at Gore (now Wilson) Street.

After about eight years in that location, Mr. Mercanti moved his auto body and auto repair business to James Street North, where he stayed five more years. In the mid-1960s, he moved to his current location, which has the latest equipment, including a down draft spray booth.

Through the years, business prospered – fortunately for Mr. Mercanti, who was supporting a family of 13, including his late wife Elaine and their 11 children.

Married at age 20, Mr. Mercanti's 11 children had all arrived by the time he was 34. "We had to do well in the business – we didn't have any choice," Mr. Mercanti chuckles.

With the assistance of his sons, Mr. Mercanti now presides over a long-established, highly successful business.

Mercanti Auto Body is also a long-standing associate member of the Hamilton Auto Club. In the mid-1990s, it was recognized by HAC for 15 years of excellent service to HAC members.

Mr. Mercanti credits success to his family and their commitment to hard work and running a clean and efficient business. "It's also important to look after the public by providing good service," adds Mr. Mercanti, whose company backs its work with lifetime warranties.

From a two-man shop back in 1952, Mercanti Auto Body today employs about 20 people, including sales manager Luigi Mason, Mr. Mercanti's brother-in-law, who has been with the company for 33 years. The group also includes five auto body and auto repair mechanics.

Pleased with the contribution made by sons Dan, Frank Jr., Adam, Patrick and Paul, Mr. Mercanti says he intends to go ahead with plans to open other outlets.

"We're doing well now," he says, "but there's always room to grow."

• Hometown fans had plenty to cheer about as both the men's and women's teams representing Canada finished on top at the World Curling Championships at Copps Coliseum earlier this year. The women's entry, skipped by Marilyn Bodogh, is pictured at left, while the men's team, skipped by Jeff Stoughton, is shown above.
– Photos by Dennis McGreal

PROCTER & GAMBLE INC.

Procter & Gamble Inc. has long played a key role in Hamilton's evolution as a major manufacturing centre. In 1995, P&G celebrated 80 years in Hamilton with the opening of new employee facilities at its Burlington Street East landmark plant.

The $10 million facilities included a meeting room, employee fitness facilities, new cafeteria, parking lot and the 'Link' – a pedestrian bridge allowing easy access to facilities the on north and south sides of Burlington Street for the plant's employees.

During the facility's opening event, Yong Quek, president of P&G in Canada, and Pat Bourque, Hamilton plant manager, joined Hamilton Mayor Bob Morrow in unveiling a plaque dedicating the facilities to employees past and present. The event marked yet another milestone in P&G's long-standing commitment to Hamilton, home of the Cincinnati, Ohio-based company's first-ever international operation.

Famous for such household necessities

• A pedestrian bridge allows easy access to facilities on the north and south sides of Burlington Street for Procter & Gamble employees.

as Ivory, Zest and Camay soaps, Pampers diapers, Crisco shortening and Tide laundry detergent, Procter & Gamble was founded in 1837 in Cincinnati by William Procter and James Gamble as a soap and candle-making business. By the early 1850s, the company was using its familiar Moon and Stars symbols on its products and had moved to an expanded plant.

The decade ended with 1859 sales of $1 million. P&G supplied soap and candles to Union Army soldiers in 1863, during the American Civil War, building a reputation for product excellence.

In 1879, James Norris Gamble, the founder's son and a trained chemist, developed an inexpensive white soap of high

quality which the other founder's son, Harley Procter, named 'Ivory.'

This famous brand would later sponsor daytime radio and television dramas that became known as 'soap operas.' And in 1915, P&G's first international plant opened in Hamilton, employing 75 people in the production of Ivory soap and Crisco oil.

Today, the plant employs 400 people making bar and liquid soap products for the North American market. It also serves as Canada's key product distribution centre.

"Hamilton is responsible for making some of the world's best personal care products and operates a world-class distribution system," says Mr. Quek. He adds, "technical mastery and strong leadership in our people ensures benchmark results."

"We are proud of Hamilton and our successes. The workplace is safe and product quality is impeccable. Cost and service exceed our customers' expectations, which helps build the business. We all win."

T here's a defining moment when you drive east to enter Hamilton's West Mountain. The drive takes you past open spaces and low-rise housing. Then, suddenly, it's before you.

Looming into view just inside the city limits on Mohawk Road West is a huge residential-commercial complex dominated by high-rise apartment buildings.

The towering buildings convey the quiet but convincing message: You've just entered a major Canadian city. Welcome to Hamilton. Known as Harvard Square, the impressive complex is also the bold corporate signature of a prominent Hamilton firm, Effort Trust Company.

Founded by Arthur Weisz in the mid-1950s as Arthur Weisz Real Estate Ltd., the company was taken over in 1979 by Effort Trust and now includes Effort Trust Real Estate, Effort Trust Property Management and Effort Trust Financial Services.

Arthur Weisz remains active as chairman of Effort Trust Co. His son, Thomas,

• *Effort Trust Company either owns or manages more than 100 apartment buildings across Southern Ontario.*

is Chief Executive Officer and President.

Thomas Weisz notes that expanding into financial services proved to be a good fit for the company: "Becoming a trust company was a logical and natural extension of our business. It was a way of providing an expanded range of services for our existing clientele."

By the mid-1990s, Effort Trust had grown to 100 employees with financial outlets at Main Street East and at the Queenston Mall in Hamilton. The outlets offer a full range of consumer banking services, from mortgages and loans to chequing and savings accounts.

The real estate and property management sides of the business also continue to prosper. Effort Trust owns, manages or is administrator for more than 12,000 residential apartment units in over 100

buildings in southern Ontario, and more than 6 million square feet of commercial property, making the company the area's largest property manager.

This includes numerous shopping malls, office and industrial buildings, and, of course, Harvard Square.

Straddling both sides of Mohawk Road West and covering two city blocks, it's Hamilton's largest high-rise apartment complex with half a dozen apartment towers, 200 townhouse units and a retail shopping centre. The complex takes its name from Harvard University, where the younger Mr. Weisz earned a Master of Laws degree in the 1970s before joining the family firm in 1979.

"Our strategy is to take care of the knitting, to manage well what we already have before expanding further," Thomas Weisz notes. "By adding value to our holdings and providing hands-on administration and good service to our customers, we're building a solid foundation for future, sustainable growth."

• *Langley Parisian owner and general manager Ken Adamson is pictured with employees Sandy Richardson, left, and Salma Mirza. The laundry-drycleaning company, with eight locations, has been in operation for more than 100 years.*
– Photo by David Gruggen

Rather than air their dirty laundry, Hamiltonians have let Langley Parisian clean up for more than a century. In 1994, the respected Hamilton laundry-drycleaning company crossed the 100-year mark – having travelled the road to success in everything from horse-drawn wagons to modern trucks.

"Household laundry used to be carted by horse and wagon when the company got going in the 1890s," notes Ken Adamson, the firm's general manager and sixth owner after purchasing the assets from his father, Ed Adamson.

"Now we mainly pick up and deliver to commercial customers and institutions, such as senior citizens residences," says Mr. Adamson. "And, it's by delivery truck of course," he adds.

The company – now known as Langley Parisian Fabricare Services – began in downtown Hamilton, where the Ramada Inn would later be built, as a branch operation of the Detroit-based Parisian laundry services chain.

In 1902, the Canadian branch moved to its current plant-headquarters location at Walnut Street. It was by that point the possession of a group of local investors headed by James Lamoreaux.

One of the investors, Walter Iredale, gained sole control of the company in 1914 and it remained in the family's hands until 1961 when it was sold to the Adamson family.

In the 1930s, Langley Parisian began offering drycleaning services and also started offering pick-up and delivery services to corporate customers.

Over the years, the company has grown from a single location and handful of workers to eight locations and around 100 employees by the mid-1990s.

Challenges of the past included getting the iron hot enough on a wood-burning stove to meet the demand for starched collars at 2 cents apiece and washed and ironed shirts at 5 to 6 cents each.

By the mid-1990s, Langley Parisian was charging $1 for laundered shirts and facing a new set of challenges in an environmentally conscious age.

For example, the once widespread use of plastic wrap has given way to reusable nylon bags, and Mr. Adamson anticipates a widespread reduction in the use of solvents in the latter half of the 1990s.

"And the solvents themselves will likely be altered to make them more environmentally friendly," says Mr. Adamson.

It's nothing less than what you would expect from Langley Parisian, a company that loves to come clean.

• The CANUSA Games, the largest and longest-running International Games in North America, brings participants from Hamilton, Ontario, and Flint, Michigan, together each year for friendly competition in 23 sports. More than 3,000 amateur athletes, ranging in age from 8 to 80, compete each year in the Games, which alternate between the twin cities of Hamilton and Flint. Some 4,000 volunteers, including directors, co-ordinators and coaches, donate their time each year to ensure the success of the Games, which were first held in Flint in 1958. The 1996 CANUSA competition will be held in Flint on August 9-11. A special Sesqui commemorative plaque will mark the occasion.

ABOVE: *McMaster University was one of the venues for the events staged as part of the 1994 World Children's Games. Here, young athletes race in the wheelchair competition.*
– Photo by Dennis McGreal

PAGES 120-121: *A blue sky and an open sheet of ice provide the perfect setting for some fun and games. Inset, a group of would-be NHLers takes advantage of the frozen harbour to hone their hockey skills. The competition is more serious in the main picture, as competitors show their stuff during the World Ice Boat Racing Championships on Hamilton Bay .*
– Photos by Dennis McGreal

C an a company constantly redefine itself and become a leader in whatever field it chooses? You can be sure . . . if it's Westinghouse.

Change has been the operative word during a century of evolution taking the firm from air brakes and appliances to its current role as a series of spokes in competitive inter-continental wheels.

Westinghouse Canada Inc. President Garry Weimer notes the turbine plant at Sanford Avenue in Hamilton – the oldest continuously running plant of the entire Westinghouse worldwide organization – is part of the power generation division that includes a number of American plants and international alliances.

"All of these plants report to the Power Generation Business Unit in Orlando, Florida," adds Mr. Weimer, who was manager of the Sanford Avenue plant prior to becoming president in 1995.

The grouping of like businesses has put the Canadian plant on the competitive front lines, much to the benefit of the local turbine plant which routinely wins major contracts in the world power generation market, notes Mr. Weimer, who oversees a corporate staff of 120 while managing branch operations in Canada.

This unique and successful corporate structure was never envisioned when George Westinghouse contemplated setting up his first operations outside of the United States in Hamilton a century ago.

The enduring relationship between Hamiltonians and Westinghouse began in the fall of 1896, when the Westinghouse Air Brake Company announced intentions to set up a branch plant in Hamilton to manufacture air brakes for trains and commenced production a year later.

The Canadian Westinghouse Company Ltd. was established in 1903 and took over control of all Westinghouse operations in Canada – steam engineering, electrical and air brakes.

In 1912, the company delivered the first electrically operated steel mill in the world to the Steel Company of Canada – known by its abbreviated name, Stelco.

The first turnover toaster was built by Canadian Westinghouse in 1914, the first low-priced gramophone in 1917 and the first electric range in 1921. The 1920s also marked Canadian Westinghouse's construction of the Queenston Generating Station of Ontario Hydro at Niagara.

And in the 1930s, the company began manufacturing the first refrigerators and washing machines to be made in Canada at the Hamilton plant on Longwood Avenue. Manufactured appliances also included vacuum cleaners, toasters and irons, and, in 1948, television sets.

For a span of more than 40 years, the

• *Westinghouse Power Generation Canada's dedicated employees are on call 24 hours a day to provide emergency repair services.*

public would recognize the Westinghouse name as a major manufacturer of appliances – even though the firm also made munitions during World War II and had diversified into lighting, gas turbines, electronics, transformers and switchgear.

After selling off its old air brakes business to Wabco, Canadian Westinghouse found its appliances business accounted for only a small percentage of sales. In 1976, the appliances division was sold to the Canadian Appliance Manufacturing Company – better known as Camco. Producing GE, Hotpoint and Moffat brand appliances, Camco remains a major Hamilton employer.

Westinghouse continued to downsize in the 1980s and 1990s and shifted its focus primarily to power generation.

Today, Westinghouse Canada Inc. is also involved in electromechanical services, nuclear services and telecommunications. More than 70 per cent of the products it manufactures are exported.

All told, Westinghouse Canada has 40 business operation locations in Canada, annual revenue of around $300 million and approximately 1,800 employees – about half of whom work in the Hamilton area where Westinghouse Canada Inc. continues to be a major employer.

• Equipped with computerized precision machining centres, advanced laser welding equipment and specialized machine tools, employees at Westinghouse's 500,000-square-foot turbine manufacturing facility produce high-quality gas and steam turbines for customers around the world.

• *Marik Pinassi owns and operates Parkway Toyota and Upper James Toyota.*
— Photo by David Gruggen

Customer satisfaction is driving the success of Upper James Toyota and Parkway Toyota. Both of these Hamilton dealerships offer full warranty programs, payment plans and financing covering a wide selection of Toyota vehicles, from economy cars to luxury sedans, trucks, vans and sport utility vehicles.

At both outlets, keeping customers happy is a source of pride.

"Customer satisfaction is our main goal," notes administrator Grace Carr. "We have a customer satisfaction program – and we work very hard at carrying it out."

And it's working: Customer referrals have kept both outlets busy serving a growing list of satisfied car buyers.

Both dealership outlets are owned and operated by businessman Marik Pinassi.

Parkway Toyota, which is located at Centennial Parkway and Barton Street East, was established in 1975.

As Toyota gained a reputation for its high-quality vehicles in the 1980s, the demand for these dependable cars increased to the extent that Mr. Pinassi established Upper James Toyota on Hamilton Mountain in the early 1980s.

Newly built in 1981, Upper James Toyota has since undergone a major expansion to keep pace with demand for its products.

Hamilton Subaru was also opened by Mr. Pinassi, in 1986.

Both dealerships also continued to build their own reputations for excellence. By the mid 1990s, customers were served by a capable staff of more than 50 people between both operations.

The two big car lots continue to boast $3 million to $4 million worth of new vehicles plus a wide assortment of used vehicles, notes Nick Taylor, general manager of the Parkway and Upper James Toyota dealerships and used car sales manager.

Between the three profitable dealerships are approximately 200 new vehicles to choose from plus an array of used vehicles.

The dealerships also believe in giving back to the community, through charitable donations and are strong sponsors with Toyota Canada of the Special Olympics.

L ike its many satisfied customers, Venetian Jewellers has acquired an eye for value and quality. "More than ever, consumers now are extremely price- and quality-conscious – it goes with the economy," notes Venetian Jewellers president Dino Tedesco.

"It makes it more challenging to succeed, but we've always emphasized high quality at reasonable prices," adds Mr. Tedesco, whose familiar store at King Street East and Ferguson Avenue has long been a source of fine jewelry.

Although major chains of jewelry stores have downsized or gone out of business, Mr. Tedesco notes independent shops such as his survive and succeed by offering personalized customer service.

"With the smaller stores like ours, you're not just a number, you're important to us and you're going to get service you'll be pleased with," he adds.

Indeed, personalized service has always been a hallmark of Venetian Jewellers. Founded in 1954 by Mr. Tedesco's father, the late Alex Tedesco, Venetian Jewellers began on York Street, between McNab and Park streets.

But the store relocated to its present location in 1969 after the City of Hamilton expropriated his former building to make way for the construction of Lloyd D. Jackson Square.

Dino Tedesco joined the business in 1967 and married in 1973. But after returning from their honeymoon, Dino and Linda Tedesco found that the elder Mr. Tedesco was terminally ill with cancer. He died in 1974.

The business needed someone dependable to assist Dino Tedesco – and his wife was a natural choice. Mrs. Tedesco left her nursing job at St. Joseph's Hospital to take on her new responsibilities as the vice-president of an established jewelry store with a loyal clientele.

Mrs. Tedesco was a dedicated jeweller, gemologist and skilled jewelry purchaser who established a friendly rapport with the store's many customers over a period of 20 years. She died in September, 1994, of a brain tumor at age 42.

Mr. Tedesco, a graduate jeweller with experience in appraisals, has continued to operate the downtown store, assisted by a staff of five. Located on the main floor of a two-storey, all-brick building more than 180 years old, the store has around 600 square feet of space – exclusively dedicated to high-quality jewelry.

"We only handle fine jewelry, gold, diamonds and genuine gems, no costume jewelry," notes Mr. Tedesco, while pointing out that his store is known for specializing in 18-karat gold items.

Boasting an array of high-quality

engagement rings, wedding rings, necklaces, ear rings and bracelets, along with watches and watch and jewelry repair services, Venetian Jewellers has a long list of clients, including many prominent Hamiltonians. The store has also attracted out-of-town celebrities. Two members of the vocal group the Platters purchased engagement rings, and Tony Randall of Odd Couple fame once stopped in to pick up a new crystal for his watch.

Beyond a selection of fine jewelry, the store's leading attraction is service. "The big chains can't always offer personalized service," notes Mr. Tedesco. "But we've always tried to treat our customers well – and provide the personal touch."

• Venetian Jewellers president Dino Tedesco says independent shops like his continue to ring in the business because of the personalized service they offer to their customers.
– Photo by Joe Bucci

A s Hamilton has grown over the years, The Bank of Nova Scotia has proven a trusted source of investment capital for business, banking services for consumers and support for worthwhile local causes.

Founded in Halifax, The Bank of Nova Scotia was, at the turn of the century, still very much a Maritime bank with 27 of its 34 Canadian branches located in Atlantic Canada. As Canada expanded westward, The Bank of Nova Scotia – or Scotiabank as we know it today – also ventured west, opening branches in Western Canada.

In 1897, the bank opened its first branch in Ontario with a location in the emerging financial centre of Toronto, a city which would later become headquarters to this ambitious financial institution, which today ranks among the nation's five largest chartered banks.

Very early in the 20th century, the bank desired a location in the bustling community of Hamilton.

In 1902, the bank opened its first branch in Hamilton at King Street East. Two other branches – one at James

• Scotiabank has 13 branches in the city, including this one at the corner of Upper James Street and Rymal Road.
– Photo by David Gruggen

Street North and the other at King Street East and Sherman Avenue South – soon followed, giving the bank a three-branch presence in Hamilton from 1903 to 1949.

In 1949, the bank opened two additional branches – one at Upper James and Fennell Avenue on Hamilton Mountain, the other at Main Street East and Kenilworth Avenue South.

Scotiabank's presence in Hamilton has continued to expand over the years.

Today, Scotiabank has 13 branches in the city along with a Mortgage Finance Centre, a Dealer Finance Centre and a Central Accounting Unit which together employ around 350 people in Hamilton.

The bank's focus is to meet the needs of businesses, particularly small businesses, in the Greater Hamilton market, while offering personal customers a full range of deposit, loan, investment and trust ser-

vices. Scotiabank is a world-wide bank with a large presence in Hamilton.

Indeed, the Hamilton branches are part of Scotiabank's far-reaching, global presence. It has 1,455 branches and offices in 46 countries to meet the financial needs of its customers around the world.

As Hamilton celebrated its Sesquicentennial in 1996, Scotiabank remained very much committed to the role in Hamilton it began nearly 95 years ago. That commitment includes an active role in the betterment of the Hamilton community.

In 1995 alone, Scotiabank provided support to such organizations as St. Joseph's Community Health Care Centre, Opera Hamilton, The United Way of Hamilton-Wentworth, Canadian National Institute for the Blind and the Hamilton SPCA. Scotiabank is also an active partner in the annual Chedoke-McMaster Children's Hospital – Jeans Day Campaign and Telethon.

Clearly, while Scotiabank continues to expand its presence around the world, it has never lost sight of its enduring, welcome role in Hamilton.

Near the Italian restaurants and outdoor tables along James Street North, you can find the heart of Hamilton's Little Italy community at Ricca's Furniture. It's here that many struggling immigrants often found their sole source of credit – and a true friend – in Guido Ricca, who founded the landmark furniture store in 1955.

"Some of these people had no money, no job, and five kids to support," recalls Mr. Ricca. "They needed beds to sleep on and other furniture right away," adds Mr. Ricca. "I could speak Italian so I told them I'd give them easy credit. I said: 'When you get a job, come in and make a payment,' and they were honest people who paid me back."

The immigrants were from all parts of Italy, including Racalmuto. Their plight struck a personal chord with Mr. Ricca, who was born in the town of Racalmuto on the southern tip of Sicily.

Mr. Ricca arrived in Hamilton in 1951 at age 18 with a diploma in cabinet making. His life soon fell into a routine of working daytime jobs and taking English language classes at night.

While at a construction job in downtown Hamilton, Mr. Ricca's carpentry and finishing skills were discovered by Dan Adler. This led to a job as furniture finisher and salesman at Adler's Furniture House for the next two years.

In 1955, Mr. Ricca acted on his dream of having his own business. He founded Ricca's Furniture in the same location, where it remains to this day on James Street North. In the beginning, the store sold inexpensive furniture and appliances. As the local market changed over time, the store would become famous for more expensive Italian furniture.

Yearly trips to shows in Milan and/or Verona resulted in Ricca's becoming an importer of fine Italian merchandise, bringing customers from across Ontario and from New York State.

A second store, Factory Furniture Mart nearby on James Street North is a division of Ricca's Furniture Limited and offers affordable and inexpensive merchandise.

Also assisting in the corporation are Mr. Ricca's wife, Ruth, and children Guy, Michael and Lisa Maria.

Aside from operating his successful business, Mr. Ricca has been actively involved and duly honoured over the years for his community work.

As a driving force in the Jamesville BIA from 1985 to 1988, he helped to turn a once-dying section of Hamilton into a thriving centre of culture and business.

A proud Hamiltonian, Mr. Ricca has been honoured several times for his efforts in fostering stronger ties between

• *Ricca's Furniture has been a fixture in Hamilton's Little Italy since 1955. Here, Guido Ricca is shown outside of his James Street North store.*
– Photo by Joe Bucci

his home town of Racalmuto and his adopted twin city of Hamilton.

In 1993, with the co-operation of Hamilton Mayor Bob Morrow, Mr. Ricca was responsible for having Murray Street named 'Corso Racalmuto.' That same year, he also planned, implemented and financially supported the Flag of Twinship, which was presented in a

special ceremony at Hamilton City Hall. And, in 1994, with the co-operation of Racalmuto Mayor Salvatore Petrotto, he was instrumental in having a street in Racalmuto named 'Viale Hamilton.'

Over the years, Mr. Ricca has received many honours, including certificates of recognition from both the city and the province. In August 1995, the title of 'Commendateur' was conferred upon Mr. Ricca by the Canadian Academy for Cultural Exchange Inc.

Now, more than 40 years later, Mr. Ricca continues to build a legacy not only for those who are part of today's life, but also for generations to come.

• Dundas has been home to Link's Food Market & Delicatessen for 33 years. Link's, famous for its kolbassa and smoked sausage, also has an 8,000-square-foot processing plant on Upper James Street in Hamilton.
– Photo by David Gruggen

Norman Link does more than bring home the bacon to food outlets throughout the Hamilton area. Going with the times, Mr. Link also brings home the Black Forest ham, lean roast beef and lean turkey.

As sales manager of Link's Food Market and Delicatessen, Mr. Link keeps up with customer requests for kolbassa, a good variety of European-style cold cuts and numerous sausages.

"We're probably best known for our kielbasa and smoked sausage, says Mr. Link of the company's famous mainstays.

These products, and others, are prepared in the firm's 8,000-square-foot processing plant on Upper James Street using high-tech, micro-processor controlled, double smokehouses.

Complete with meat-curing machinery, automatic slicers, vacuum packagers, and tumbler units which seal natural juices in prepared meats, the modern facility is a striking example of how this mid-sized

family business has evolved from its beginning as a mom-and-pop operation.

Mr. Link notes that the business was started by his parents Alois and Agnes Link, who immigrated to Montreal from Germany in the mid-1950s. The couple, both trained in the specialty meats industry, moved to Kitchener in the early 1960s, where they opened their business in a cramped downtown shop.

After relocating to the Hamilton area, Alois Link, who remains company president, helped his company grow into a firm that by the mid-'90s was celebrating more than 30 years in business and

producing tons of specialty meats a week for customers across southern Ontario.

Consistency of product and a willingness to prepare custom orders are among the reasons for the family firm's success, suggests Norman Link, who works alongside his brother Peter, general manager and designer of the sprawling plant.

Further family ties can be found at the company's popular Dundas store run by Agnes Link with the able assistance of Peter's wife Marlene and other brother Bernard. The Link family is also a longtime supporter of local food banks.

Despite some impressive successes, the Links aren't about to strive for fast growth. "We've got one of the most modern facilities in Canada now and we want to grow further by expanding our customer base," notes Norman Link. "But we haven't tried for rapid growth because that might mean sacrificing on quality. It's better to grow steadily but slowly so you maintain the right level of quality."

At the age of 66, when most men are retired, European winemaker Andrew Peller travelled to the Niagara Peninsula to realize his dream of creating premium quality wines.

These wines would proudly bear his family name and rival any fine wine in North America.

Drawing on his knowledge and his experience as a maker of fine wines, Andrew Peller realized the best wines invariably start with excellent grapes.

Searching for the best grapes and best vineyards became a priority after Mr. Peller acquired the former Beau Chatel winery on South Service Road in the Winona area of Stoney Creek in 1970.

Mr. Peller felt the newly acquired winery needed a French name – and Andres Wines was born, buying its grapes from more than 100 local vineyards in the fertile Niagara Peninsula. With its rich, sandy loam soils mixed with gravel for the right drainage and a natural acidity, the peninsula is the perfect location for growing excellent wine grapes.

In a temperate location between lakes Ontario and Erie, the Niagara region also benefits from longer days and more sunlight than many European regions

In these ideal conditions, Andres Wines grew into one of Canada's largest wineries, with more than 90 different wine and wine-based products and employing around 150 people.

As the years passed, Mr. Peller's son Joseph and grandson John continued the family business, which would eventually acquire Hillebrand Winery, run as a separate company controlled by Andres Wines. Today, the Andres name is gradually giving way to the family's real name as the company's Peller Estates group of high-quality wines continues to experience sales growth.

Peller Estates has a fine selection of wines that are a tribute to the dedication, patience and craft of everyone who has given their all to help Andrew Peller realize his dream of creating premium quality Ontario wines that rival any great wines for taste and quality.

Josie Yachetti, a sales representative at the company's head office wine store, notes that 91 wines and wine products of both Andres and Peller Estates vintages are offered at her store.

"Some of our popular Andres brands are Domaine D'or and Hochtaler white wines," adds Ms Yachetti, "while Peller Estates has a very popular French Cross dry white wine that's really going over

well with the wine-buying public."

Other Peller Estates vintages gaining attention are Chardonnay Sur Lie 1994 VQA, with its rich and subtle aromas of sweet butter, vanilla and light oak; Merlot 1993 VQA, with its immense depth and generous robust finish; and Muscat Ottonel 1995 VQA, with its fragrant spicy aroma and clean, dry finish.

The Andres winery at the gateway of wine country attracts approximately 30,000 people annually on wine tours.

Hillebrand at Niagara-on-the-Lake is deeper into wine country and attracts as many as 75,000 tourists annually.

Wines from Peller Estates, Andres or Hillebrand can be purchased at any of hundreds of specialty outlets in grocery stores and malls, and at LCBO outlets.

Given the growing quality of Ontario wines, these wineries offer excellent value for even the most discerning palates.

• *Winemaker Barry Poag raises a glass to Andres Wines, the winery founded by Andrew Peller in 1970.*
— Photo by David Gruggen

Chapter 5

Arts & Entertainment

Curtain up, light the lights,
we've got nothin' to hit but the heights;
Startin' here; startin' now;
Honey, everything's comin' up roses.
– From Gypsy

Move over, Ethel Merman. Because we have put a brand new spin on the old standard, "There's no business like show business." And we have done it Hamilton-style; with our own medley of hospitality, hits and ingenuity.

We may not be an exotic port of call, but Hamilton benefits from tourism to the tune of $200 million annually, with over a million visitors a year, and hundreds of conventions.

We have sung for our supper and then some, staging the Junos, for the first of back-to-back years at Copps Coliseum in March of 1995, and beating out both the O'Keefe Centre and SkyDome for the honours.

Performers on that nationally televised awards show were a who's who of the Canadian music scene – Celine Dion, with David Foster; the Barenaked Ladies, Crash Test Dummies, Prairie Oyster with Charlie Major, Michelle Wright, Sarah McLachlan, Moist and hometown talent, Jim Witter.

In an emotionally charged tribute, Buffy Saint Marie was inducted into the Juno Hall of Fame.

With a change in venue, fans were allowed to purchase tickets – a first for the 24th annual Canadian Academy of Arts and Sciences ceremony. Based on our spectacular debut, we earned honours for the Silver Anniversary of the Junos in March of 1996. Because as CARAS president Lee Silversides said: "With 10,000 fans of Canadian music roaring their approval, the show was elevated to a level never seen before. Many inside and outside of the industry called it the best Junos ever."

Getting equal time, the Canadian Country Music Awards had their day when they kicked off a four-day festival in the fall of 1995. Amid rhinestone jackets, cowboy boots and ten-gallon hats the stars of "hurtin' songs" staged the best of western twang with George Fox, Patricia Conroy, Shania Twain, Lisa Brokop, One Horse Blue, Joel Feeney, as well as our cross-over artists Charlie Major, Prairie Oyster, Jim Witter and the host of these televised awards ceremony at Hamilton Place, Michelle Wright. Said Tom Tompkins, the president of the CCMA, one reason for the locale was "they like to party down here in Hamilton."

And in 1995 we raised our voices in worship and praise at the Canadian Christian Festival. By year's end, we will have hosted the world competitions in basketball, judo, children's games, gymnastics and curling. We're the official alternative venue and training camp for the Toronto Raptors of the National Basketball Association and neutral site for the National Hockey League.

And we've done our homework with the International Science and Engineering Fair, an experiment which attracted 1,000 entrants from some two dozen countries, as far away as Argentina, Africa, Brazil, and China.

Marking the first time that the ISEF had ventured beyond the U.S. border in its 46-year history, the distinguished team of judges included Nobel laureates such as McMaster University's Dr. Bertram Brockhouse, Toronto's Dr. John Polanyi and Cambridge, England's Dr. Anthony Hewish.

The national Chambers of Commerce will plot their strategies on these banks.

Speaking of water, the International Great Lakes, St. Lawrence Mayors' Conference was held in 1995 on our fair shores.

Under the invitation of the group's president, Mayor Robert Morrow, some 150 mayors and their representatives – including Chicago Mayor Richard Daley and James Blanchard, U.S, ambassador to Canada – attended the three-day conference; and after a boat tour of the harbour, praised our Remedial Action Plan.

Courted by Canada's Deputy PM Sheila Copps, the environment ministers of the G-7 nations mapped an international cleanup in the port of Hamilton. It was the most prestigious summit ever to gather round the table in Hamilton; an event certainly, on a par with any first world financial discussion.

The influential Group of Seven; namely Canada, the U.S., Germany, Japan, Britain, Italy and France, centred debate on global warming, and greenhouse gas emissions – the deadly carbon dioxide waste from machinery, cars and industrial belts that spews into the atmosphere, and punches a hole in the ozone layer.

Regulation is a hard sell on the North American marketplace – where an anarchy of entrepreneurial spirit, often dominates the environmental streak; especially in a recessionary climate, with a Republican dominated Congress south of the border and a stance clouded by votes and lobby groups. Not since Reaganomics and the hardline Margaret Thatcher era had sustainable development fallen into such political disfavour. Thus unable to harness noxious CO_2 substances, they settled for studies on tax incentives for other fuels.

More palatable, on a menu of agenda items, was a five-course Canadian meal, served with panache in the dining room of Dundurn Castle. Here on the bluffs of the Hamilton Bay, with its panoramic view of the harbour and its own restoration efforts, the entourage feasted on smoked British Columbia salmon, roasted farm elk, as well as a strawberry and rhubarb mousse – washed down with Stoney Ridge 1993 Reserve Chardonnay and Inniskillin Icewine.

On a sad note, the city lost a marquee talent and luminary of the local stage in 1994. Peter Mandia, the heart, soul and inspiration behind Theatre Aquarius, passed away in October, after a blockbuster 22 seasons shaping a regional troupe into a national treasure. The co-founder, executive and artistic director nurtured the ensemble until it outgrew its cramped quarters, and then raised the curtain on the show-stopping $11.8 million, 750-seat duMaurier Centre on King William Street downtown.

One less light glows on King William. But his fire will never be extinguished. Because, as Mandia himself would have said, the show must go on.

ABOVE: *With Anne Murray hosting, Canada's best were honoured at the 1996 Juno Awards at Copps Coliseum.*
– Photo by Dennis McGreal

FACING PAGE: *Soprano Linda Roark-Strummer is shown in a scene from Opera Hamilton's production of Giuseppi Verdi's Nabucco, staged at Hamilton Place.*

PAGES 132-133: *The Hamilton Ballet Youth Ensemble in a performance of Snow White at Hamilton Place. The first major ballet ever produced in Hamilton, the performance was an official Sesqui event. It was choreographed by the company's founder and artistic director, Vitek Wincza. A non-profit charitable organization, the Youth Ensemble is open to dancers ages 12-19 who wish to gain first-hand experience by performing with professionals.*
– Photo by Dennis McGreal

A t first glance, it seems like any other neighbourhood. You hear the voices of children as they play hide-and-go-seek. You see neighbours washing cars, others sitting on their porches discussing sport scores, while "power walkers" wave as they pass by.

But right in the middle of this east Mountain street sits a house like no other. History says that about 100 years ago this was *the* farm house in the area, before neighbourhoods became commonplace.

The house stood alone back then, among running creeks and overgrown trees. Today, it's surrounded by 1950s-style homes. But once again it stands alone, for a number of reasons.

As you pull into the only orange driveway on the block, you can't help but notice the old, white-stucco house, which recently has been re-sided, actually stands sideways to the street, with its red front door facing north, rather than west.

You wonder why anyone would buy such a "different" place. But then, that's the exact reason why the Britt family chose this building in the late 1980s.

"After being in 10 different homes in Hamilton, and a business office downtown, this was ideal for both home and business," says Linda Britt, owner and creative director of Jinsu Productions.

Linda and husband Tom, (a Hamilton-Wentworth Regional police officer, as well as the Region's 1994 Police Officer of the Year and recent recipient of the Ontario Police Bravery Award) are both graduates of Mohawk College. They began their careers in Elliot Lake.

"I started at the only radio station in town," explains Mrs. Britt. "I learned to appreciate the radio business, because I literally did everything," she says. "At first I answered phones, then I was scheduling commercials, writing copy, voicing, producing – and at the end of the day I even took out the garbage."

After five years, the Britts returned to Hamilton to raise their new infant son. Almost immediately upon their return, Linda was hired by CKOC Radio.

"It was another great learning experience, but after a number of years I realized there wasn't much chance of advancement for a copywriter."

After much persuading by family and friends, Linda tried it on her own.

"At first I freelanced, then took on a partner. It didn't work out, but I learned a lot fast, and the hard way," she says. "I think I'm better for it now. I know Jinsu is, that's for sure," she adds.

Jinsu – which by the way "doesn't mean anything," according to Linda – today provides its customers with both creative and business services.

• *Jinsu Productions owner Linda Britt is shown in-studio, putting the final touches on one of her company's latest projects, a radio commercial.*
– Photo by David Gruggen

"At first I was handling only media buying and copywriting, but it expanded to include all printed materials and promotions," Linda explains, adding that she helps other companies stand out from the crowd, through the use of "logos, commercials, campaigns or promotions."

Jinsu clients have included Mountain Plaza, Fiesta Mall, Sweet Trays by Elizabeth, Kimberley's Costumes, and Avestel Credit Union, as well as others outside of the Region, such as Niagara Square and Ed Learn Ford.

"Radio is my medium of choice," notes Linda, with heightened enthusiasm.

"When you combine the written word with a unique voice, the imagination takes over, creating a particular mood."

In '92, it was again time for Linda and Jinsu to tackle another business addition when she got into the administration and information game. "I've considered myself creative, but administration and information were things I never really felt comfortable with." Both now make up 50 per cent of Jinsu's business.

"Designing personal systems for local business has really balanced my creative side," Linda explains.

In fact, today it's commonplace to see Linda working on at least two computers at one time, or running to one of the many others scattered throughout the house producing either the latest radio, print designs or databases.

And all from a little old farmhouse on the east mountain in Hamilton!

Visitors to Southside men's clothing store sometimes feel as though they've just walked into a warm and friendly gentlemen's den.

High ceilings, upholstered chairs and wood panelling add to the den-like ambience of this downtown tailored clothing and casual apparel store on the south side of King Street East.

"People feel we're halfway between a men's club and clothing store," chuckles Dave Lee, co-owner and proprietor of the store, situated between James and Hughson streets, opposite the site of the new Gore Park Fountain.

"We're very laid-back – there's almost a 'Cheers' atmosphere here," adds Mr. Lee, who has a table and chairs at the back of the store for impromptu lunches and dinners with staff, customers and friends. Newcomers are sometimes treated to a bite to eat while frequent visitors to the store contribute some food or drink to the meal "because there's no such thing as a free lunch," he adds with a laugh.

Adding to the informal approach is a habit among many customers to park at a rear parking lot and enter through the back door of this 3,000-square-foot store, which was founded in 1983.

Once inside the store, visitors are greeted by Mr. Lee and partner Rob Wills, who are both co-owners and sales staff of this business, which is equally divided between clothing for tailoring and casual and sportswear items such as golf shirts and slacks and deck shoes.

Tailoring is performed on-site by tailor Enrico Guglielmo "and we're known for our tailored clothing," notes Mr. Lee, whose best-selling tailored suit retails for $550 while jackets often run from $350 to $400 and trousers from $120 to $150.

The owners are assisted by two part-time salespeople. Mr. Lee's wife Nancy does book keeping while children, Dave, 27, Andrea, 24 and Craig, 20, often clean the store on Sundays.

The Lees also join gatherings of friends in painting and redecorating the store. Mr. Wills helps with these efforts while his wife Nancy watches their young children Katie and Jennifer.

Mr. Lee was a former Canadian Football League punt returner and defensive back who spent a season with the B.C. Lions in the early 1970s.

After a stint on the Hamilton Tiger-Cats practice roster, Mr. Lee left football and got into sales, managing the former Stag, and Tyner & Shorten men's clothing stores in Hamilton.

Since 1983, he's been an equal partner in Southside, a store which prides itself in building customer loyalty by finding the right clothes at the right price.

• At Southside, co-owners Dave Lee, left, and Rob Wills stand by their tailor Enrico Guglielmo, whose talents have helped to earn the downtown store a reputation for its tailored clothing.
— *Photo by David Gruggen*

"We'll pour the customer a cup of coffee and chat with them to get an idea of the price range, type of suit and occasion or function it's being purchased for," explains Mr. Lee, who goes through a tin of coffee each week while conducting this relaxed interview process.

"A lot of the time we can find someone clothing they're really happy with – at a lower price than they had expected to pay," adds Mr. Lee, a former director of the Downtown Business Improvement Area and Hamilton Thistle Club who has coached amateur football and hockey.

Mr. Lee notes his store takes a value-added approach by not charging for alterations and by guaranteeing everything sold. It's an approach that draws customers well past business hours.

"People often make appointments to come into the store on holidays or after hours," explains Mr. Lee, "and we encourage that because we want them to feel comfortable as possible."

Palmese PHOTODESIGN Group Inc.

• *Robert Palmese combined his skills with his camera and a computer to create this image of himself with the other members of the PhotoDesign team. Shown from left: Robert, Perry, Mara and Lisa.*

In 1993, after 15 years of providing in-house graphic communications for Westinghouse Canada Inc., Senior Designer/Photographer Robert Palmese and his small team of talented graphic arts professionals set up shop under a new name: Palmese PhotoDesign Group.

Their mandate was to assure Westinghouse the same level of graphic services, while offering their high calibre photography, graphic design and digital imaging skills to other businesses in the Hamilton/Toronto area.

"In launching this venture, we looked at two significant developments that were impacting the graphic services market," points out Robert. "First, most companies were reducing their communications budgets. They expected the dollars they did have available to go as far as possible.

"Secondly, with the ongoing advances in digital imaging, it was feasible for a small group of hard-working people, with the right skills, to achieve the same range and quality of graphic services previously available only through large outfits with much higher overheads," he explains.

"Our goal was to offer our customers the very best photographic and design solutions within their budget limitations."

Judging by the company's continually expanding client list, this approach has been extremely successful.

The four talented individuals who make up PhotoDesign are a close-knit bunch. Their genuine enthusiasm and fresh, creative outlook is a tangible element of their work. Together, they bring a variety of skills to the business.

Robert has years of commercial and industrial photography experience, and a flair for corporate design. Mara, a Sheridan College graduate, specializes in typesetting and layout. Perry is the resident digital illustration and pre-press technology whiz. With a degree in Political Science, Lisa's field of expertise is communications and public relations.

Proud supporters of their community, this year they put their creativity to work as the designers of the Official Event Guide of the Sesqui Celebrations.

"PhotoDesign's contribution and dedication to the Sesqui cause far exceeded our greatest expectations," said Carmen D. Rizotto, Executive Director, Hamilton Sesquicentennial Celebrations Inc.

Combining talent with technical skills, the PhotoDesign team continues to score victories in a highly competitive field.

I t's a small business known for its big business. Gilbert's Big & Tall Men's Shop, specializes in tailor-made clothing for men of generous proportions.

Hamilton's famous big-sizes clothing store was founded in 1952 by Gilbert Lazich, a professional tailor and amateur wrestler. Mr. Lazich, six-foot-one and tipping the scales well past 200 pounds, wasn't exactly small himself and he appreciated clothes tailor-made for his own oversized frame.

"And some of Gilbert's wrestling and football friends were just huge," recalls his wife, Stella Lazich. "So Gilbert started making their clothes – and we decided oversized clothing was the line of business we wanted to specialize in," adds Mrs. Lazich, secretary-treasurer of the successful business.

Predictably, Gilbert's Big & Tall grew too big for its original Kenilworth Avenue location and moved to its current King Street West building in 1954.

Perhaps just as predictably, Gilbert's Big & Tall also outgrew the century-old King West building, so in 1966 they built an addition, doubling the store's size.

And in 1973, a second addition again doubled the shop's size to its current dimensions, rivalling that of a small department store.

• Gilbert Lazich decided to make it big when he started out in business and he's never looked back. Shown here with his wife Stella and son Tom, he founded Gilbert's Big & Tall in 1952.
— Photo by Joe Bucci

The building has literally been home to the Lazichs since the early 1950s. The couple raised a family in the second-floor, three-bedroom apartment.

Their sons, Tom and Ted, work as salesmen in the store, where they are joined by professional tailors at the store, which employs a total of 10 people.

Located directly across the street from CHCH TV11's Telecentre, Gilbert's Big & Tall has had its share of famous clientele over the years.

There are, of course, famous wrestlers from the 1960s-1970s era, including Killer Kowalski, Gene Keniske, Whipper Billy Watson, Dick Beyer, the Tollis Brothers, and Benny and Billy McGuire, brothers, who each tipped the scales at more than 700 pounds.

Mrs. Lazich recalls the day the shop was visited by a very large and friendly young man named John Candy.

The late actor-comedian had stopped by to check out their sports apparel,

including jogging suits, T-shirts and pants.

"He walked in one day to see what we had and to get measured up," recollects Mrs. Lazich. "And from then on, his people would regularly place orders on his behalf. He was a nice young man."

Another celebrity who's both big and tall is Sweet Lou Dunbar of the Harlem Globetrotters. The 6-foot-11 basketball player has easy-to-remember measurements: 40-inch waist, 40-inch leg inseam and 40-inch arm length.

Another visitor was of average stature – but a show business giant.

"Bob Hope came in and bought six pairs of black, executive knee-high socks," recalls Mrs. Lazich with a laugh. "I told him I wanted to get into show business and we joked around a bit."

Another famous individual of average stature, former Prime Minister Pierre Trudeau, ended an interview being conducted at the Telecentre and visited the shop to pick up an expensive silk tie.

Although the store also sells suits in average sizes, it specializes in providing great-fitting, tailored, oversized clothing from pajamas and night clothes to suits, sportswear and casual attire. "More than ever, people are looking for perfection,," says Mrs. Lazich, "and we do our very best to give them the perfect fit."

• Hamilton Place has been a cultural showpiece ever since the curtain first went up in September of 1973. Catering to a smorgasbord of tastes, the Great Hall has attracted the brightest stars from the entertainment world.
– *Photo by Dennis McGreal*

It opened with a flourish that evening in September of 1973, as members of the Hamilton Philharmonic Orchestra stuck up their instruments. Then, the flamboyant Maestro Boris Brott whirled on the carpeted podium and raised his baton to conduct the audience in "O Canada."

In the front row, Mayor Vic Copps wiped tears from his eyes, as did Hamilton Place General Manager George MacPherson, standing in the wings. The 2,000 people in the capacity crowd swelled and almost burst with civic pride.

There were waves of applause – reaching a deafening crescendo as an emotional outpouring thundered and roared through the seats and crashed onto the stage.

Because this was the home that Hamilton built.

Today, two decades later, George MacPherson is vice-president of ATP/Dodger Productions, based on Broadway, New York. He is one of the biggest names in the business. Recently, Variety magazine, the bible of the industry, awarded him the stature of the best road show manager in all the United States.

But even that can't compare to the thrill of that night in the theatre he helped launch. And, while George admits to having had many successes in his career, "I still consider the opening of 'The Place' as the highlight of my life," he says.

The moment capped a trio of victories, recalls Marnie Paikin, former chairman of the building's board of directors. In '71, we celebrated our 125th birthday. A year later, we hosted and won the Grey Cup. In '73, the curtain went up on Hamilton Place. We soared in self-confidence. "And, we said to ourselves, My Gosh! We're a terrific people around here," with a spirit of determination "to create our own destiny," she says. That's the kind of legacy that Hamilton Place brought to the citizens.

The city had seriously discussed an entertainment facility as far back as the 1950s. One proposal called for a trio of buildings – an auditorium, athletic centre and planetarium.

In 1963, the Hamilton Downtown Association spearheaded a drive to create a cultural showpiece.

Among members of the newly formed committee was The Hamilton Spectator's Business Editor, Milford Smith, whom some credit as being the "sparkplug" for the theatrical home.

Other key players were Colin S. Glassco, vice-president and general manager of the Appleford Paper Products Company; Jack McNie, president of Russell T. Kelley Advertising and Martin Luxton of the legal firm, Martin and Martin – as well as F.W. (Ted) Daikin, executive vice-president of the Robinson's stores and the chairman of the first campaign committee.

Behind it all was Mayor Vic Copps, who rallied the troops – politicians, industry and the people – to support the cause. The office workers signed up for payroll deductions, and housewives dipped into their pockets to pay nickels, dimes and half-dollars weekly to what was then only an artist's conception of a theatre-auditorium.

One senior citizen endorsed and handed over a pension cheque, while school children donated proceeds from lemonade stands and penny sales. Together, they raised more than $3.2 million. It was a supreme act of faith in a factory town.

The rest was supposed to come from three levels of government – municipal, federal and provincial. But both Ottawa and Queen's Park backed out, leaving us to pick up the tab. (Interestingly enough, Toronto's fund-raising drive to raise $4.8 million for the St. Lawrence Centre for the Arts, fell hopelessly short of its goal. It raised a paltry $1.7 million.)

Our $10.9 million showpiece for the arts, erected by what was then a smokestack and steel-mill citizenry, still stands as one of the most successful fund-raising ventures in North America. (Wayne Strongman of the Bach-Elgar Choir probably put it best when he enthused: "Talk about the triumph of the common man!")

There have been many triumphs since then, though perhaps none so powerful as that of September, 1973. Ask 100 people about their own memories, either a play or a concert, and you'll probably come up with 100 answers. And there, in itself, lies the true beauty of the theatre; that it serves a smorgasbord of tastes.

That stage has held every star from Harry Belafonte to Celine Dion, everything from Sesame Street to Stompin' Tom. The list has been a who's who of the industry: Liberace, Jack Jones, George Carlin, Tom Jones, David Copperfield, Rita MacNeil, k.d. lang, Anne Murray, Howie Mandel, Victor Borge, Bill Cosby, Nana Mouskouri, The Bolshoi Ballet, La Traviata, Don Giovanni, A Chorus Line, Hometown, Jesus Christ Superstar, West Side Story, Les Miserables, Evita and Cats. But more than that, we've nurtured our own homegrown talent.

Our orchestra has been music to the ears of international critics. Opera Hamilton has soared to star-studded heights under Maestro Daniel Lipton. The Bach-Elgar Choir has sung a new tune, as one of Canada's best amateur group of choristers.

The Hamilton Ballet School has stepped into the spotlight, and added another move to our communal repertoire. Then, there is the Geritol Follies, which attracts hundreds of busloads of tourists from across the United States and Canada. Graduates of New Faces, the theatrical group, have a role in every major production in the country, from Miss Saigon to Showboat.

No one knows precisely how much money these events create for the community. "The return is enormous," says Gabe Macaluso, the General Manager of Hamilton Entertainment and Convention Facilities Inc. One study by McMaster University suggested $145 million is generated annually by the Hamilton Convention Centre, Hamilton Place and Copps Coliseum, enriching the region both financially and culturally.

What began as a vision, became the reality, and paid off, big time. "It was a dream, forever," recalls Geraldine Copps. "It was such a community success story."

"It's an example of what can happen when you get enthusiastic support from the community," says Jack McNie, former chairman of the Hamilton Place co-ordinating committee. It's a building that, he says, "turned out to be a bargain in terms of the cost. It's still an outstanding theatre."

We'll end with the words of George Macpherson, who extols the designs of architect Trevor Garwood-Jones.

"I probably spend 300 days a year in and about theatres throughout the world," says the former Hamilton Place GM.

"I can see in the new buildings many design innovations that came from Hamilton Place. There are a couple that have even copied the Great Hall's colour scheme," he adds.

"But no matter where in the world or on what stage I am standing, there is only one Hamilton Place.

"While bricks and mortar and paint can be copied, the spirit and love from the citizens of Hamilton that went into the creation of Hamilton Place can never be copied or repeated."

ABOVE: *Hollywood star and hometown hero Martin Short strikes a pose with members of the New Faces theatre group.*
– Photo by Dennis McGreal

Their kids have grown up and moved away. Now they're left with a lot of memories – and an oversized, multi-bedroom home that needs a lot of upkeep.

They're empty-nesters. They're among a growing number who no longer live with their family – but still have the work of maintaining a family home.

And they've found a friend in Micor Developments Inc., a company which specializes in meeting the needs of an aging population of empty nesters.

Tired of trudging up and down stairs? Welcome to Micor. The firm's trademark is a staircase with a line drawn through it. It proudly boasts the slogan: No More Stairs. "We specialize in building single-storey, executive townhouse bungalows for empty nesters and people over 50," says Micor President Michael Corrado.

His company brought to the forefront the advantages of one-floor living and was the first in the area to really promote the single-storey townhome.

"It's the answer for a lot of people," says the president of Micor, a firm which derives its name from the first few letters of Michael Corrado's first and last name.

Founded in 1986, Micor Developments has led the way in bringing not only new

Michael Corrado, president of Micor Developments, is shown at his first development, Loyalist Green, located on Wilson Street West in Ancaster.
– Photo by David Gruggen

homes to empty nesters, but entirely new lifestyles as well. Micor's one-floor executive townhomes leave homeowners to enjoy themselves while their condominium fees pay for snow removal, lawn-cutting, garden upkeep, water, property insurance and most other maintenance.

For homeowners long accustomed to devoting their spare time to such property chores, to have this time freed up for pleasurable pursuits is a welcome change.

Nor do they have to settle for cramped living space. These outstanding one-to-two bedroom homes feature eat-in kitchens and large master bedrooms with ensuite bathrooms. Generous principal rooms with cathedral ceilings and skylights add to a spacious atmosphere.

With so many beneficial features, along with privacy and superb locations, the Micor homes are also attracting busy younger professionals with little time for yard work. "And you have the security of living in a private enclave with a private

drive," notes Mr. Corrado, a first-generation builder who has risen to prominence in the Hamilton area.

"You've also got the peace and quiet of an adult community," adds the second vice-president of the Hamilton-Halton Home Builders Association. The homes can be seen in developments such as The Bungalows of Ancaster in the Meadowlands subdivision, Loyalist green, Wilson Woods and The Gables of Fiddlers Green in the heart of Old Ancaster.

As it celebrated its 10th anniversary in 1996, Mr. Corrado formed a partnership with the Pica/Calzonetti Group to undertake some impressive projects in Hamilton, including redeveloping the former Cathedral Girls High School into a state-of-the-art retirement complex.

Another Pica/Calzonetti/Corrado project – one Mr. Corrado is particularly exited about – is The Bungalows at Chedoke, an executive townhouse development north of Mohawk Road in an older Mountain Brow neighbourhood, close to Chedoke Hospital and shopping. "It's a great opportunity to buy a new home in an established area that hasn't been built in for decades," says Mr. Corrado.

"Where else can you can make a brand new beginning in an old neighbourhood?"

From large subdivisions to major projects of large firms, surveying and engineering services have been provided by Hamilton-based Ashenhurst Nouwens Limited for more than 40 years.

Ashenhurst Nouwens has built a solid reputation as a provider of professional engineering and land surveying services to various levels of government and to such major corporations as Stelco, for its continuous caster, and Dofasco, for its No. 3 Blast Furnace reconstruction.

Founded in 1956 and incorporated in 1982, Ashenhurst Nouwens Limited is the successor to H.B. Ashenhurst, a Consulting Professional Engineer and Ontario Land Surveyor. Since its incorporation, the company has experienced steady growth in the volume, range and size of the projects it has undertaken.

"Our prime work has centred on subdivision development, both in short and long-term projects," notes Peter Ashenhurst, company secretary-treasurer.

"Projects have included complete engineering and land surveying services for 20 Place Estates, a condominium development of more than 600 units by the Spallacci Group and phases two, three, four and five of Dewitt Heights subdivision, developed by George Sinclair Construction," adds Mr. Ashenhurst, who has more than 30 years' experience in the engineering and surveying field.

He was previously project engineer co-ordinator for the sub-structure construction at McMaster Medical Centre and provided legal survey work for the Department of Highways for various 400 series of highways for land acquisitions, construction surveys and supervision.

Ashenhurst Nouwens, with a branch office in Grimsby and a consultation office at Jordan Station, has also performed detailed engineering and survey work for some development phases of such Hamilton subdivisions as Wellington Chase, Abbey Hill Farm and South Hill.

The company is also a major player in the surveying and engineering design of townhouses and condominiums, including the actual architectural design of many projects, and single-family houses.

Work with various government levels has included involvement in providing airport and navigation surveys to the federal Ministry of Transport, ongoing work on the Red Hill Creek Expressway for Hamilton-Wentworth and work on projects for conservation authorities.

A complete range of planning, surveying, engineering and building design services are available from initial stages of conception, to feasibility studies, planning, pre-engineering and design work, to project supervision, including legal surveys and construction layout – all under the personal direction of a company executive or senior staff member.

Company president John Nouwens takes pride in his firm's ability to produce high-quality work within the confines of a given project. "The company puts a high priority on its ability to complete projects within the required time and budget constraints," says Mr. Nouwens, an Ontario Land Surveyor who previously worked eight years in Holland as a town planner and surveyor-engineer.

"We have the personnel, equipment and resources to produce the successful completion of any assignment."

"In the normal course of the work program, our multi-disciplined staff are able to work either in the office or field environment," he adds. "Such flexibility enables the most efficient use of our resources as the moment requires."

• *Peter Ashenhurst, seated, is shown with partner John Nouwens, O.L.S., on right, and Ashenhurst Nouwens' chief engineer Donald Senft, P.Eng.*
– Photo by David Gruggen

Superman is a cameraman's nightmare. When moviedom's Man of Steel leaps over tall buildings or flies faster than a speeding bullet, Warner Bros. Inc.'s helicopter-mounted cameras are pushed to superhuman limits.

The chances of capturing these heroic feats on clear film footage free of motion distortion would appear remote when the movie camera is shooting from a swaying, vibrating helicopter.

This is a job for WESCAM – a progressive world leader in the design and manufacturing of stabilized aerial camera, image capture and video transmission systems used in public safety and surveillance and entertainment services industries.

Living up to its 'Rock Solid. Worldwide' logo, WESCAM employs gyro-stabilizing technology developed by company founder Noxon Leavitt.

WESCAM camera mounts encase, isolate and suspend the movie camera, keeping it motionless, despite external jarring and shifting.

Using WESCAM technology, cameras are able to shoot remarkably clear footage, free from any motion distortion – even if the camera and WESCAM mount are attached to the side of a lurching train, truck or helicopter.

This advanced equipment is so sensitive, in fact, that it can detect the earth's rotational movement.

Not surprisingly, WESCAM, which was formerly known as Istec (short for Isolation Technology), has seen its camera mounts used in the Olympics, the Tour de France, police surveillance work, the Pope's Tour of Canada, and numerous Hollywood epics, including Goldeneye, Judge Dredd, Braveheart, Seven, Runaway Train, Star Wars, The Fugitive, Patriot Games, the huge Imax Systems Inc.-National Film Board of Canada films and, of course, the Superman movies.

In 1995, WESCAM became listed on the TSE and a successful sale of 4.4 million shares netted the company close to $30 million.

That same year, WESCAM acquired 100 per cent of Versatron Corp., giving the Flamborough company greater penetration into the American market for unmanned air vehicles.

WESCAM, with an October 31 year end, reported a 181 per cent rise in fiscal 1995 net earnings to $1.7 million on revenue of $32.4 million.

In March 1996, WESCAM reported fiscal first quarter net earnings of $305,000 – an increase of 455 per cent over $55,000 for the first three months of fiscal 1995. Revenue rose by 125 per cent to $10.8 million and it bought 100 per

• Mark Chamberlain went to work for WESCAM in 1984 with a goal of one day owning the company. Today, he is the president of the company, which in 1995 was listed on the TSE and netted close to $30 million through a successful sale of 4.4 million shares.

cent ownership of WESCAM-USA.

That same month, WESCAM announced a $6.2 million military subcontract to build high accuracy pan and tilt platforms to hold surveillance equipment on behalf of the Canadian Armed Forces.

The contract was just another example of WESCAM's innovative approach.

Mark Chamberlain, WESCAM's confident president, anticipates using the military contract as a platform leading to other contracts.

Mr. Chamberlain's strategy of finding and utilizing new applications for his company's constantly evolving technological know-how is a driving force behind its impressive growth.

"We capture and enhance visual information acquired from moving platforms," notes Mr. Chamberlain. "And there appears to be no limit on future growth."

The company spun off from Westinghouse Canada in 1974 when Noxon Leavitt, the former head of advanced electronic research and electro-optics at Westinghouse Canada, went into business on his own after Westinghouse

decided to divest itself of the gyro-stabilizing technology he had developed. Istec would later rename itself after its best-known product, WESCAM.

The company grew rapidly, quadrupling sales in five years to $1 million by the mid-1980s through the sale, leasing and servicing of its gyro-stabilizing WESCAM technology.

In 1984, the firm experienced another pivotal point in its corporate history with the arrival of Mr. Chamberlain, then a young engineering consultant and entrepreneur in his 20s, who recalls going to work for the company "on the understanding I would be buying it."

And the years leading up to the buyout provided Mr. Chamberlain with valuable experience, thanks to Mr. Leavitt, who has since left the company.

"Noxon Leavitt was my mentor," says Mr. Chamberlain. "I gained a lot from Noxon's honest approach to business and his never-say-die attitude was inspiring," he explains. "He wasn't afraid to try anything. And you have to take risks to succeed at anything."

• *WESCAM has earned worldwide acclaim for its gyro-stabilizing technology, which has been used in the coverage of sporting events such as the Olympics and the Tour de France. The firm's technology has also been embraced by Hollywood, where WESCAM camera mounts have been used in the making of numerous movies, including Star Wars and Superman. Success in Hollywood has resulted in WESCAM receiving an Oscar from the Academy of Motion Picture Arts & Sciences, and WESCAM personnel have also been honoured with five Emmy Awards for technical excellence and personal achievement.*

"Over the next two years," recalls Mr. Chamberlain, "I put together a management and financial team, and we bought the company in February 1987."

Then in his late 20s, Mr. Chamberlain sold his house and put everything he had on the line to buy the company.

But the calculated risk paid off.

The business grew from 17 employees and $1 million in revenue in 1987 to a total of 60 employees and $12 million in revenue in 1993, when Mr. Chamberlain brought in a new partner, Jefferson Partners Capital Corp., headed by

Jack Kiervin, who is now WESCAM's chairman. "We merged with Jefferson and became a technology company with capital," explains Mr. Chamberlain, while adding that in 1993 the company began to make the transition from an entrepreneurial entity to a professionally managed organization.

Mr. Chamberlain remains a minority owner of WESCAM, which by the mid-1990s employed 250 people – 150 of them working in the Hamilton area – serving the public safety and surveillance, and entertainment services industries.

• It's the audience that's usually asking for more when Theatre Aquarius stages one of its productions. Shown here are actors David Walden and Gordon Woolvett in a classic scene from the Aquarius production of Oliver. Theatre Aquarius productions are staged at the duMaurier Centre in the heart of downtown Hamilton.

• *The Disney On Ice production of Aladdin was one of the many shows to make a stop at Copps Coliseum. Over the years, Hamilton audiences have also been thrilled by performances by top stars from the figure skating world.*
– Photo by Dennis McGreal

Anthony DeSantis was a young man with a mission when he arrived in Hamilton in 1951. Far from enjoying the relatively carefree life of many teenagers, the 17-year-old immigrant from Italy focused on work from the moment he arrived in Canada.

Mr. DeSantis was determined to earn enough money to send for his parents and family to join him in Hamilton.

He achieved this goal by spending long days working construction and manufacturing jobs and driving a bus for the Hamilton Street Railway while taking English language classes in the evenings.

In 1957, while in his early 20s, Mr. DeSantis met prominent real estate broker Bill Kronas and began selling houses on behalf of the brokerage. The late Mr. Kronas became a mentor to Mr. DeSantis, schooling him in the ways of real estate sales as the two developed something of a father-and-son relationship built on mutual admiration and respect.

Within just a few months, the enthusiastic young salesman was one of the Metropolitan Hamilton Real Estate Board's top producers.

Convinced that the real estate market offered a wide array of opportunities, Mr. DeSantis began purchasing lots, houses and land parcels as far north as Timmins in hopes that the mining centre would develop gold mines. Although a gold rush did not materialize, the real estate holdings still sold for a profit.

In 1963, Mr. DeSantis bought a dilapidated house on Chestnut Street by paying the City of Hamilton for taxes owed on the land. He then co-built his first house.

It was the start of a developer role he would expand over the years by building and selling thousands of homes in subdivisions in Hamilton-Wentworth and Halton regions and Brant County.

Mr. DeSantis' most recent project is a just-completed 82-house development on Stoney Creek Mountain. He is now working on Millbrook Village, a 300-home subdivision in Burlington, valued at more than $60 million. In addition to

residential townhouses, condominium apartments and single-family homes, Mr. DeSantis has also built a number of commercial and industrial projects.

Today, various aspects of Mr. DeSantis' real estate and development businesses are controlled by a number of companies that he runs as president, including A. DeSantis Holdings Ltd., DeSantis Group Inc., A. DeSantis Real Estate Ltd., HGH Developments Ltd. and A. DeSantis Developments Ltd.

After three decades on Ottawa Street in a building Mr. DeSantis built himself, he

has now moved his operations to 8 Main Street E., a property he has just acquired and is in the process of renovating.

Active in the community, Mr. DeSantis is a member of the Metropolitan Hamilton Real Estate Board, Canadian Real Estate Association, Hamilton and District Chamber of Commerce and the Hamilton-Halton Home Builders' Association.

He's also a member of The Order of Sons of Italy of Ontario; The Hamilton Club; Glendale Golf and Country Club and St. Luke's Parish.

Although his hard work and determination earned him success, Mr. DeSantis admits much of this success would not have been possible if not for a supportive

family, including wife Vicki, vice-president of the family firms; daughter Andrea, in her second year of law at Osgoode Hall; and son Anthony Jr., who joined the family business in the spring of 1995.

Today, with Anthony DeSantis Jr., who holds a BA from the University of Toronto and an MBA from McMaster University, also playing an active role in charting the future of the DeSantis companies, this successful family business is well-positioned for continued prosperity as it builds on an enduring reputation for value and service.

• *Anthony DeSantis is pictured with son Anthony DeSantis Jr., who joined the family firm in the spring of 1995.*
– Photo by David Gruggen

• Mario Nesci is owner and president of Mario's Tile and Carpet. His office and warehouse is located at Mountain Industrial Park on Nebo Road.
— **Photo by David Gruggen**

P eople are literally 'floored' by Mario Nesci's services. And the owner-president of Mario's Tile and Carpet couldn't be happier.

Mr. Nesci was destined for the flooring business since his youth in the Calabria region of Italy as a 13-year-old apprentice tile installer. On arriving in Hamilton in 1976 as a certified tile installer, he stayed with his sponsoring uncle Frank Stancati in Stoney Creek and he initially worked for tile installation companies.

After-hours, Mr. Nesci ran a tile service of his own while nurturing dreams of one day having his own business.

Mr. Nesci moved into an apartment in Hamilton with his brother Frank about eight months later where he continued to build his own client base from after-hours tile installation work. In 1978, Mr. Nesci married and moved to a house on Stella Court in Hamilton, where he made the decision to go into business for himself.

"I felt I had enough customers at that point to justify going into business on my own," recalls Mr. Nesci, adding his wife,

Maria, did the books and some customer relations work while he used his garage as a warehouse for imported Italian tiles.

"We had a couple of workmen who would come to my house to pick up the tile," recollects Mr. Nesci. "And I'd give them an espresso to start their day right," he adds with a chuckle.

In 1980, Mr. Nesci gave his business a formal name: Mario's Tile and Carpet. The company soon outgrew the household garage and Mario's Tile moved to roomier quarters in a 2,000-square-foot location on Hamilton Mountain in 1983.

Then, in 1992, the growing company moved again, this time to quarters five times larger at Mountain Industrial Park, where Mario's Tiles and Carpet continues to occupy a 10,000-square-foot office and

warehouse unit on Nebo Road, between Stone Church Road East and Highway 53.

The company, which recently added a new computer system, now employs five people – including a couple of the original espresso-quaffing workers – plus a pool of workers who are employed on a contract basis for specific projects.

"We supply a lot of builders and stores with imported Italian tile," notes Mr. Nesci, adding that his business is evenly divided between wholesaling to business and retailing to the general public. In addition to expertly cutting and laying ceramic floor and wall tiles, the company also lays carpet and hardwood flooring.

"Tiles are still the biggest part of our business – but hardwood floors are coming back in popularity," asserts Mr. Nesci, whose firm supports a number of charities and sponsors a minor hockey team at the Chedoke Twin Pad Arena.

"We help out the customer the best we can," says Mr. Nesci. "Either we'll install the flooring or we'll provide advice if the customer wants to do it himself."

Getting taken to the cleaners can be a rewarding experience if you're going to Wright's Cleaners and Laundry.

Since 1872, Wright's has provided exemplary service to its customers.

Generations of the Wright family ran their successful drycleaning business until 1990, when brothers Doug and Allan Wright sold the business.

Wright's Cleaners was subsequently acquired by the current owners, Feroz Mithani and his wife, Noorjehan.

Although relatively new to Wright's, Mr. Mithani brings more than 20 years of professional drycleaning managerial experience to the venerable company.

Since taking over Wright's Cleaners in 1991, the Mithanis have increased the number of pick-up and drop-off outlets to 16, half of them in Hamilton, the rest in a number of other centres, including Waterdown, Ancaster, Dundas, Stoney Creek and Oakville.

Annual revenue for the company has increased by 50 per cent since the takeover. Wright's now drycleans 1.5 million garments and provides laundry services to 130,000 shirts annually.

The Mithanis have also increased the number of employees to 65 from 30, most of them at the Hamilton Wright's outlets and at the drycleaning plant and headquarters located on Dunsmure Road at Reid Avenue, Hamilton. They've also invested heavily in modern, environmentally friendly equipment.

"We changed all the machinery in 1995," Mr. Mithani explains with pride, "and we now have some of the most energy-efficient, environmentally friendly equipment in the industry."

The Mithanis also have an innovative approach that embraces the latest quality-enhancing technologies and processes.

Mr. Mithani notes that his company is employing the unique Master Drycleaner cleaning process which was patented by the American firm Fabritech.

"With the Master Cleaner method, the whites turn whiter and the dark colours turn brighter," explains Mr. Mithani.

Wright's, he adds, also uses the Adjust-a-Drape drapery cleaning process.

"With the Adjust-a-Drape process, we can guarantee the length of the drapes and an even hemline," asserts Mr. Mithani, who notes that the process can involve stretching drapes back to their original length after inevitable shrinkage and the evening-out of wavy hemlines.

For higher levels of satisfaction, the company offers customers its Custom Deluxe service, featuring hand-washing and drycleaning and hand-pressing.

"The Custom Deluxe service costs a little more, but it's worth spending a little more for garments requiring extra care," says Mr. Mithani. "These garments will last longer, there will be no shrinkage problems and you won't discover any missing sequins or buttons."

With this much emphasis placed on guaranteed results and quality cleaning, it's hardly surprising that the drycleaning chain is growing due to referrals.

Wright's larger customers include the municipalities of Hamilton and Hamilton-Wentworth region; area fire and police departments and boards of education, National Steel Car, Copps Coliseum and the downtown Hamilton Armoury.

"We're very pleased that people come to us with their wedding gowns and most valued, expensive clothing," says Mr. Mithani. "People trust us with their very best clothing and we do our very best to make sure our customers are satisfied."

• Wright's Cleaners and Laundry, with a workforce of 65 people, has a total of 16 pick-up and drop-off outlets in the area, half of those in Hamilton.

CODY'S HOME DECOR INC.

Neil Cody isn't one to paper things over – not when a fresh coat of paint can have you convinced you're gazing at marble or antique wood.

The president of Cody's Home Decor Inc. is transforming the venerable Hamilton paint and wallpaper business into a leader in the lucrative field of home decorating. "You've got to be nimble – and be very customer focused," says Mr. Cody as he wanders through his landmark store, warehouse and headquarters on East Avenue at Barton Street East.

The company is a major distributor of wall stencils, gold paints, an array of decorative paints, crackling compounds, specialty applicators and brushes (including a $150 badger fur brush) and other home decor craft products.

Mr. Cody notes the former Cody's Stores Ltd. went through a financial re-organization in the spring of 1996 to emerge as Cody's Home Decor Inc., a firm specializing in home decorating products. He continues to build the wholesale and retail sides of the business.

Yet this innovative leader in the home decor business was initially reluctant to join his father, Keith Cody, in running a family firm that has been home to generations of Codys since 1921.

"After I graduated from high school, my dad was keen on my getting into the business – but I didn't want to come in on dad's coat tails," recalls Mr. Cody, who cites his father and designer-decorator wife Margaret among major influences shaping his entrepreneurial growth.

Instead, the young high school grad set off to see the world, backpacking his way across Europe, the Middle East and Asia for three years. When he returned to Canada, Mr. Cody was ready to commit to going into the business "provided I could make my own mark."

Mr. Cody received that opportunity in 1980 as general manager of the company's then newly opened Western Canada division. After seven years in Calgary and Vancouver, he returned to Hamilton in 1988 as national sales manager. A year later, he was named president.

Keith Cody remains chairman and store manager of Cody's, while son Peter is a distribution clerk and son Andrew operates the Western Canada division.

Founded in 1921 by brothers Basil and Douglas Cody, the business was initially focused on hardware, with paint and wallpaper mere sidelines.

During the Depression, the business pared back to sell basic clothing and home decorating goods along with ingredients for making one's own paint. It was a forerunner of the do-it-yourself home decorating business that would more fully emerge 60 years later.

In 1945, Basil Cody's 18-year-old son Keith left school to work at the store, selling light bulbs for 10 cents each, wallpaper for 14 cents a roll and paint for $5.50 a gallon.

Keith Cody acquired full ownership of the company in 1970 and sold it to his son, Neil in 1996, the year Cody's marked its 75th birthday. The private firm is now a major distributor of home decor specialty products, while its retail store continues to sell paint and wallpaper.

Neil Cody notes the company's evolution has accelerated during his presidency.

"We've had more change in the past six years than the previous 30," he says. "Our primary direction now is to continue building the home decorating business with specialized home decor products."

Chapter 6

Sights & Sounds

PAGES 152-153: *The Battle of Stoney Creek comes to life each summer during a weekend celebration of the War of 1812 at Battlefield Park in Stoney Creek. The site is also home to the Stoney Creek Monument and historic Battlefield House, which was built in 1794.*
– Photo by Dennis McGreal

ABOVE: *Young performers entertain during It's Your Festival, a four-day multi-arts and ethnic cultural showcase for all ages, held annually at Gage Park.*

FACING PAGE: *Dressed in period costume, a trio entertains on the grounds of Whitehern; the Town Crier and Queen Victoria make an appearance during Waterdown's Victorian Days; and dancers take a bow after performing at Earthsong, a celebration of cultures through music and dance, food and arts and crafts.*
– Photos by Dennis McGreal

Murray Hogarth's decision 40 years ago to open his own independent gas bar flew in the face of conventional wisdom.

The major oil companies owned the streets, and would surely crush any challengers. But Mr. Hogarth saw an opportunity to carve out a unique niche based on delivering service excellence at the pumps, and took advantage.

At 25, he sold shares to an investor, borrowed money from family members, and opened the first Pioneer gas bar on Upper James Street in Hamilton. He later repaid the loans, bought out the investors and assumed full control of the company.

With 26 stations in the Hamilton area today, Pioneer Petroleums provides one out of every five fill-ups to area motorists. The original Upper James site has since been expanded and includes one of Canada's first automated car washes.

Pioneer's additional 220-plus retail gas sites, most of them in Ontario, make the company Canada's largest independent gasoline marketer – and the only major gas retailer to continue growing over the last three years. The aggressive independent, founded on a spirit of service, has been winning customers through its commitment to delivering top-quality products and the highest level of customer service and convenience.

"When I opened the first location on Upper James in 1956, I saw an opportunity the major players were overlooking and took advantage of it," says Mr. Hogarth, who had previously worked as a sales and marketing representative for British American Oil Co., a predecessor of Gulf Canada later acquired by Petro Canada.

"By making customer service our main focus, we gave our customers something they couldn't find anywhere else."

Mr. Hogarth placed his attendants in a kiosk at pump islands, giving customers instant service at a time when most gas stations were serviced by mechanics who responded when customers drove over a bell cord. Then he introduced Bonus Bucks – Pioneer cash that gave customers another reason to return to his service stations. Bonus Bucks remain as successful today as ever.

Next came the Pioneer Pledge – an assurance that every windshield would be cleaned, that the attendant would offer to check under the hood and that every customer would receive Bonus Bucks. If not, Pioneer would give them $10 worth of Bonus Bucks – no questions asked.

This spirit of service brought steady growth for the fledgling company.

Today, Mr. Hogarth is Chairman and Chief Executive Officer of The Pioneer Group Inc., a Burlington-based family

holding company that has fostered his entrepreneurial spirit in others through the creation of various partnership companies.

Many of those companies have been born out of Mr. Hogarth's desire to deliver even higher levels of customer convenience at Pioneer gas bars, starting with a company that designs and builds car washes and later evolving to include dry cleaners, Tim Hortons and fast-food franchises, real estate development and even bagged ice.

It's a winning combination that finds

many motorists pulling in to have their tanks filled and their cars washed while they sip a cup of Tim Hortons coffee, and pick up a bag of ice or their dry cleaning to take home.

"The strategy of The Pioneer Group is to continue to find retail uses for our commercial real estate," explains Mr. Hogarth, adding that the company sometimes adds strip malls to its sites.

"Multiple-use sites generate more consumer traffic, benefitting each of the businesses while giving the consumer

• *Murray Hogarth is Chairman and Chief Executive Officer of The Pioneer Group. He opened his first Pioneer gas bar 40 years ago. Today, he has 26 Pioneer gas stations in the area, including this one at the corner of Fairview Street and Guelph Line in Burlington.*
– Photo by Bob Chambers

the convenience of a one-stop location to meet their needs," he adds.

Sales through the The Pioneer Group's office exceed $350 million, not including $150 million of business it manages through a unique strategic alliance Mr. Hogarth negotiated with Sunoco more than two years ago.

Through its alliance with Sunoco, Pioneer also developed its own high-performance premium gasoline – Magnum 93 Octane – giving the company an edge over most majors who were offering 91

Octane as their premium product.

The pioneer spirit that founded the business 40 years ago has been continuously fostered, allowing The Pioneer Group to rise to any challenge even in tough economic times.

"We have nearly doubled our size in the past three years, even though the size of the Ontario petroleum market has actually decreased," notes Mr. Hogarth.

Much of that growth, he explains, has been achieved through improved efficiencies and through the acquisitions of other

less-efficient retail gasoline networks including Top Value and Olco.

Pioneer's Burlington head office employs about 50 people, most of whom are long-service, experienced employees who have been largely responsible for Pioneer's success. The Pioneer Group collectively is responsible for employment of more than 2,000.

With its aggressive, imaginative and diversified approach, The Pioneer Group is preparing to take advantage of further opportunities as they are identified.

ABOVE: *A unique learning centre, the Children's Museum is designed especially for children ages two to 13. Each exhibit at the museum, on the grounds of Gage Park, offers creative and interactive experiences to be shared by the whole family.*
– Photo by Dennis McGreal

FACING PAGE: *Canada's largest outdoor wave pool is part of Wild Waterworks at Confederation Park. Featuring water slides and areas for younger children, Wild Waterworks is open daily from June through to Labour Day.*
– Photo by David Gruggen

• An modern indoor swimming pool with a giant water slide is one of the many features of Hamilton's Royal Connaught Howard Johnson Hotel.
– Photo by David Gruggen

From the elegance of a bygone era to contemporary music and modern recreation facilities, the Royal Connaught Howard Johnson Plaza Hotel offers a memorable stay.

Officially opened more than 80 years ago by the Duke of Connaught, the venerable hotel has played host to an array of notable guests, including Prime Minister Lester B. Pearson, Ontario Premier Mike Harris, country music stars Shania Twain and Michelle Wright and comedian Martin Short.

Margaret and Pierre Trudeau were also among the many well-known guests to enjoy a quiet escape from the public eye in the comfortable confines of the hotel.

"It's still the Grand Old Lady of Hamilton and it's truly one of Canada's great hotels," notes hotel manager Louis Jaketic, who is emphasizing the old and the new at this landmark establishment which overlooks Gore Park in the heart of downtown Hamilton.

Mr. Jaketic says the hotel's stately old charm will imbue celebration events designed to evoke a sense of nostalgia and commemorate the Connaught's central role in Hamilton's social life.

He points out that the hotel also offers such modern features as a large indoor swimming pool and giant water slide.

There are also several popular in-hotel attractions, including Yuk Yuk's comedy club, Fran's Restaurant and Larry's Hideaway, a restaurant-bar facility featuring live music and entertainment. The in-hotel attractions operate from space leased from the hotel.

In addition, the hotel offers seasonal family packages featuring price discounts and free accommodations for children under the age of 18 sharing a room with their parents. The packages are a terrific bargain, both for visitors to Hamilton – and for native Hamiltonians, who can indulge in an escape to a nearby source of entertainment and pampering.

And, area residents don't have to travel very far to take a dip in the pool and enjoy a rejuvenating weekend getaway.

Mr. Jaketic says the Royal Connaught Howard Johnson's 207 comfortable rooms, meeting halls and main ballroom were to undergo a general upgrading in 1996 in preparation for increased business from tourism and conventions.

"With the number of conventions that are coming to Hamilton, we're looking forward to a great year," says Mr. Jaketic.

"We're very confident in Hamilton. The area has the lowest unemployment of any centre in Canada – and the outlook is great for tourism and conventions."

Mr. Jaketic says the change to Howard Johnson ownership has brought additional benefits, including the big hotel chain's reservation system, name recognition, international marketing and advertising programs and quality assurance program.

Noting that hotel guests are guaranteed a consistent level of quality in facilities and service, Mr. Jaketic explains that the Connaught takes great pride in meeting and exceeding standards to make every stay a memorable one.

"We want our guests to be as comfortable as possible, to make themselves at home and to really enjoy their stay in one of our country's great hotels."

• *Overlooking Gore Park in the heart of downtown Hamilton, The Royal Connaught Howard Johnson Hotel remains one of the great hotels in Canada.*
– Photo by David Gruggen

• The corner of West Avenue and Barton Street is a much brighter place, thanks to a group of students who put their artistic skills to work as part of a government program. The young artists painted a mural highlighting Black history on the outside walls of the former West Avenue School, which is currently the Rotary Club of Hamilton Self-Help Centre.
— *Photo by Dennis McGreal*

LEFT: *Festitalia, an annual celebration of Italian arts and culture, serves up food and fun for everyone. Festitalia's furry mascot, Amico, a hit with young and old alike, can be seen at the various events throughout the annual month-long extravaganza.*

BELOW: *Good food is a part of Festitalia each year and there's plenty to be had during the popular Regional Food Nights. Here, a volunteer cook from one of the local Italian clubs works her kitchen magic prior to a dinner.*
— Photos by
Brian Carnahan

ABOVE: A parachutist makes a perfect landing during the Hamilton International Air Show. Held annually at the Hamilton Airport, the show is one of the best expositions of historic and contemporary aircraft from the Canadian and U.S. forces and from other countries of the world.

LEFT: The spectacular new Canadian Warplane Heritage Museum, located at the Hamilton Airport. The world-class, state-of-the-art, wing-shaped building is home to one of the largest flying vintage collections in the world, which has been expanded to include jets. Among the exhibits is an 'indoor flying' T-33 jet trainer that allows visitors to pilot the aircraft through the innovative use of micro technology. Built at a cost of $12 million, the museum was designed by architect Brian Chamberlain. Featuring one of the largest aviation gift shops in the country, it was officially opened in April of 1996 by Prince Charles.

— Photos by Dennis McGreal

• *The Graham Restorations team, from left, front: Marietta Ciavarra, Elizabeth Graham, Diane Killins, Jennifer Graham. Back: Phil Ball, Terry Bolan, Allan Graham, Ben Graham, Pete Demmans, Steven Jovanov, Jeremy Belanger.*
– Photo by Joe Bucci

A fire damaging your home can be a traumatic experience, leaving you and your family to struggle with the loss of treasured possessions.

As you sift through the charred remnants of memorabilia, you are often in a state of confusion. You wonder whether you can salvage furnishings or anything of value from the ashes.

In such difficult situations, a growing number of people turn to the expert advice and assistance offered by Graham Restorations and Cleaning Services.

"It's a very stressful time for most of our clients, whether they're coping with loss from a fire or a break-in or some form of property damage," notes company president Ben Graham, president of the East Mountain business housed in distinctive greenhouse glass encased offices on Unsworth Drive.

"We do our best to assess the situation and then do everything possible to restore their property," adds Mr. Graham, who previously operated the general contracting company B.K. Graham Ltd.

A general contractor and carpenter by trade, Mr. Graham entered the restoration business in 1976 when he answered a request for assistance from an old friend

whose home was damaged in a fire. As he helped his friend salvage furniture and possessions, he found this line of work to be interesting and challenging.

Two years later, Mr. Graham was in restoration work full-time with a steady workload following the tornado which swept through Waterford. In 1985, he again had his hands full restoring buildings and furniture damaged by a tornado. This time, it was the infamous Barrie tornado doing the damage.

A few years later, some management changes were made. Elizabeth Graham, who had performed bookkeeping services for her husband for more than 20 years, was made a full partner in the company.

The couple's daughter Jennifer, a Carlton University student majoring in Biology and Psychology, works summers at the company.

Their son Allan, who's a graduate of Mohawk College's three-year Business Administration program and a carpenter by trade, joined the growing company on a

full-time basis in 1996 as an estimator.

Allan Graham had celebrated his 14th birthday in the 1980s at his parents' most unusual job site to date: a storage warehouse and aircraft hangar at Brevoort, a radar station on a little remote island in Canada's high Arctic, east of Baffin Island.

"That was an unusual, one-shot restoration job and it's the farthest we've ever gone to a job site," recalls Ben Graham. "Our usual market area is from Niagara region around to Mississauga and points north and south, essentially the greater Golden Horseshoe," he explains.

Mr. Graham, in the class of the first 100 Certified Restorers in North America, takes satisfaction from the positive role that his family business plays in putting back the pieces of customers' lives.

"There's a lot of satisfaction in restoration work, in the form of putting homes and damaged items the owner feels are lost forever, back to acceptable condition."

When the dishwasher can't dish it out, Sutton & Son may save it from being a wash-out. The Hamilton firm has been a trusted name in appliance repairs and parts since 1928.

"We fix refrigerators, washers, dryers, dishwashers, stoves, microwave ovens and just about any other major appliance you can think of," notes Sutton & Son general manager Steve Henderson.

"We've got a good reputation for our service and parts and we're pleased that people have come to rely on us," adds Mr. Henderson, whose company is located on Gage Avenue North, just south of Barton, near Ivor Wynne Stadium.

Sutton & Son's service work is also relied on by such firms as Hamilton Appliance & Fireplace Centre, Home & Rural Appliances and Burlington Appliance Centre.

The business is located in a century-old building which became the original home of Sutton & Son, a company which was founded in 1928 by Maurice Sutton and his son John.

"We became known for our service, parts and advice on fixing appliances,"

• Sutton & Son has been a trusted name in appliance repairs and parts in Hamilton since 1928. The company is located in its original home in a building on Gage Avenue North.

___

says Helen Sutton, widow of John Sutton.

The company weathered the Great Depression of the 1930s and prospered during the 1940s, investing $500 in a brand new truck for making service calls at five cents a visit.

Maurice Sutton continued to run the business until he suffered a stoke in 1957.

Then John Sutton took over the firm, running it until his death in 1982.

His widow kept the business going until 1988, when it was sold. The business changed hands again in 1993, when it was purchased by Steve Henderson's parents, Liz and Boyd Henderson.

Today, you can still find walls lined with electric stove elements and other appliance parts at the Sutton & Son office. But there have been changes over the years. Steve Henderson notes the company now offers delivery of parts

throughout Niagara, where it intends to establish a branch location.

Mr. Henderson explains that another change to his company was a decision to provide installation services for dishwashers and gas dryers.

The firm is an authorized service agent for Maytag appliances, "and yes it does get a little lonely sometimes," chuckles Mr. Henderson, in reference to Maytag's dependability advertisements.

Sutton & Son is also the parts agent for another dependable manufacturer of appliances, Camco, the Mississauga-based firm with a major manufacturing plant in Hamilton. Camco produces Hot Point, Moffat, McLary and GE brand appliances.

Yet some things, it seems, will never change. "We still get one or two calls a week to fix or supply parts for old wringer washers," says Mr. Henderson.

"It's surprising how many of those old washing machines are out there. But we're happy to do whatever we can to keep them in good working order."

However, many parts are no longer available, he says. "It's been a steady part of our business for years."

• With everything from boat races to a unique children's play area complete with an authentic tugboat, there's plenty of fun for the entire family at the new Bayfront Park in Hamilton's North End. And, there's plenty of dry-land fun for the family each year at It's Your Festival in Gage Park. The Festival features dancers, singers, musicians, magicians, clowns, and other colourful characters.
                    – *Photos by Dennis McGreal*

W hether serving professional contractors or the private homeowner, Turkstra Lumber Co. Ltd. lives by its popular slogan 'Always on the Level.'

"Our slogan is our governing philosophy – to be as honest, straight-forward and helpful with people as we can be," says company president Carl Turkstra.

Turkstra Lumber's origins date back to 1951, when company founder Peter Turkstra ran a contracting firm which began buying lumber in bulk to build warehouses for clients. When the elder Mr. Turkstra found that by bulk buying he could resell at a profit, he decided to go into the lumber business.

He established Turkstra Lumber on Upper James Street on the Hamilton Mountain in 1953 and gradually switched from contracting to focus purely on the lumber business. Then, in the early 1960s, the company relocated its lumber yard and headquarters to its current two-acre location on Upper Wellington Street between Mohawk and Limeridge roads.

During this time, Carl Turkstra moved to Montreal where, for 17 years, he would work as a professor of Civil Engineering at McGill University. In 1981, he moved to New York City to work as Professor and Head of the Department of Civil Engineering at Polytechnic University.

• *Turkstra Lumber has several lumber yards in the area, including this one in Dundas. Turkstra also has a lumber yard and headquarters at a two-acre location on Hamilton Mountain.*
– Photo by Joe Bucci

In 1990, Peter Turkstra was in his early 80s and looking to retire, so son Carl was invited to return to Hamilton to run the family business. He was named president in 1991 and today presides over a growing family business with lumber yards in Hamilton, Dundas, Waterdown, Stoney Creek, Brantford, Smithville, Dunnville, Fort Erie and Ridgeway.

In Smithville, Turkstra operates a mill producing wood moulding, cedar siding, window parts and parts for furniture makers. Also in Smithville is a plant manufacturing wood roof trusses. Windows are manufactured by a subsidiary known as Fairfield windows in Stoney Creek. J.R.'s Hardware sells architectural hardware to non-residential construction customers, a major source of revenue growth.

Already the largest lumber business in the Niagara peninsula, Turkstra plans to expand with additional outlets in Southern Ontario by the end of the decade.

By the mid-1990s, approximately 70 per cent of the company's business was in

sales and service to professional contractors. The remaining 30 per cent was in retail sales to consumers. Through revamped stores and increased service and selection, the company hopes to increase the retail side of the business.

Carl Turkstra notes his company's success has been built on providing expertise as well as product, a tribute to Turkstra Lumber's 160 employees, including his son Peter, a management trainee. Mr. Turkstra's well-known brother, lawyer Herman Turkstra, is a director on the board of this family business while cousin Ron Turkstra is vice-president of sales.

"Our salespeople are very experienced and knowledgeable in the contracting business, so we're able to provide advice and problem solving to our contractor customers," says Carl Turkstra.

"We know the contracting business, our salespeople know the business, our whole staff knows the business and we stay current with changes in the industry," he adds. "It's a mutual support relationship between ourselves and contractors. This is the way all good supply houses work. You give a lot of attention, service and support to the professionals."

Mr. Turkstra says this commitment to service has helped the company weather recessions. "We're a very strong company – and we're ready to grow."

G.S. WARK LTD., GENERAL CONTRACTORS

• *The Wark brothers, John, Michael and George at the latest G.S. Wark project, an addition to the Children's Aid Society of Hamilton building.*
— Photo by Dennis McGreal

N ot many of us can leave a lasting monument behind when we retire from our life's work. And that's a source of quiet pride to George Wark and his brothers John and Michael of G.S. Wark Ltd., General Contractors.

The business was started by their father in 1955, and has thrived in Hamilton ever since. "My father was a carpenter, and so was my grandfather," George Wark says. "So it was inevitable that my brothers and I would work in the business. We were exposed to it from the time we were kids."

G.S. Wark was initially involved in residential construction, but in 1960 switched over to Industrial, Commercial and Institutional work, George explains.

Among the best-known examples of their construction efforts are the new Henderson Hospital Boiler Plant, The Greater Hamilton Technology Enterprise Centre, and additions and renovations to the Children's Aid Society building on Wentworth Street.

In 1989, G.S. Wark moved into the construction of non-profit housing, an area where it found great success.

One of the biggest difficulties facing his business is keeping tight control on costs, George says. One way to do that, he explains, is to pick the appropriate sub-trades at time of tendering.

"It's a challenge, but so far we're succeeding better than others have over the last five or six years," he points out. "The secret is in identifying a niche, such as with non-profit housing. Now we're getting involved in the design/build process. We'll go to an owner, meet with him, discuss his needs, then choose an architect for the project."

One of the strengths of G.S. Wark is that it is a family business, George says, but that doesn't mean anyone has it easy.

"Your expectations of family members are much higher," he explains. "We're quite demanding of each other."

He says the philosophy of G.S. Wark is to treat people fairly and to do the best job. "We're not coming here from out of town, we're here for the long haul. So we have to do a good job, because if we don't, it will come back to haunt us.

"Over the years, we tend to work with the same groups of people in Hamilton," he adds. "When you do a good job, the word gets around."

The Wark brothers have gold seal certificates recognizing their high level of qualification in the construction business, but George says the real satisfaction comes when his wife drives by a building with his two young children and points out a project that their daddy built.

"For example," he explains, "we did a couple of sets of stairs going up the mountain, one at the end of Dundurn and the other at the Chedoke Golf Course. My brother did some innovative work at getting the excavating equipment to the location while keeping the damage to the escarpment to a minimum.

"No one else knows what it took to do that job, but we do," he adds. "And those stairs will still be there long after we're gone. Things like that mean a lot."

• With Gore Park sparkling in the night, the spirit of the season is captured in this Christmastime scene of the downtown area.
– *Photo by Bob Chambers*

• Hamilton Harbour provides the perfect vantage point as the sky explodes with colour during Victoria Day celebrations.
– *Photo by David Gruggen*

The roots of today's Canadian Imperial Bank of Commerce run deep in Hamilton. In 1833, Hamilton had just been incorporated as a town when a group of citizens led by Job Loder and supported by Sir Allan McNab applied to form The Gore Bank, a fore-runner of today's CIBC. Approval was granted two years later.

With a population of just 1,350 people, Hamilton in the early 1830s had only a few dirt roads, 18 stores and 10 taverns when The Gore Bank was established in a stone building on King Street West near McNab Street.

In 1844, The Gore Bank relocated to the south-west corner of King Street East and Hughson, a site which would later house the Main Hamilton branch of the CIBC. The Gore Bank elected 31-year-old Colin Ferrie as bank president in 1839 and Mr. Ferrie continued to rise in prominence to later become the first mayor of Hamilton.

By 1846 when Hamilton incorporated as a city, The Gore Bank boasted branch offices in Simcoe, St. Thomas, Guelph and other Ontario centres.

To improve its financial stability, in 1869, The Gore Bank merged with The Canadian Bank of Commerce based in Toronto.

Just three years later, another ambitious bank – The Bank of Hamilton – was founded in 1872 by dry goods store owner Donald McInnes and other prominent Hamilton businessmen in downtown Hamilton offices previously occupied by The Canadian Bank of Commerce.

That same decade, The Bank of Hamilton opened branch offices in Listowel, Milton, Clarksville, Beeton, Georgetown and even one in Port Elgin, a branch run by F. A. Colquhoun, who would later become mayor of Hamilton.

In 1887, The Bank of Hamilton purchased new downtown headquarters at the south-west corner of King and James streets – the site of today's twin CIBC towers – in the heart of the city overlooking the Gore. A year later, The Bank of Hamilton opened another branch office, this one in Toronto.

When the Bank of Hamilton celebrated its 25th anniversary back in 1897, it had profit of $145,000 plus financial resources of $10 million and additional branches located in Grimsby, Kitchener (then known as Berlin), Winnipeg and at other centres in Western Canada.

By the year 1905, The Bank of Hamilton boasted 64 branches, most in

Ontario along with 15 in Manitoba, five in Saskatchewan and Alberta (then part of the Northwest Territories) and two in British Columbia. It was a truly national bank based in Hamilton.

Just three years later, The Bank of Hamilton employed 600 people in 95 branches, 43 of them in Western Canada.

By the end of World War I, the Bank of Hamilton had a total of 157 branch offices (including one at Locke and Herkimer streets, now a CIBC branch) and $70 million in assets.

However, the burden of high taxation and increasing competition were among the factors resulting in The Bank of Hamilton merging with the Canadian Bank of Commerce in 1923.

In 1928, the 55-year-old Standard Bank of Canada merged with the Canadian Bank of Commerce. Finally, in 1961, The Imperial Bank of Canada merged with The Canadian Bank of Commerce to form The Canadian Imperial Bank of Commerce – today's CIBC.

With so much of its history deeply rooted in this city, the CIBC continues to play a vital role in contemporary Hamilton.

Mark Brooks, district manager for CIBC Hamilton Centre Branches, notes the bank has a high concentration of 37 branches employing more than 700 people in the greater Hamilton area, 550 of them in Hamilton alone.

Mr. Brooks adds that two branches – one at Rymal Road and Upper James Street in Hamilton and the other at Fairview Road in Burlington, opened in 1995 while a third branch, near Home Depot at the Meadowlands in Ancaster, opened in 1996.

With this large presence in Hamilton has come a large role in supporting local charities. "Both the bank and the employees are major contributors to the United Way," notes Mr. Brooks.

"We also support the Civic Hospitals – St. Joseph's and Chedoke-McMaster; Ronald McDonald House, Opera Hamilton the Royal Botanical Gardens and many other worthy causes."

Mr. Brooks says that the CIBC will continue to play an active role in supporting worthwhile causes in Hamilton "and we'll continue to offer quality financial services to our many clients in the Greater Hamilton Area."

ABOVE: *The CIBC stands tall at the corner of King and James streets.*
– Photo by Dennis McGreal

FACING PAGE: *A bird's-eye view of the inside of the CIBC building.*
– Photo by David Gruggen

• *St. John The Baptist Roman Catholic Church is just one of the many projects built by Frisina Construction in the Hamilton area during the past 42 years.*
– Photo by David Gruggen

F ew business leaders can claim to have forever changed Hamilton's skyline in the manner Alfonso Frisina has. As the builder of Century 21 – the city's tallest building – Mr. Frisina's unique business signature towers 45 storeys above Main Street and dominates the downtown Hamilton landscape.

And the high costs of erecting such a skyscraper along with subsequent building height restrictions make it a virtual certainty no one will ever match this impressive accomplishment.

Yet the monolithic apartment complex is only the most striking reminder of the remarkable impact this successful developer has had on the Hamilton area.

Mr. Frisina has also built numerous schools, apartment complexes and public buildings, even turning his hand to single-family home construction.

Mr. Frisina's charitable work includes participation as chairman of the Hamilton fund-raising efforts for flood relief in Florence, Italy; and more recently, two Frisina Dream Homes at Rymal Estates on south Hamilton Mountain. They were raffled separately to raise needed funding for hospitals under the auspices of the Hamilton Civic Hospitals Foundation.

How Mr. Frisina became such a prominent local developer is a story that begins in Italy. Born at Delianuova, Reggio Calabria in January, 1926, he was among the fourth generation of a respected family long active in carpentry and the construction industry in Italy.

Our story might also have ended in Italy – except that in 1949, Mr. Frisina's fiancee Antonia Giorgi left Italy to live with her father in the United States.

Mr. Frisina followed soon after.

However, he was unable to gain access to the U.S. since he did not have any of his own family ties for sponsorship. Since nearby Canada was more welcoming, Mr. Frisina headed north and began working as a farm hand, a term required through a contract with the federal government in order to gain admission as an immigrant.

"I lost a lot of weight getting up at 5 a.m. to milk cows," recalls Mr. Frisina, "and I wasn't used to the food so I didn't eat much. I was like a toothpick . . . I wasn't a farmer."

After leaving the first farm and toughing out a few more months on a second farm, Mr. Frisina went to the U.S., where he married his childhood sweetheart Antonia in 1950.

And despite his rough introduction to Canada, Mr. Frisina found he had taken a shine to the northern country.

"Canada has more potential than the U.S. for anyone who wants to work," says Mr. Frisina, who recalls promptly extending an invitation for Antonia to join him in Hamilton. She has been his greatest supporter and lifelong partner.

Hamilton has been their home ever since. They have six children and seven grandchildren – all of whom live in Hamilton and vicinity.

Mr. Frisina quickly began pursuing his carpentry trade in Hamilton, working long hours for local contractors – and then dedicated even longer hours undertaking jobs of his own on the side.

Although he progressed quickly, becoming foreman for a number of contractors, Mr. Frisina, then in his 20s, was eager to strike out on his own.

In 1954, Mr. Frisina established his own company, Frisina Construction Company Ltd., which immediately took on the daunting task of a major project – Strathcona School in Burlington.

A string of major Hamilton area projects followed, including:
• Mount Albion School (Saltfleet Township)
• Tappleytown School (Saltfleet Township)
• St. Patrick School (Hamilton)
• Saltfleet High School (Stoney Creek)
• Rousseau School (Ancaster)
• Ancaster High School (Ancaster)
• St. John the Baptist Roman Catholic Church (Hamilton)
• Postal Station (Ancaster)
• Postal Station B (Hamilton)
• Water Works Offices building in Burlington.

And there were many more such projects undertaken by Frisina Construction, which also built a number of residential apartment buildings in Hamilton, including the following:
• Filfrin Apartments
• Chedoke Towers
• Delta Towers
• Benvenuto Apartments
• Sorrento Apartments

In 1963, Mr. Frisina became the first developer to convince the city to change its highrise bylaw to allow for the construction of buildings exceeding six storeys. Following this change, he completed the construction of the Clarendon, the city's first highrise apartment complex – a 25-storey apartment building with 265 units built on a city block of rezoned land acquired by Mr. Frisina.

And in 1972, Mr. Frisina developed Century 21, the striking 45-storey landmark that would become the city's tallest building ever on its completion in 1974. With the repeal of the highrise bylaw allowing such skyscrapers, Century 21

• *Al Frisina is pictured with his sons, from left, Ralph, Dan and Al Jr., at Frisina Construction's Rymal Estates site. The development is located on a 36-acre parcel of land at Highway 53 between Garth Street and Upper Paradise Road.*
– Photo by David Gruggen

appears destined to remain Hamilton's tallest building for generations to come.

After donating a new, 2,400-square-foot luxury home at Rymal Estates to 1994's Dreams and Miracles fund-raising campaign to raise funds for Henderson General Hospital, Mr. Frisina generously donated a second luxury home to the 1995 campaign.

Assisting Mr. Frisina in developing Rymal Estates are three of his six grown children. Son Ralph, the president of Mainstone Realty; son Danny, who directs

the construction company's job site; and son Al, a computer specialist, all play major roles in the ongoing development of the 36-acre parcel of land at Highway 53 between Garth Street and Upper Paradise Road in Hamilton.

Although he's determined "never to retire," Mr. Frisina can take comfort in knowing that a new generation continues to enhance the tradition of building excellence he has established with his many successful projects across the greater Hamilton area.

• When Coldwell Banker sought out compatible brokers in Hamilton, the company was sold on Rob McDowell, a veteran realtor who had operated his own realty firm for 15 years.
— *Photo by David Gruggen*

Taking a traditional approach, Coldwell Banker Elite Realty has evolved into a major Hamilton area realtor – with expectations of more heady growth in years to come.

"There are bigger companies out there, but we're one of the major players in the local marketplace," notes David Pauls, the general manager of all three of the Coldwell Banker offices in Hamilton-Wentworth region.

"And our game plan is to continue growing and gain more market share," adds Mr. Pauls, whose outlets are owned by Coldwell Banker Elite Realtor with headquarters on Hamilton Mountain.

"We're more of a traditional broker, offering our sales representatives support services such as education, training and use of our facilities," he explains.

Mr. Pauls suggests that by devoting effort and resources into developing the potential of its sales representatives, Coldwell Banker ends up with highly professional, knowledgeable representatives "and that's a benefit to ourselves and to the people who use our services."

"Our philosophy is that we believe in developing the synergy of good people working together and prospering together . . . using a traditional broker support approach." That traditional approach has long been used in the United States, where Coldwell Banker originated in the early 1990s and is today the largest realtor in the United States.

In 1990, Coldwell Banker arrived in Canada to establish a presence here and become a truly North American firm.

The company set about finding compatible brokers in major Canadian cities. In 1991, Coldwell Banker chose Rob McDowell for a Hamilton presence.

A veteran realtor-entrepreneur with a vision, Mr. McDowell had operated R. McDowell Realty for 15 years and was eager to explore the potential for growth inherent in merging with a larger entity.

Growth wasn't long in coming: By October 1993, when Mr. Pauls joined the new Coldwell Banker office, it had grown from a handful of representatives to more than 30. "A month later, the Canada Trust Real Estate offices were merged into Coldwell Banker and we were up to 70 people," recalls Mr. Pauls, adding that Coldwell Banker Elite Realty continues to enjoy a vibrant cross-sales relationship with Canada Trust.

The growing Coldwell company next took over some former Alec Murray and Barry Kelly real estate offices.

All told, in just three years, Coldwell Banker Elite Realty grew from 30 representatives to 120 representatives in 1996, operating out of offices on Hamilton Mountain, in Westdale and at Queenston Road in Stoney Creek.

And Mr. Pauls sees further growth ahead. "While some of our competitors have been downsizing and closing offices, we've been expanding to meet the growing demand for our type of broker operation," he observes.

"The consumer of the 1990s is looking for the more-knowledgeable sales representatives that we can provide. We intend to continue developing our people and earn further gains in market share."

"Funeral services have been veiled in past years," says Leigh Hall, assistant manager of Dodsworth & Brown Funeral Home.

"We're lifting the veil to educate the public," adds Mr. Hall, whose funeral home has chapels in Ancaster and Burlington in addition to L.G. Wallace Funeral Home, located on Ottawa Street North in Hamilton, and Robinson Chapel, one of the larger funeral homes in downtown Hamilton.

Founded in 1867, Dodsworth & Brown merged over the years with L. G. Wallace, founded in the 1920s, and the recently renovated Robinson Chapel, founded in 1896.

Mr. Hall says the funeral homes are committed to taking the mystery out of the funeral service while providing families with the information on what to expect and carefully tailoring funerals to meet the individual needs of every family.

Part of that approach includes a resource centre featuring an array of books and videos on death, grief, funeral pre-planning and pre-arranging. The homes make this information available to the public along with children's colouring books, developed by the funeral home staff, depicting scenes from a funeral.

Although the use of colouring books may sound unusual, Mr. Hall notes the books have proven effective in aiding a child's understanding of the funeral.

By colouring pictures of flowers or a funeral director and family gathered around a casket, children are made aware, in a friendly way, of what they can expect to see inside a funeral home.

"It's important that we educate all members of the community, young and old, so there are no surprises or misconceptions," asserts Mr. Hall, while adding that the more knowledgeable families become, the more likely they are to know exactly what they want in the way of a funeral service, including services, pricing procedures and characteristics of caskets.

"Our goal is to tailor these services to meet their needs," says Mr. Hall. "Some families want a long service, others want a short service, others want a memorial service they designed. It's important that their wishes are communicated so we can do everything possible to assist them."

Mr. Hall notes that the homes also offer an after-funeral program known as Arborcare. Families are assisted by Support Co-ordinator Helen Humphreys,

week. Many of the staff members are actively involved in sponsoring baseball and hockey teams and in supporting community organizations.

The funeral homes even lend their spacious premises free of charge to non-profit organizations for meetings.

"As part of the community, we feel we must take an active role in community life," says Mr. Hall.

who helps them adjust to life after the funeral by putting them in touch with various support groups in the community.

"We believe this type of care should be part of the service and we promote it at no extra charge," explains Mr. Hall.

"Our commitment to the family isn't over when the funeral ends," he adds.

Nor does the commitment of staff to the community end at the close of a work

• The Dodsworth and Brown Funeral Home staff is committed to providing caring and professional service.
– *Photo by Joe Bucci*

Chapter 7

Local Landmarks

ABOVE: *A beautifully appointed 35-room mansion, historic Dundurn Castle was the home of Sir Alan Napier MacNab, Prime Minister of the United Provinces of Upper Canada from 1854-1856. As part of the city's Sesqui celebrations, the Castle's exterior was repainted in its original colours for a visit by the Governor General of Canada, His Excellency, Romeo LeBlanc.*

RIGHT: *An historical restoration in the heart of Hamilton, Whitehern Mansion offers visitors a glimpse into the life of three generations of the prominent McQuesten family.*
– Photos by Dennis McGreal

ABOVE: *The Cathedral of Christ the King was opened for worship in December of 1933. Built by Pigott Construction Company, it is a magnificent structure serving Hamilton's Roman Catholic population.*

LEFT: *St. Paul's Presbyterian Church, with its Gothic Revival style of architecture, was first opened for worship in March of 1857. The church, on James Street South, was designed by architect William Thomas and features one of the finest stone spires in Canada. The spire, which was restored in 1989 at a cost of $1.3 million, rises to a height of 55 metres above ground level. The church has been designated a provincial and a national historic site.*

PAGES 180-181: *Looking east at the downtown area with Copps Coliseum, foreground, the Stelco Tower behind it and Century 21 in the distance.*
— Photos by Dennis McGreal

ABOVE: *A night-time shot of the Hamilton Farmers' Market, with the central branch of the Hamilton Public Library in the background.*

LEFT: *The Hamilton Eaton Centre, which opened in May of 1989, is a major part of the cornerstone of Hamilton's downtown core.*
          *– **Photos by Dennis McGreal***

• *Contractors Machinery & Equipment is headquartered on Heritage Road in Burlington. A distributor of industrial cranes, the firm was founded in 1946.*
– Photo by David Gruggen

For the past 50 years, Canadian companies who have needed a lift have relied on Contractors Machinery & Equipment Ltd.

The distributor of industrial cranes, founded in 1946, is owned and operated by Bernie J. Faloney Sr., Chairman, and son Wally Faloney, President and C.E.O.

CME is the oldest and largest distributor of Grove hydraulic cranes. CME Industries, a division of the company, is also National Crane's largest telescoping crane dealer in North America. The National crane is assembled at the firm's head office in Burlington.

The company also represents such well-known products as Grove/Manlift aerial work platforms, Taylor forklift trucks and container handlers, American Crane conventional and locomotive cranes, Gradall excavators and boom forklifts, Ross batching plants and Fassi articulated boom cranes.

CME also operates a rental division with more than several hundred rental products, specializing in the lift industry only, to meet its customers' requirements.

Recently, the Hamilton Harbour Commission contracted CME to provide all of the crane and material lift requirements for the Port of Hamilton.

On average, some 12 million tonnes of cargo pass through the harbour each year,

including steel, containers and locomotives. CME works closely with A Crane Rentals, which operates CME's two 250-ton crawler cranes for loading and unloading cargo from all over the world.

CME was also awarded the contract to supply Grove cranes, National boom trucks and Grove manlifts to link the Northumberland Strait. Strait Crossing Joint Venture, a construction consortium of four companies, has committed to the rental of 22 Grove rough terrain cranes, 12 National boom trucks and 21 Grove manlifts from CME, a total of 55 units which are currently at the job site.

This $840-million project will see SCJV construct a 13-kilometre bridge across the stormy Northumberland Strait linking Borden, P.E.I., to Jourimain Island, New Brunswick, in addition to 16 kilometres of road approaches.

The enormous structure will be the world's longest continuous marine-span bridge, and the project is expected to be completed in 1997.

CME also won the contract to supply

equipment on the Highway 407 project in Toronto. The $1-billion, 69-kilometre highway is being built by Canadian Highways International Constructors.

The company is able to provide parts and service back-up across the nation from its Burlington head office and its branches in Montreal and Edmonton, along with its sub-distributors who are strategically located across the country.

Sales and parts personnel are available seven days a week, 24 hours a day, to deal with any problems which may arise.

Staff members, who are all factory-trained and attend numerous courses annually, specialize in providing service for material handling and lifting, and their work is fully guaranteed. The company stocks more than $1 million worth of parts in its inventory at all times.

Another area of growth for CME is in the articulated crane industry. Any business requiring assistance in the picking up and delivering of material has found the articulated crane a valued tool.

The Fassi product CME carries is second to none in quality and provides more that 400 variations to support the many needs of material handling customers.

Committed to enhancing the quality of life in the community, CME has earned a reputation for honesty and for providing the best construction equipment available.

• Located in a stately home on Main Street, Cattel, Eaton & Chambers Funeral Home has been a part of Dundas' heritage for nearly 160 years.

– Photo by David Gruggen

Surrounded by majestic shade trees, the Cattel, Eaton & Chambers Funeral Home offers a comforting tradition of service, steeped in local history. The funeral home has been a proud part of the Valley Town's heritage for nearly 160 years, making it one of Canada's oldest funeral establishments.

That heritage is very much in evidence upon entering the stately Main Street building in the heart of Dundas.

Just inside the funeral home, visitors are met with a winding oak staircase. As they proceed through the home they can be found casting admiring glances at the original woodwork and marble fireplaces.

Even the basement in this building, dating back to 1872, retains its original plaster walls and fireplace.

Since 1953, gray stone has covered the original brickwork, and in 1960, a rear addition was built to house a chapel, funeral home offices, casket display area and spacious visitation room.

The funeral home's origins date back to 1837, when Isaac Latshaw began a funeral business on King Street, not far from today's Cattel, Eaton & Chambers Funeral Home.

Mr. Latshaw operated the business until his death in 1881. His son, Fred Latshaw, inherited the business and it remained in his hands until 1912.

The business passed through several owners over the years until it was purchased by Wallace Cattel in 1939.

Mr. Cattel was joined by Irwin Eaton in 1945 and the Cattel & Eaton partnership operated the funeral home and ambulance services for many years.

During these years, the funeral home also enriched its reputation as a caring member of the Dundas community by supporting a number of charities and local worthy causes, including the construction of such projects as the Dundas arena and public swimming pool and the formation of local lacrosse teams.

In 1968, Mr. Eaton bought out his former partner and continued operating the funeral home until 1983, when it was sold to the Chambers family.

The funeral home – which continues to be operated by the Chambers family – has maintained its commitment to the Dundas community as a sponsor of local sports teams and community events.

Indeed, Cattel, Eaton & Chambers takes pride in its enduring tradition of community support.

And the funeral home continues to build on a remarkable heritage of service to area families.

TOP: The Canadac sculpture at the Art Gallery of Hamilton is a unique downtown landmark.

LEFT: The Canadian Football Hall of Fame's Touchdown Statue is a testament to the gridiron greats who helped make Hamilton the home of the Tiger-Cats. City Hall is in the background.

ABOVE: *The Hamilton Board of Education building was opened in November of 1967 by the Honourable William G. Davis, then Ontario Minister of Education.*
– Photos by Dennis McGreal

ABOVE: With four Corinthian columns on James Street, and six pilasters on Main Street, this landmark building has the look of a Roman temple. Since the early part of the century, it has been home to various financial institutions, including the Landed Bank and Loan Company, Canada Permanent Mortgage Company and the Mercantile Bank of Canada.

FACING PAGE: Recognized as one of the finest showplaces in all of Canada, Hamilton Place is conveniently situated in the heart of downtown Hamilton. The spectacular facility, built by Frid Construction in 1972, has hosted everything from rock shows to opera and Broadway productions.
                    – Photos by Dennis McGreal

FACING PAGE: *Once the home of the Tuckett family, this magnificent mansion at the corner of King Street West and Queen Street, is a base for the Scottish Rite. Renowned for its craftsmanship, the building features a Gothic stone entrance and a huge auditorium similar to those of the ancient cathedrals.*

LEFT: *Century 21, built by Frisina Construction, is the tallest building in Hamilton. The 45-storey landmark was completed in 1974.*
– Photos by Dennis McGreal

ABOVE: *Officially opened in 1914 by the Duke of Connaught, the Royal Connaught Howard Johnson Hotel is regarded as the Grand Old Lady of Hamilton.*

FACING PAGE: *The lobby of The Sheraton Hamilton Hotel features a winding staircase and spectacular 16-foot, 1,600-pound spiralling crystal chandelier. The hotel is a five-star, four-diamond facility connected to Jackson Square and the Hamilton Convention Centre. It is the official hotel of the Sesqui celebrations.*
— Photos by David Gruggen

It was a pivotal moment in Hamilton's modern history. Unable to secure sufficient financing, some local developers had reluctantly pulled out of a major, 1970s $30 million downtown urban renewal project – Lloyd D. Jackson Square. Fortunately, the Bank of Montreal was prepared to take a chance on Hamilton's downtown.

The bank brought some of its vast resources to bear and became one of the new mall's anchors, with its main Hamilton branch right at the primary entrance to the downtown mall. In gratitude, Mayor Victor Copps presented a Builder of Hamilton plaque to the bank in 1972 for its participation as a key part of the project and for its contribution toward making Jackson Square a reality.

"Bank of Montreal was instrumental in getting Jackson Square going," recalls Don Marr, the bank's vice-president, community banking for Hamilton-Wentworth region.

"We anchored the mall and really made a commitment to its success."

Such a commitment to the improvement of Hamilton was nothing new for the bank, which has also been involved in the restoration of the Gore Park Fountain, is an active member of the Renaissance Committee revitalizing Hamilton and was leading financial sector donor – with a grant of $350,000 – to McMaster University's last fund-raising campaign.

Bank of Montreal is also sponsor of High Winds on the Skyway, an exhibition of paintings depicting Hamilton and environs through the ages. This special Hamilton Art Gallery attraction was part of the February 1996 kick-off of the city's Sesquicentennial festivities.

As well, the bank has long supported other cultural attractions, including Theatre Aquarius, the art gallery and the Hamilton Philharmonic Orchestra.

This sponsorship helps keep admission costs of these attractions at reasonable levels, making the arts more accessible for ordinary citizens.

Bank of Montreal is also a major supporter of Junior Achievement, Chedoke-McMaster hospitals Mother's Day Telethon, Kid's Help Phone Line and many other worthy causes.

Locally, the bank has 20 branches in Hamilton-Wentworth and Burlington which together employ over 500 people.

And the roots of such involvement run deep. Bank of Montreal saw Hamilton's rich potential and opened for business here in 1843, three years before Hamilton incorporated as a city. It was Hamilton's first bank – and it remains the oldest continuously operating bank in the city.

"We've been a very active part of

half of its income outside of Canada. It has assets exceeding $150 billion and customers around the world.

While Bank of Montreal has grown to become one of the 10 largest banks in North America, it has never lost sight of its commitment to Hamilton, asserts bank spokesman Joe Barbera.

"What was true in 1843 remains true today," he says. "Hamilton is a city with potential and Bank of Montreal remains positioned to assist in its continuous development and growth."

Hamilton's heritage for over 150 years," notes Mr. Marr. "Our Hamilton-Wentworth employees together put in 25,000 hours of volunteer work in 1995 alone and we're very proud of that community involvement," he adds.

The bank is also a major lender and active partner in the success of small business. Local Bank of Montreal representatives sit on Hamilton and District Chamber of Commerce committees and the Business Advisory Council.

The oldest bank in Canada, Bank of Montreal is a diversified financial services institution that earns about

• Bank of Montreal has been a part of Hamilton's heritage for more than 150 years. After years of doing business from its downtown Main and James streets location, the bank relocated to Jackson Square in the 1970s.
– Photo by David Gruggen

With its lush gardens, carpets of flowers and clusters of trees, Bayview Cemetery provides a peaceful place to reflect on the passing of a loved one. Walking along its winding paths, through gentle breezes and the sun-dappled shade of majestic trees, visitors are filled with a sense of serenity.

Adjacent to the Royal Botanical Gardens and offering an inspiring view of Burlington Bay, the cemetery is truly one of the most beautiful memorials in Canada.

Its carpets of flowers and park-like setting, reminding one of the nearby RBG, are a peaceful celebration of nature. Here, on Spring Garden Road, in dignified surroundings of great beauty, families begin the healing process that must follow a loss.

"We offer many options for both at-need and pre-arranged programs," notes Ross Hutchison, manager of Bayview Cemetery, Crematory & Mausoleum Inc., which is owned and operated by Patrick J. Markey. "Our goal is always to provide as many options as possible so families can choose the one that is most comfortable for them," adds Mr. Hutchison, whose cemetery, established in 1925, also features a classically designed mausoleum, the first of its kind in Canada.

To assist in finding the right option, Mr. Hutchison advises pre-planning, which allows for peace of mind. With pre-planning people make their own wishes known to family and friends.

Options can be examined with a clear mind, allowing a meaningful choice to be made. This approach avoids the pressure and confusion families may face when pre-planning is not undertaken.

Mr. Hutchison observes that cremation has become a more popular avenue in recent years with more than 40 per cent favouring this option in the mid-1990s compared with 18 per cent in 1985.

Families decide whether to place cremation urns in a bronze, marble or glass niche inside the mausoleum or in Bayview Cemetery's new Carillon Tower offering visitors a view of the bay and Hamilton skyline. At the base of the tower, there is space for 5,500 names to be eventually etched into granite tablets.

Cremation urns can also be placed in a niche in Bayview's outdoor granite columbaria or remains can be scattered in one of the Scattering Gardens with the option of a bronze memorial marker also available. Mr. Hutchison says another popular option is an above-ground burial, where the casket or urn is placed in a crypt or niche compartment which is then sealed in the mausoleum or columbarium.

Filled with the warm atmosphere of light reflected through stained glass, the marble-lined mausoleum provides a serene setting where families can choose entombment, including private family crypts, or niches where cremation urns are placed. With every option there are dedication plaques bearing names of deceased.

Mr. Hutchison says the mausoleum option is now comparable in price to in-ground burial and that its popularity has necessitated an addition to the mausoleum. "Whatever option families choose, Bayview offers a living memorial in a beautiful setting that people can visit and spend quiet moments of reflection."

• *Bayview Cemetery, adjacent to the Royal Botanical Gardens, features a classically designed mausoleum, the first of its kind in Canada.*
– Photo by Joe Bucci

ABOVE: Built back in 1835 on what is today Sulphur Springs Road in Ancaster, Griffen House was the home of Enerals Griffen, a Virginia slave who made his way to freedom via the Underground Railroad.

LEFT: Dating back to 1855, the Hermitage ruins are located in the Dundas Valley. The site was the summer home of George Leith, a gentleman farmer and Scottish aristocrat who came to Canada in 1834.
– Photos by Dennis McGreal

ABOVE: *The Hamilton Military Museum is located in Dundurn Park. The museum houses an impressive collection depicting Canadian military history from the War of 1812 to World War I.*

LEFT: *The Hamilton Museum of Steam and Technology lets you experience the grandeur of the Victorian steam era. The site preserves two historic 70-ton steam engines, the oldest of their kind in North America.*
– Photos by Dennis McGreal

• Recognized throughout the world for horticulture, research and education, the Royal Botanical Gardens is one of the largest botanical gardens in the world. The Rock Garden and Tea House are among the attractions at the RBG, which features more than 125,000 spring flowering bulbs, the world's largest lilac collection, a quarter-million iris blooms and two acres of roses. In total, the RBG boasts five major garden areas and more than 1,000 hectares of forest, field and marsh.
– Photo by Dennis McGreal

C lub members know enough to skip breakfast and lunch – and loosen their belts a notch – when they visit the Venetian Club of Hamilton for dinner. "We like to provide a good meal," chuckles Venetian Club Past President Luigi Mason.

"Afterwards, people like to walk around a bit, to wear some calories off – and make room for dessert."

One of the ways to wear off some of those calories is to have a friendly game of bocce. There are three bocce lanes located in the basement of club.

Mr. Mason says a typical dinner can consist of several courses, including lasagna followed by prime rib of beef, then lemon chicken breast, followed by a generous fish platter, all accompanied by vegetables, rolls and wine – and followed up with coffee and dessert. "Better still, don't eat for a couple of days if you're coming to the Venetian Club," he adds.

Founded in 1947, the successful club was enjoying nearly half a century of a tradition of dining excellence during

• Luigi Mason, past president and currently a director at the Venetian Club, is pictured in front of a plaster mural at the club. The mural depicts the Rialto bridge, spanning the Grand Canal, a famous landmark in Venice.
– Photo by Joe Bucci

Hamilton's Sesquicentennial. Located in the north end at John Street North and Barton Street, the Venetian Club features two large air-conditioned halls, the largest of which has seating for 300 people while the other seats around 200 people.

There is also a meeting room at the club which accommodates 25 people.

With its full kitchen facilities, the Venetian Club specializes in Italian cuisine such as manicotti and lasagna along with its famous fish platters. A North American menu is also offered by renowned club chef Marcella.

The three-level club facilities are also rented out for weddings, showers, stags, baptisms, communions, meetings or any

other occasion. There are often as many as 400 to 500 guests between the two halls at this bustling club. The club provides catering and guests can either arrange their own disk jockey or have a DJ arranged through the club.

A non-profit organization, the Venetian Club uses the funds it raises through meals and events to fund its ongoing operation. Club members elect an executive body which in turn elects the club president, vice-president, manager, treasurer and secretary.

The club also keeps its food prices at a very affordable level. For example, in 1996, a dish of pasta with home-made sauce, chicken, sausage and vegetables cost just $12 per plate. It's little wonder the club's business continues to grow through repeat business and referrals.

"People will come here for a stag or a wedding and they're happy with the prices and the atmosphere and they come back again and again." notes Mr. Mason.

"It has helped to make us one of the most successful clubs in the area."

J.B Marlatt Funeral Home Ltd.

• *J.B. Marlatt Funeral Home is one of the oldest and largest funeral facilities in Hamilton. It features a beautiful chapel, with seating for 250 people.*
— Photo by Joe Bucci

The J. B. Marlatt Funeral Home (1985) Ltd. tradition began in the Hamilton area more than 150 years ago with its founder, Ezekial Marlatt a cabinet maker from Grimsby.

His grandson, James Bertram Marlatt, opened the doors of its present location on Main Street East, Hamilton in 1939.

J. B. Marlatt Dundas Chapel on King Street West opened in 1959.

After five generations, the Marlatt heritage ended in 1985 with the sale of the funeral home business to the Loewen Group, a Canadian funeral company based in Burnaby B.C.

The home is one of the oldest and largest funeral facilities in Hamilton.

Since its latest renovation, families are offered an on-site private reception facility, the first of its kind in Hamilton, and a beautiful chapel which provides seating for 250 people.

The staff of dedicated and caring employees are committed to the individual and personal needs of the family.

"Community involvement is something we really try to focus on," states David Culgin, manager of the J. B. Marlatt Funeral Home.

"We take great pride in the ongoing commitment and involvement we have to our community and its causes with our support of various organizations, charities and hospitals," he adds.

"The funeral home has undergone many changes over the years, but our high standards of service, tradition, dedication and abiding commitment that we have for the families, friends and community we serve, will not change," says Mr. Culgin. "We will only continue to grow stronger."

Chapter 8

Industry & Technology

• A red-hot steel slab, 8.5 inches thick by 30 feet in length, emerges from one of the two reheat furnaces at Dofasco. The slabs are rolled to thicknesses of less than a half-inch.
– Photo courtesy of Dofasco

S teel is inseparably linked to Hamilton's identity. It's virtually impossible to think of steel in Canada without thinking of the nation's steel capital, Hamilton. Despite diversification into medical, services and high-technology industries, steel and related industries remain the major components of Hamilton's economy, employment and identity.

Indeed, while the health sector may have edged its way into becoming the biggest source of jobs overall, steelmakers Stelco Inc. and Dofasco Inc. remain the city's two largest individual employers. Add on the employment rolls of the area's many steel fabricators and service centres and the enormous contribution of the steel industry to Hamilton becomes even more apparent.

Nor should anyone continue to think of our steel giants in terms of old industry. Smokestacks obscure the more realistic view of Hamilton's high-tech steelmakers. The reality is that Hamilton's big steel companies have invested many billions of dollars in computer-driven high technology to produce the expensive, high-strength, thin-gauge, corrosion resistant steels sought by automotive and other customers.

Gone is the old steelmaking technology involving the pouring of molten steel into ingots for storage in inventory before being reheated and then fashioned into basic steel products.

Now, both of the big steelmakers continuous cast their steel, pouring it directly into slabs which are then rolled in thinner widths for the production of steel coils.

The extensive investment in technology – necessary to remain competitive with foreign steelmakers – has also meant a redundancy of jobs and both big steelmakers have virtually cut their workforces in half over the years to approximately 7,000 employees each in the mid-1990s. However, even if both hit their eventual targets for 6,000 employees each they will still remain the area's largest individual employers.

The organizational and technological changes leading to these workforce reductions have also made the steelmakers stronger and more competitive. That in turn has gone a long way to making the thousands of remaining jobs more secure.

Right-sizing, technological investments and a strategy to concentrate on higher market end value-added products have all paid off, with Stelco and Dofasco enjoying a return to financial health. And both steelmakers rank highly among North America's most cost-competitive, high-quality steel suppliers of choice to a wide array of customers.

The local steel industry's return to profitability in the mid-1990s, its investment of many billions of dollars in new technology, its core position in the reindustrialization of Ontario, its successful restructuring and its integral importance to the Canadian economy are all evidence of the central role played by this remarkable industry in Hamilton, now and in years to come.

ABOVE: *Each of the seven 'finishing stands' at Dofasco's #2 Hot Mill rolls the strip of steel progressively thinner until it reaches the desired thickness for sale or for further processing and coating operations.*

PAGES 204-205: *The operator's pulpit of Dofasco's Continuous Pickle/Line Cold Rolling Complex is an example of the technological advances that have been made within the steel industry. Process computers control a number of quality parameters to help ensure that the finished product matches the customers' specified needs.*
– Photos courtesy of Dofasco

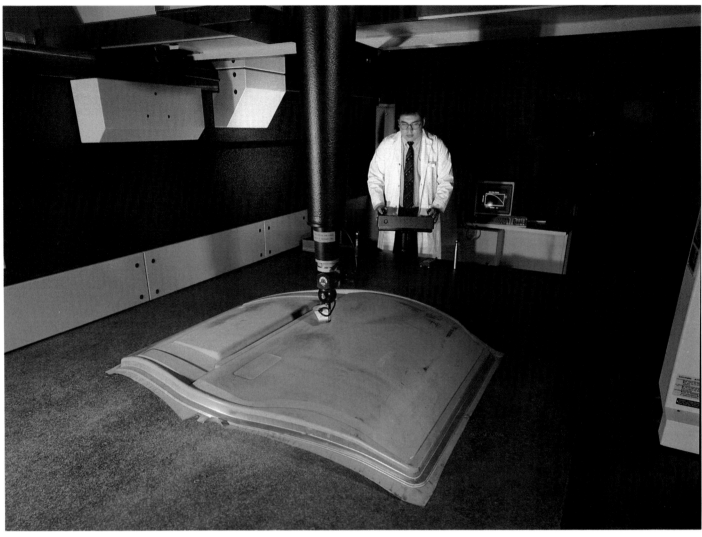

• *Dofasco's advanced research facilities provide knowledge and understanding of how the company's steel products perform at customers' plants. Results of research information are fed back to production where steel specifications are altered or new steel products developed to meet customers' exacting needs.*
– Photo courtesy of Dofasco

O ur product is steel. Our strength is people. Those two simple statements of fact within Dofasco's slogan epitomizes what the company is all about.

From the start, Dofasco's dedicated people have been a major factor behind the company's rise to become North America's most profitable steelmaker.

In 1912, Clifton W. Sherman came to Hamilton from the United States and built Dominion Steel Castings Co. Ltd., a foundry employing about 100 people on a five-acre site by the city's natural harbour.

The harbour provided easy access to raw materials to feed foundry production of steel castings for a then-vibrant Canadian rail industry.

A year later, the company amalgamated with the Hamilton Malleable Iron Co. Ltd. and was renamed Dominion Steel Foundry Ltd. with an expanded workforce of about 260 people.

By 1914, Mr. Sherman's brother, Frank A. Sherman, joined Dofasco which was then involved in military production to support the First World War effort.

"It was their spirit of innovation, combined with a special sense of how people deserved to be treated, that characterized the company," current Dofasco President John Mayberry says of the Sherman brothers.

In 1917, a plate mill was purchased and activated along with a forging department and rolling mill. A year later, there

were 11 open hearth furnaces producing 750 tons of steel per day. The company was renamed Dominion Foundries and Steel Ltd. with a workforce of 2,283.

By the early 1920s, Dofasco had built and commissioned the $2 million Universal and Sheared Plate Mill, the only one of its kind in Canada, producing previously imported steel plate.

While weathering the Great Depression of the 1930s, Dofasco continued to achieve new milestones, including the installation of 20-inch cold reducing mill in 1935 to produce the first Canadian-made tin plate. Two years later, a 42-inch cold mill was added and Dofasco's cold rolled steel capacity was increased to 100 tons per day.

The 1930s also marked some important 'people' milestones, including the start of various recreation clubs which today number more than 70. This emphasis on recreation also led to the creation of the 100-acre F. H. Sherman Recreation and Learning Centre, a complex with multiple recreation facilities enjoyed by Dofasco employees and their families today.

In 1936, Dofasco held its first massive company picnic. The same year, it held its first Christmas Party, a tradition that continues today. Open to all Dofasco employees and their families as well as retirees and their spouses, the annual Christmas Party is North America's largest.

And in 1938, Dofasco took the truly innovative step of introducing a profit sharing plan which recognized the importance of each employee's contribution to the company. Used for savings and pension creation, the plan remains an important benefit to Dofasco employees.

Numerous expansions continued in the 1940s and, in 1951, Dofasco's first Blast Furnace was lighted, making it the nation's fourth fully-integrated steel producer making steel products from raw ore.

In 1954, Dofasco poured North America's first batch of steel made in a basic oxygen furnace, which remains leading edge technology. A year later, Dofasco completed a 56-inch cold mill and started up Canada's first continuous galvanizing line.

By the early 1960s, Dofasco was rolling 1 million tons of steel per year. By the late 1970s, Dofasco started up its No. 2 Melt Shop, bringing the annual output to around 4 million tons.

In the early 1980s, the company, now officially renamed Dofasco Inc., started up its $380,000 No. 2 Hot Strip Mill and No. 4 Galvanizing Line.

By the mid-1980s, Dofasco built its fourth continuous Pickle Line for $75 million and made its biggest single expenditure ever when it embarked on a $750 million continuous slab caster program. It also began a $450 million continuous pickle line cold rolling complex.

In 1995, Dofasco started up a mini mill in Kentucky, a joint venture project with Toronto-based Co-Steel. Around the same time, Dofasco announced construction of a $200 million electric arc furnace and slab caster in Hamilton with a capacity of 1.3 million tons.

After weathering some lean years, Dofasco returned to its traditional role as a profitable steelmaker in the 1990s. The company reported 1995 profit of $195.8 million and provided a record profit sharing payout to employees.

Dofasco has always contributed to worthy causes in good times and bad.

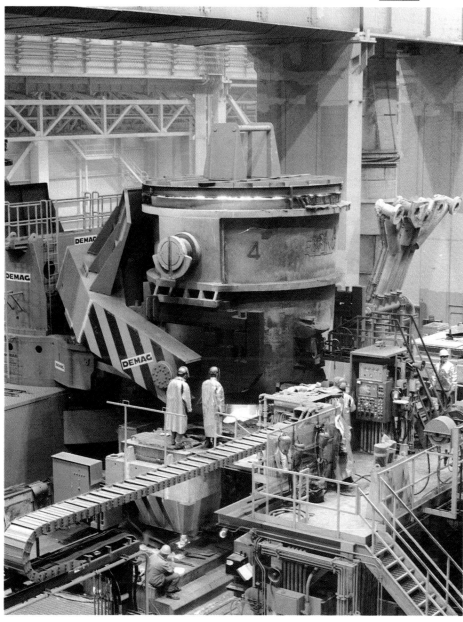

• *A 300-ton ladle of molten steel is positioned at the No. 1 Continuous Slab Caster, where the steel is formed into slabs for rolling flat into steel products.*
– Photo courtesy of Dofasco

Employees donate more than $1 million annually, as does the company. It has also donated its Sherman Centre, a meetings-social events facility, to Hamilton East Kiwanis for youth development.

Mr. Mayberry says success will still come to mills which can rely on highly skilled and dedicated people along with investments in technology.

Dofasco's strategy is to find and dominate market niches in which few rivals can compete – and to create stronger customer relationships. "As long as you can produce lower-cost, higher quality

products with better service, you will succeed," says Mr. Mayberry.

While the Hamilton steelmaker has invested more than $3 billion in technological improvements over the past 15 years, a major reason for the company's success has always been its "bright, competent and dedicated people," acknowledges Mr. Mayberry.

"And while there are those who may think our advertising slogan about our strength being people is just that – a slogan – believe me, it's a heartfelt statement of fact," he says.

O ffering living proof that anything old can be made new again, a restructured Dominion Castings Ltd. is preserving a piece of Hamilton's industrial past – and future.

Founded in 1912 as Dominion Foundries Co., the company was the original core of Dofasco Inc., the steelmaker which owes its contracted name to its foundry beginnings.

But as Dofasco grew into one of the nation's biggest steel companies, the foundry played an increasingly diminished role while its high steel industry wages made it uncompetitive with other foundries.

And the foundry appeared finished when Dofasco closed it and terminated its jobs in the fall of 1992 following years of losses. But NACO Inc. of Downers Grove, Illinois, bought the foundry assets in early 1993, restructured the Hamilton plant as Dominion Castings and began one of the most impressive turnarounds in the city's history.

"We started up from zero," recalls Andy Mikalauskas, a vice-president of Dominion Castings. "We're just now becoming profitable," he adds, noting that by the mid-'90s sales had more than doubled while the workforce had grown to 700 hourly rated and 120 staff and supervisory personnel.

"We're not out of the woods yet," adds the general manager, pointing out that a third

• This group of Dominion Castings employees has plenty to smile about as the company continues to forge ahead after getting new life in 1992.
– Photo by Bob Chambers

of the foundries across North America have gone out of business. "Fortunately, Dofasco had the foresight to sell the assets and allow us to continue the deep roots we have in this community – but in a restructured format."

"We still have to make sure we remain competitive," cautions Mr. Mikalauskas.

"But we're in a better position now than we've been in a long time. And NACO has made the difference."

Not only did NACO make the rebirth of Dominion Castings possible, he says, the American company's focus on the steel casting business, markets and customers has allowed its wholly owned Hamilton subsidiary to focus sharply on its own future.

"It helps being part of a company that focusses solely on its core business because we can all concentrate on the same objectives," explains Mr. Mikalauskas. "Towards the end with Dofasco, the foundry was only about 1 per cent of its business, so Dofasco couldn't devote many resources to it – and it would have been wrong if they had."

"Their business," he says, "was, and is, flat rolled steelmaking first and foremost."

Accounting for 90 per cent of Dominion Castings' sales is the railroad industry, which it supplies with locomotive and freight car undercarriages. The other 10 per cent goes to steel mills, mining and other customers. "Railroads are by far our primary market – and we're now the only major railroad foundry in Canada," notes Mr. Mikalauskas.

Dominion Castings is the only Canadian foundry in the NACO group which has worldwide production capability.

And with wages now in line with other foundries, a low-valued Canadian dollar and a cyclical upturn in foundry markets, Dominion Castings is winning its share of contract allocations. That's good news for Hamilton, which has gained a solvent, taxpaying company and more than 800 jobs – primarily labour-oriented positions which have gone to previously unemployed labourers displaced by industry downsizing.

Not that this company deserves to be labelled as an old labour industry.

"Casting is becoming a much more technical industry with computer-assisted design technology, solidification modelling and finite element analysis," Mr. Mikalauskas says. "And this emphasis on improving technology is also a big part of our future."

Peace is winning the war. Overcoming severe market conditions after suffering the loss of major customers, pattern-maker Dan Peace has battled his way back to prosperity.

Mr. Peace, president of Dominion Pattern Works, lost his biggest single customer – accounting for 25 per cent of sales – in the early 1990s when Dofasco Inc. closed its steel castings division foundry.

The Dofasco foundry closing worsened a then-bleak local market which had experienced similar foundry closings by International Harvester, Otis Elevator, Westinghouse Canada, Slater Steel, Canada Iron and others.

As foundries closed, several smaller pattern shops went out of business, leaving Dominion Pattern Works alone as the dominant player in a shrinking local market.

But Mr. Peace fought back with aggressive marketing in the United States, broadening his customer base and finding fresh sources of sales.

The American Midwest proved a lucrative market for the wood, metal and plastic patterns Dominion Pattern Works sells to foundries for use in moulds to cast an impressive array of railway and industrial equipment parts. The company also has non-ferrous customers making copper and aluminum castings for pulp and paper, mining and manufacturing industries.

"Our long-distance telephone bill started to get pretty big – and it still is," chuckles Mr. Peace, adding that U.S. sales have been growing steadily and to go after sales further afield, Dominion Pattern Works has devoted considerable resources to staff training and new equipment.

Higher production tooling and computer assisted design work along with a versatile, skilled staff helped 1995 sales revenue exceed 1994 revenue by 20 per cent. After laying off much of his staff, Mr. Peace was able to recall all of them and increase his workforce to a dozen people.

Dominion Pattern Works' skills base was also broadened during a learning period in which the firm focused heavily on maximizing customer satisfaction while consistently achieving on-time delivery, recalls Mr. Peace.

"We've made some real strides – and the credit goes to our staff team," Mr. Peace says of the firm's highly-skilled pattern-makers who boast a combined total of more than 400 years experience.

And just as the company had managed to more than recover lost business, it reaped the windfall of recapturing its old major customer: Dofasco's former foundry, which was sold to foundry operators who then reopened it as the successfully restructured Dominion Castings. Other major customers for the firm include Westinghouse Canada,

• *Dominion Pattern Works president Dan Peace, left, shown with his father Gord Peace, has lots to smile about as his company continues to prosper.*
— **Photo by David Gruggen**

General Motors and General Electric.

Dominion Pattern Works, with its 80th anniversary in 1996, has achieved new levels of prosperity with sales in the mid-1990s one third higher than those of prior years.

His company's turnaround is a source of satisfaction for Mr. Peace, who represents the third generation of Peace pattern-makers to head Dominion Pattern Works.

The small business was founded in 1916 by his grandfather, Harold Peace, and was later run by the founder's son, Gordon Peace, until Gord retired in the mid-1980s and turned the keys over to son Dan.

Dominion Pattern Works still operates out of its original 5,000-square-foot building, located on Princess Street in north-east Hamilton, creating customized tooling for industrial customers.

"This is very specialized work – our people can make just about anything," says Mr. Peace. "Pattern-making goes beyond science and skill. It's more than craftsmanship. It's an artform and there's a lot of heart in the work we do."

• *President Mario DiPietro (wearing tie) and plant superintendent Hal Gimmer are shown in the test room at Hamilton Wire Products. Also pictured are Sam Stephan, the company's quality inspector and employee Alan Gosnay, far left.*
– Photo by David Gruggen

No one ever doubted spring-maker Hamilton Wire's ability to bounce back from adversity. Blessed with ideal labour relations, a committed workforce and a successful takeover by an American giant, the Gage Avenue North company has emerged from the past recession larger and stronger than ever.

"We've grown a lot in the past couple of years," says general manager Mario DiPietro, who estimates sales have "almost doubled" at the company, which turns thick steel wire into chair control springs for office furniture.

The company also produces wire forms and springs for auto parts firms. It buys 80 per cent of its steel – some 3 to 4 million tons annually – from Stelco Inc.

"And while we like to operate with a lean office staff, we've doubled our hourly staff," adds Mr. DiPietro, whose company, by the mid-1990s, employed 30 hourly workers and seven office staff.

Mr. DiPietro notes the company enjoys "excellent labour relations," and regularly holds meetings with the employees and a representative of the United Steelworkers of America. It's at these monthly meetings that the employees are encouraged to raise concerns and all parties attempt to resolve issues amicably.

"We're proud of these sessions," says Mr. DiPietro, "because we're able to nip problems in the bud – it's very rare that things ever progress to the point of a grievance being launched."

This co-operative approach helps to explain why the company, founded in 1931, has experienced only a very short strike, in the 1950s.

"People feel comfortable with this company," says Mr. DiPietro, "because they know they're being listened to and that the company cares about them."

Adding to this comfort level is Leggett & Platt Inc., the Carthage, Missouri-based giant which, in 1993, bought Hamilton Wire from the Harrison family, who had owned and operated it for generations.

Although a local ownership connection was severed, Leggett & Platt was able to bring enhanced financial stability, a centralized accounting system, access to a wider customer base and considerable resources to the Hamilton company.

Initial plans for Hamilton Wire Products focussed on establishing a stable source of component supply for Leggett's chair control companies. Building on that foundation, Hamilton Wire has been able to expand sales to many companies outside the Leggett Family of businesses.

Mr. DiPietro feels the American parent has been able to expand on Hamilton Wire's traditional labour harmony by devoting substantial time and finances towards health and safety programs.

"We're committed to health and safety in a big way. We feel it's a quality of life matter and we want our people to feel good about working here. And there's a positive outlook at this plant."

Then there's the impressive investment in plant equipment – including a grinding machine using German technology – installed by Leggett & Platt, a mid-ranked Fortune 500 company with annual sales well in excess of $2 billion and yearly growth rates of 15 per cent or more.

"I'm proud to be part of such a winning company," says Mr. DiPietro. "We've joined up with a stable, long-term growth company. The employees feel more secure and that's boosted morale."

Hamilton Wire, run as part of Leggett & Platt's No-Sag division, was committed to achieving ISO 9000 certification from the International Standards Organization by the end of 1996, making the company's products immediately accepted throughout world markets. "We've kept the teamwork approach going – in fact we've built on it," notes Mr. DiPietro.

• *General manager Livio Rattner, right, and Vince Valeri, one of the owners of Dynamic & Proto Circuits Inc., display a high-tech telephone switching device which the Stoney Creek company produced for Northern Telecom.*
– Photo by David Gruggen

Dynamic & Proto Circuits Inc. is growing rapidly by confining itself to a small – but challenging – market for rigid, prototype circuit boards. And with its large new plant, expanded workforce and rising revenue, the Stoney Creek circuit board maker has found it's nice to have a niche.

General manager Livio Rattner attributes the company's success to its practice of sticking closely to its core business as the Canadian quality manufacturer of prototype circuit boards.

Staying with what they do best has paid off for Dynamic & Proto Circuits, a company formed by Vince Valeri in the mid-1970s from the merger of Dynamic Circuits Inc. and Proto Circuits Inc.

After acquiring its new location on Barton Street in the mid-1990s and investing many millions of dollars in equipment – including a state-of-the-art water treatment system – the company continues to invest heavily in new technology and machinery.

"We're involved in a fast-changing industry and we have to keep up with the latest developments in technology and equipment," notes Mr. Rattner, adding that market demand is increasing for complex circuit boards.

This new generation of circuit boards often feature smaller dimensions and are made up of multiple layers.

Driving Dynamic & Proto Circuits' success is the company's commitment to ensuring customers receive fast delivery of high-quality prototype circuit boards.

Dynamic & Proto Circuits' customers place a strong emphasis on receiving prototype circuit boards quickly and the company takes great pride in its ability to meet these fast delivery demands.

The company also provides training for its workforce, which has grown to 120 and continues to grow at a steady rate.

In addition to a highly trained workforce and tight quality control processes, the company is also certified by the International Standards Organization under ISO 9002-1994, providing it with fast product acceptance and credibility in foreign markets. Dynamic & Proto Circuits is also certified under U.L. (Underwriters Laboratories) and military standards. About half the firm's products are exported, mainly to the United States.

With an emphasis on cutting edge technology, high quality and fast delivery, Dynamic & Proto Circuits' boards are an integral component of computer systems serving telecommunications, medical, scientific and military industries.

• The Control Pulpit at Stelco Inc.'s Hilton Works is a state-of-the-art operation, geared to producing superior bar quality. Hilton Works is an integrated steelmaking and processing complex situated on 1,100 acres in Hamilton. Products include semi-finished slabs and blooms; and finished products include Plate, Hot Rolled Sheet, Coated Sheet, Rod and Bars. Products are sold in a variety of markets, with major penetration in the automotive, steel service centre, construction, pipe and tube, and wire and wire products sector.
— **Photo courtesy of Photo Services, Stelco Hilton Works**

Quietly, almost imperceptibly, Hamilton has evolved into a high-technology centre. The city is as comfortable today with the latest computer-driven advancements as it is with its enduring steel industry – an industry which has also joined the high-tech revolution.

Evidence of high-tech machinery and processes can be found everywhere. You can find a glimpse of the future today at Westinghouse Canada's Sanford Avenue turbines plant, which competes globally for power generation customers.

And you can find advanced manufacturing at such Westinghouse spin-off companies as WESCAM, makers of gyro-stabilized camera mounts embraced by Hollywood for filming an array of movies, including Judge Dredd and the Superman flicks. Floating in its own gyro-stabilized world, the camera can film from moving helicopters and trains without vibration.

Of course there are other companies arising from businesses divested by Westinghouse, including Stern Laboratories in Hamilton, specializing in meticulous research and nuclear reactor safety testing; and Gennum Corp. in neighbouring Burlington where components are made for hearing instruments and electronic sound equipment.

Another Burlington firm, CRS Robotics, uses robot arms to perform the dull, dirty and dangerous jobs which are shunned by people. Industry has welcomed these robot arms, which seem to delight in performing highly repetitive tasks or working in toxic environments.

Then, there's Fell-Fab in Hamilton, which has provided high-tech insulation for satellites and for the Canadarm robotic arm on NASA's Space Shuttles. The insulation allowed the robotic space arm to stay within NASA weight limitations while providing the correct temperature for it to operate.

There's also Comtronic Computer Centre, which is meeting the specialized needs of customers through its computer clone systems and expert advice.

And, there's Dynamic and Proto Circuits, which serves a growing export market with its array of technologically advanced prototype, rigid circuit boards.

Of course, there's also McMaster University with its advanced robotics research facilities, high-tech product testing capabilities and in-house nuclear reactor.

Robotic arms can also be found in the steel mills, where steelmaking has become a computer-assisted, high-tech process utilizing billions of dollars worth of specialized equipment.

The list goes on and on in a city where the formation of new high-tech companies is frequently accompanied by the high-tech conversions of more established firms.

"A lot of what we think of as advanced manufacturing is process-laden as much as technology-driven," points out Len Sharpe, manager of the Westinghouse turbine plant, who notes high-tech advancements are only part of the equation.

"It's a matter of making your operations as efficient as possible, giving your people ownership of the decision-making process, getting everyone working together as a team and going in the same direction," he says, adding that high-technology assists this progressive approach.

The move to high-tech is a direction Hamilton is taking with confidence as the community embraces futuristic technology to achieve gains for present day – and future – generations.

• This robotic skimmer at Stelco Inc.'s Hilton Works is the only one of its kind in the world, removing impurities from the ceramic-lined zinc pot. The induction-heated zinc pot at Hilton Works' Z-Line is the largest in the world.
– Photo courtesy of Photo Services, Stelco Hilton Works

I f you're looking to find the top executives at BartonAir Fabrications Inc. – you can probably find them on the shop floor, engaged in some of the hands-on work that built their success.

"I still, after all these years, can't resist getting directly involved, rolling up my sleeves, working alongside one of the company's skilled employees and getting the job done together," says Andy Di Cristofaro, president of the custom steel fabricating, welding and industrial machining firm at Niagara and Burlington streets.

"I still spend more time at the shop than the average employee," admits Mr. Di Cristofaro whose roots in the metal working industry date back to his youth as a tradesman in Italy.

After arriving in Canada in the early '60s, Mr. Di Cristofaro went on to establish Barton Metal Works Ltd. in Stoney Creek. From its modern facilities, the successful company would supply machining services to industry for more than 20 years until its assets were eventually sold to a subsidiary of Westinghouse Electric Corp.

And when Mr. Di Cristofaro decided to expand the BartonAir Fabrications business he founded in 1987, he formed a partnership with some key Barton Metal employees, including son Vince Di Cristofaro and general manager Art King.

"Placing my full trust in Art was a very easy decision for me, considering Art's unquestionable loyalty to me for so many years," Mr. Di Cristofaro says of his decision to make the general manager a business associate.

For Mr. King, the expanded role allows greater scope for furthering the business success achieved with Mr. Di Cristofaro over a period of more than 20 years.

"Working with Andy has been a great experience," says Mr. King, "but more than that, it is also a tremendous opportunity, for myself and my associates."

That sense of satisfaction is shared by Vince Di Cristofaro, executive vice-president, who points with pride to office walls lined with photographs of successful company projects he's been involved with while growing up in the business.

"A measure of the company's ability can be gained by viewing these," he says, noting that many of the photos depict intricate work, demonstrating the firm's expertise in performing custom plate work fabricating and industrial machining

for steelmakers, mining companies and other industrial customers.

The company made a momentous decision in 1993, when it left its cramped Stoney Creek plant for its current location at Niagara Street, Hamilton.

The 66,000-square-foot building is nearly three times the size of the old plant and is situated in Hamilton's industrial heartland, nearby major steelmakers.

The company had been turning away

• A move to a new 66,000-square-foot plant in the heart of Hamilton's industrial heartland sparked an increase in business for BartonAir Fabrications.
– Photo by Bob Chambers

potential business and contracting out work it would rather have done on its own – all because it lacked physical capacity at its old Stoney Creek plant.

But all that changed with the move to a larger, completely refurbished and modernized building – and with the company's investment in conventional and computer-controlled machine tools and fabricating equipment, says Mr. King.

"Having such a large variety of metal working equipment in our shop has negated the necessity to subcontract work to a large degree," he explains.

"When we do the work ourselves," Mr. King says, "we have ultimate control

over delivery schedules, cost and quality."

It's a clearly successful formula: With its vast array of overhead cranes, metal working equipment and machine tools the modern plant boasted a workforce of 70 people in the mid-1990s, compared with barely a dozen in the late 1980s.

And the manufacturing floor is a beehive of activity, with skilled workers diligently fabricating, welding and machining a variety of components from a palm-sized steel shaft to large fabrications weighing over 40 tons, as BartonAir demonstrates again its ability to offer a wide range of services.

The company also provides design and engineering services and solutions to industry through an on-staff engineer and a department that's responsible for maintaining the firm's Canadian Welding Bureau certification.

And a mechanical department boasting skilled machine fitters can disassemble whole machines, then refurbish worn pieces of equipment following computer-assisted inspections. Any components requiring replacement are custom produced at the sprawling plant.

Citing his associates, employees and customers for BartonAir's success, Mr. Di Cristofaro sums up his determined approach, noting that "if you persist, insist and resist, you will not fail in your attempt to do anything you wish."

John Bruzzese is very much at home with steel-framed houses. The president of Hamilton-based Armour Steel Supply Ltd. started manufacturing and supplying steel framing for homes in the early 1990s – and business is booming.

While his company has traditionally been a supplier of structural steel products, Mr. Bruzzese notes that steel framing products accounted for 25 per cent of sales by the mid-1990s.

"And within another year or so, the steel framing business could be as much as seven times larger than the structural steel side of our business," suggests Mr. Bruzzese, who also exports millions of dollars worth of steel framing products to Mexico, the United States and Europe.

Founded in 1964 by Ozzie Palmieri, a friend of the Bruzzese family, the company was from the beginning a manufacturer and supplier of structural products such as steel I beams, posts and concrete reinforcing bar used in residential, light industrial and retail mall applications.

Armour Steel is also something of a family business. Mr. Bruzzese's brother Pat is the company's operations manager while his brother Perry oversees the structural components business.

Armour Steel has reached a crossroads in its corporate evolution, notes Mr. Bruzzese. "There is an incredible global opportunity we are focusing on with a patented automated wall panellizing system that is causing the residential builders to make the transition to light gauge steel framed houses."

"The product is very light-weight and easy to handle," says Mr. Bruzzese, who provides pre-cut framing products featuring pre-punched holes for wiring.

"Two framers can easily carry a 20-foot by 8-foot-high wall," he adds, pointing out that steel framing is comparable in price to traditional wood but has the potential of generating significant savings for home builders because of the pre-assembled wall sections reducing on-site labour costs.

"And you don't have the call-back costs you have with wood, which can warp and shift, causing nail pops, squeaky floors and cracked walls," he explains. "Steel stays perfectly straight all the time."

Other steel framing advantages include its uniform quality and durability, zero risk of insect infestation or damage and superior strength. Also, it doesn't burn. And, using steel saves trees.

With so many benefits to steel framing, Mr. Bruzzese is winning over a growing number of builders whose customers are demanding steel framed homes.

"The biggest push for steel framed homes is coming from home buyers," he notes, "and we're going to see steel used in a lot more houses in the years ahead."

• John Bruzzese is the president of Armour Steel Supply Limited. The Hamilton-based company started manufacturing and supplying steel framing for homes in 1990.
– Photo by Joe Bucci

• An electric arc furnace is shown being assembled for Dofasco at McCabe Steel's new plant, which is located on Invandi Court in Stoney Creek.

The versatile approach has earned enduring success for McCabe Steel. "We do a lot of work for our customers that these companies used to do themselves in-house," notes Norm McCabe, president of the growing Stoney Creek steel processing, manufacturing and fabricating company.

"We're the beneficiary of a lot of contracted-out work," adds Mr. McCabe, whose Arvin Avenue plant produces structural steel and custom-built machinery products for steel, mining and transportation industry customers.

"Out-sourcing by our customers is a major source of growth for us."

McCabe Steel has produced everything from motor frames, steel mill components and blast furnace components to massive ship loaders and a 200-foot-long rail car to transport massive steam boilers to South Carolina. "We even built a crash barrier system for the Ford company to use in measured test crashes of its vehicles," says Mr. McCabe.

It's all a long way from the little two-man welding shop Mr. McCabe founded with his older brother Fred on Cathcart Street, Hamilton, in 1969. The steel fabricating firm began landing contracts with Stelco Inc. and Dofasco Inc. and soon outgrew its original premises.

By the mid-1970s, the company employed half-a-dozen people and had relocated to a 4,000-square-foot building on Seaman Avenue, Stoney Creek.

A series of expansions followed, taking the plant to 15,000 square feet and more than 50 employees when Fred McCabe left in 1984 to found a similar business, A&F Fabricating, with his brother Andre.

Norm McCabe continued growing the McCabe Steel business and in 1990 relocated to the current 28,000-square-foot plant on 2.5 acres at Arvin Avenue.

Then, in 1996, it also acquired a 55,000-square-foot building on 13.5 acres on nearby Jones Road. This multi-million-dollar acquisition gave the company an impressive total of 83,000 square feet of

space between the two plants.

The workforce also grew, to 70 people in 1995 and an estimated workforce of 100 by spring of 1996. Mr. McCabe notes his company has continued to operate the Arvin Avenue plant after relocating its headquarters to Jones Road in the spring of 1996.

He readily admits he enjoys the challenges and variety of work that come with being a versatile provider of a wide array of products to customers in steel, mining and transportation sectors.

McCabe Steel uses its own design and drafting people while contracting out most engineering work to bring in the specialized skills needed for specific projects the company undertakes.

"The demand is certainly out there and it's growing," adds Mr. McCabe.

"More and more companies are looking to reduce or eliminate fixed costs associated with in-house services. They look to us to provide those services – and that's where our growth is coming from."

• A section of waste gas duct, for an electric arc furnace at Dofasco, is set for delivery at Dynamic Steel.
– Photo by David Gruggen

Working under pressure is working wonders for Dynamic Steel Inc., a company which has engineered a remarkable turnaround. The pressure vessel manufacturer found itself in a fight for survival during lean years in the early 1990s.

Used to working with pressure of a different sort, Dynamic Steel president Matt Di Tomasso faced the added pressure of trying to find new sources of sales revenue to keep his firm in production. Pressure vessels resemble oversized oil tanks but feature thick steel walls and welded seals that meet stringent anti-leaking requirements.

Mr. Di Tomasso was clearly up to the challenge: By the mid-1990s the pressure vessel maker and custom steel fabricator had more than tripled its annual sales revenue to $5.5 million while quadrupling its workforce to 40 people. Behind the turnaround was Mr. Di Tomasso's early recognition that Canada's slower recovery meant needed growth had to come from exports.

"We needed sales, and we weren't getting enough of them from around here," he says.

To assist with a sales push south, Mr. Di Tomasso brought in exports expert Dwayne Wanner, who lined up a number of lucrative contracts in the U.S., including a deal supplying pressure vessels to the Navy.

And to sustain growth, Mr. Di Tomasso also beefed up service while shoring up domestic sales in a gradually recovering local market. "We knew it had to be a combination of things – exports, local sales and service – to grow healthy again," he recalls, adding his Hamilton firm broke even in 1994, recorded profits in 1995 and expected to surpass those profits in 1996.

"Now we've got a 50-50 split between exports and domestic sales. We're also doing more service work. Boiler repair is expected to pick up . . . It's all starting to even out."

Mr. Di Tomasso is now happily grappling with a new problem – keeping up with demand. "It's been very busy. We've got a backlog of orders for several months."

Local work includes providing pressure vessels, pressurized with nitrogen, plus duct work to Eichleay Engineering Co. for work on Stelco's pulverized coal injection system blast furnace modernization program.

"We're really getting in pretty good shape," notes Mr. Di Tomasso, whose skilled workforce produces some of the world's highest quality pressure vessels from the company's plant at Lake Avenue North.

"One key factor is that economic conditions have improved and we're benefiting from an improved economy," he observes.

"But we've also hired some very good salespeople and we've teamed up some local environmental companies in a network – and as their business has picked up, our business has picked up as well," adds Mr. Di Tomasso. "By reaching out for new sales, we've not only replaced lost business but we've grown as a result. We're now increasing our exports and local business – and we're determined to continue growing."

• The Port of Hamilton is one of busiest ports in the country. With approximately 8.6 million tonnes of cargo handled from January to September of 1995, Hamilton's port ranked eighth overall among the most active ports in Canada. As expected, steel industry-related shipments continued to make up a large portion of the port's activity.
— *Photos by*
Glenn Lethbridge

Agunshot in Europe turned the course of Hotz family history. In 1920, Jewish Lithuanian general merchandise salesman Max Hotz was confronted by armed robbers while driving his horse and wagon through a forest near the German border.

A struggle ensued, and part of Mr. Hotz' ear lobe was shot off. He managed to escape home, where he told his wife Shanna to gather their four children and possessions. They were going to Canada.

In 1921, the Hotz family arrived in Hamilton, where a nearly penniless Mr. Hotz became a 'ragman,' driving a horse and wagon down city streets, calling out for rags, bottles and scraps of metal he could resell as raw material to paper mills, foundries and steelmakers. It was the birth of a recycling company decades before the word 'recycling' was invented.

From their home on John Street North – owned by Mrs. Hotz's father Zorrach Takefman, who arrived in Hamilton in the mid-1890s – the couple raised a family of six children, two of whom were born in Canada. Their eldest son Abe dropped out of high school in the 1930s to help his father in the family business, and son Louis followed, giving rise to the company name Hotz & Sons Co.

The late Abe Hotz introduced trucks to their business and helped it expand into a diversified recycling and disposal firm, recollects younger brother Louis, 73.

"Abe brought in around 15 big trucks, expanded the reach into a wider market area and really helped it grow," recalls Louis Hotz, former company chairman, in an interview from his Ravenscliffe Avenue home, where he was joined by Yetta, his wife and family historian.

From Max Hotz's death in 1954 to his own death in 1982, Abe Hotz brought about a tenfold increase in business by utilizing larger trucks capable of carrying up to 200 drums and serving customers as far away as Detroit, notes Louis Hotz.

"At one time or another, just about every member of the family has had some involvement in the business," Mr. Hotz adds. Other family members include his sisters Anne, a bookkeeper; and Lillian, founder of the Canadian Association of Retired Persons; along with brothers Dr. Harry Hotz, a prominent pediatrician; and the late Jack Hotz, a lawyer.

The Hotz group of companies now includes Hotz Environmental Services, with its Household Hazardous Waste Division and Industrial Hazardous Waste Division; Hotz Ferrous, a scrap metal recycling company; and Hotz & Sons Co., with its Metals Division and Drums & Wipers Division.

Headquartered on Lottridge Street, the company employs some 50 people in diversified operations ranging from scrap metal recycling to the recycling of paints and management of hazardous materials. The company owns a fleet of 15 specially outfitted, large capacity vehicles plus cranes, tow motors, loading docks and various acquired properties.

Louis Hotz now serves as general manager of the Drums & Wipers Division of Hotz & Sons, while his son Martin Hotz, 34, is overall company president.

"Just as Abe brought the company to a new level of growth by introducing trucks, my son Martin is bringing the company into its next stage by introducing computer systems and new ways of doing things," Louis Hotz says with pride.

"And, perhaps years from now, another generation will take it to the next stage."

T he steady, determined clatter of a horse-drawn buggy routinely announced the arrival of Jacob Goldblatt and Louis Takefman at Hamilton factories in the late 1890s.

The brothers-in-law had immigrated to Canada from Lithuania in search of opportunity – and found it in the collecting of scrap metal. Mr. Goldblatt's son Frank, with greater proficiency in English, helped the older men build a successful business reselling scrap metal to Hamilton's burgeoning steel and manufacturing industries.

Frank Goldblatt – Mr. Frank as he was affectionately referred to by employees – would become company chairman, forging from modest beginnings the modern-day business dynasty that is Intermetco.

Now the nation's largest recycler of metal products, Intermetco is a major manufacturer and distributor of spiralweld pipe, a diversified firm with 17 operating subsidiaries and divisions across North America.

The company's well-known Intermetco 73 logo symbolizes the success achieved at its 73 Robert Street, Hamilton corporate headquarters where the company began.

By the mid-1990s, Intermetco – the International Iron and Metal Company of Hamilton – was approaching a century in business, with multi-million-dollar profits and a workforce of approximately 300 people across North America.

"When we went public, it opened up a whole new vista for us," notes Marvin Goldblatt, who was president of the firm when it became listed on the Toronto Stock Exchange in 1969. He would later replace his father Frank Goldblatt as chairman of the fast-growing company.

"We're sticking to our core metals recycling and pipe businesses now," notes Marvin Goldblatt, "and from 1970 to today we've had steady growth."

Fiscal 1994 profits of $1.3 million on sales revenue of $168.2 million marked a 47 per cent revenue gain over 1993 and Intermetco's third straight year of continuous financial improvement, notes Ed Fraser, the firm's vice-president, finance.

More impressive, the company earned profits of $2.2 million on revenue of $153.8 million for just the first nine months of fiscal 1995. The company's common shares are held by institutional and individual investors and by members of retired president Abby Goldblatt and Marvin Goldblatt families.

Intermetco president Bernie Poplack attributes the company's improving fortunes to the maintenance of high steel scrap prices and an improving economy in the mid-'90s.

And chairman Marvin Goldblatt agrees that "as the steel industry goes, so we go."

"Stelco is a major customer, as well as Slater Steel, Dofasco and other steel companies, including Ivaco and Sydbec-Dosco in

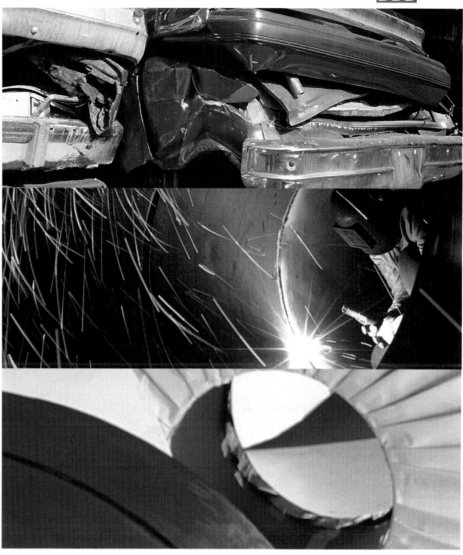

• *Intermetco Limited is the country's foremost recycler and processor of scrap metal products. In addition, the company also manufactures and distributes pipe, structural pipe and tubular products across North America, and it also warehouses, processes, and packages galvanized steel in Canada*

Quebec and Sydney Steel on the East Coast."

Underscoring a commitment to the environment, Mr. Goldblatt notes that his firm has an environmental protection expert on staff. The chairman also notes that "recycling of materials to conserve our dwindling resources and anti-pollution programs of all types are examples of activities in which progress is essential and in which Intermetco can contribute to achievement."

The modern metals recycling division, the largest in Canada, features advanced shearing, shredding, crushing and baling equipment, even a 'fragmentizer' which can reduce a car to fist-sized chunks of steel in a matter of seconds.

After metal recycling, the company's second biggest business is in the manufacturing

of spiralweld pipe products in the U.S. and the distribution of pipe piling, tubular pipe and beams as part of a burgeoning pipe business established after the Second World War.

Another growing source of revenue for the company is the slitting and warehousing of galvanized steel at its Coilpac division which was established in the early 1990s.

As Intermetco considers its future role in cyclical markets, it's clear the company intends to take a thoughtful, measured approach to growth.

"We intend to pursue expansion and diversification of our company on clear, logical lines," notes Mr. Goldblatt. "The new fields we seek will be activities in which we will be able to apply our experience and take advantage of our collective expertise."

Munro Metal Products Limited couldn't say no to its customers, so the sheet steel fabricator found added success as a growing wholesaler of others' products.

Metal fabrication of ductwork, pipe and fittings now accounts for about 20 per cent of annual business. The remaining 80 per cent is derived from wholesaling heating, air conditioning and ventilation equipment.

Munro Metal president John Rayworth says the wholesale side of the business has opened up new opportunities for his company, which was strictly a metal processor when it began in 1924. Overall sales rose more than 20 per cent in 1995 over 1994, with continued heady growth expected through the remainder of the 1990s.

Company controller Peter Cauchi notes that Munro Metal's move into wholesaling began in the 1960s, when customers who were buying ductwork for heating equipment began asking Munro Metal to supply the equipment itself. The company wasn't about to say no to its customers.

"We started out in sheet metal and got more and more into (wholesaling) equipment as our customers asked us to expand our product lines," Mr. Cauchi explains.

With wholesale now making up the bulk of sales, the company finds itself in an extremely competitive marketplace.

"The way we do business today is completely different than the way we did business 10 years ago," notes Mr. Cauchi.

"We are now more market-driven and more customer-focused. The customer has so many choices in the marketplace, we now know we have to offer more than our competitors," he adds.

Among Munro Metal's advantages is a one-stop shopping approach: The company is the only wholesaler in the area that also manufactures sheet metal products, allowing it to provide clients with custom-designed solutions. A full service department also gives the company an edge over competitors who often have to send customers back to the manufacturers for service.

"There is no doubt that we have taken a value-added approach to satisfying our customers," asserts Mr. Cauchi.

Mr. Rayworth notes the Middle East has also emerged as a potentially lucrative market for gas-powered cooling equipment his company distributes. "The Middle East looks good for several reasons," says Mr. Rayworth. "They have lots of gas, lots of money and lots of hot days."

The company, which today has more than 70 continuous operating years under its belt, was founded by Murdo John Munro, who gave the firm his name.

Munro Metal was subsequently sold to the partnership of Richard Lord and Norm McCarthy before being sold in 1972 to Mr. Rayworth's father, Lawrence Rayworth, now company chairman.

The younger Mr. Rayworth bought the business from his father in 1988 and, after weathering the recession, he has positioned Munro Metal Products to reap benefits from the subsequent recovery.

The Tim Hortons chain opened its first store on Ottawa Street in Hamilton in 1964, and is proud to have played a role in the continuing development of this fine community throughout the years.

"I have always taken a great deal of pride and satisfaction in the fact that Hamiltonians have taken the Tim Hortons chain so much to their hearts," says Ron Joyce, co-founder of the chain. "The chain's success has come very much as a result of the acceptance and loyalty shown within this city."

Tim Hortons store owners throughout the Hamilton area have committed a great deal of time, energy and funding to local events and programs that have benefitted numerous children within the area. The store owners have participated in local charity drives and worthwhile causes on an ongoing basis. And they have demonstrated a strong support and encouragement for the performing arts in Hamilton.

The Tim Hortons chain currently has more than 1200 locations from coast to coast in Canada, including each province and both territories. The chain stays on the leading edge of the industry by implementing such innovations as drive-thrus, double drive-thrus, smoke-free locations and separate glassed-in smoking rooms.

In 1964, the chain sold only coffee and donuts, but today its menu includes a vast array of baked goods such as muffins, tarts, pies, specialty cakes and bagels. The popularity of the phenomenally successful Timbit, introduced in 1976, continues

today. Tim Hortons also provides a strong luncheon menu which includes soups, sandwiches and chili, clearly reflecting today's consumer preferences.

While Tim Hortons stores offer an enjoyable retreat for their many loyal customers, today's lifestyles demand the convenience of accessibility. Tim Hortons has answered this demand by expanding into various non-traditional locations.

Outlets in the form of kiosks and carts can now be found in hospitals, universities, retail outlets, tourist attractions, gas bars and sporting arenas.

Probably the most significant contribution to the community made by the Tim Hortons store owners comes from their continuing support and funding of the Tim Horton Children's Foundation.

A non-profit, charitable organization, the Foundation operates summer camps for deserving children from each community. Store owners work with schools, churches, local agencies and organizations such as Big Brothers and Big Sisters to

select appropriate children to attend one of the six 10-day sessions each summer.

The Foundation currently operates camps in Parry Sound, Ontario; Quyon, Quebec; Tatamagouche, Nova Scotia; and Kananaskis, Alberta, allowing well over 2,000 children each year to enjoy a once-in-a-lifetime experience.

Hamiltonians have played a major role in helping to expand the Foundation's work with children by giving generously throughout the year to the counter coin boxes at each Tim Hortons store. Customers also take part enthusiastically in the annual Camp Day Canada fundraiser, the day set aside whereby all proceeds from all coffee sales during this 24-hour period at all locations are donated by the store owners to the Foundation. Additional customer donations on Camp Day have made this the single most important fund-raising event for the Foundation throughout the year.

Tim Hortons store owners and operators share a great pride in Hamilton and are confident that a positive future lies ahead for this caring community.

"We anticipate a continued steady growth with Hamilton and surrounding areas over the next several years, and hope that we can maintain the levels of quality, service and success that our customers within the area have come to expect," says Mr. Joyce.

• *There are over 1,200 Tim Hortons across the country. Store #1,000 (top) is on Golf Links Road in Ancaster. Store #1,104 is in the Right House building in downtown Hamilton.*

• Mobile Cartage founder Mel Johnson snapped this photo of his Model T Ford in 1930, with four-year-old son Doug shown at right. The original steering wheel and licence plate from the Model T are to this day proudly displayed at the Mobile Cartage offices. The successful company is operated by Ed and Mark Johnson, the founder's grandsons, making Mobile the oldest cartage and transport firm in Hamilton still being operated by the original family owners.

Mel Johnson went from carrying fellow soldiers on the battle-fields of World War I to carrying general cargo by truck through the streets of Hamilton.

The dedicated Great War stretcher-bearer returned to Hamilton in 1919 and founded a company familiar to all Hamiltonians – Mobile Cartage.

After buying a brand new black Ford Model T Truck, he operated Mobile Cartage from his home on Forest Avenue as a one-man operation.

It was the beginning of an enduring legacy: Mobile Cartage would go on to become a large, thriving business, the oldest cartage and transport firm in Hamilton which is still operated by the original family owners.

"We still have the original steering wheel and license plate from my grandfa-

ther's Model T truck," notes Ed Johnson, president of Mobile Cartage, which now employs 45 people at its Nash Road offices, truck terminal and distribution warehouse facilities.

"We keep the steering wheel and plate on display," adds Mr. Johnson, 32, whose office walls are lined with old black-and-white photographs and memorabilia dating back to the family firm's early years.

His brother Mark Johnson, 37, is vice-president, finance. The family firm's first dispatcher was the brothers' great aunt Grace, who died in 1995 at the age of 96.

Also involved in the running of the family business over the years were the founder's only child, Doug Johnson, and his wife Beatrice, who both retired in 1989 after many years of service.

As a child Doug Johnson did his part to help out, starting off by making deliv-

eries on his bicycle and then eventually working alongside his father and his mother Ethel, who took her turn doing the office work at Mobile Cartage.

Doug eventually took over as company president and the family tradition continued with Beatrice in the office and the couple's three children – Mark, Betsy and Edward – all helping out at Mobile Cartage in one way or another during their school years.

Mobile Cartage trucks are today a familiar sight across Hamilton and beyond. The trucks are also a memorable sight as they're often adorned with a large illustration of the company's famous insignia: a unique, humourous cartoon character pushing a wheelbarrow.

"My great uncle Ted Johnson came up with our cartoon character in the 1920s and he was quite a character himself, with

a great sense of humour," says Ed Johnson. "If you take a good look at the illustration, the cartoon character is running full tilt with a wheelbarrow and he's headed for disaster. The front wheel is about to collide with a brick."

Over the years, the growing company expanded into roomier locations, moving out of the founder's home to a business site at Wellington and Wilson streets.

But an industry transition to big tractor trailers left little manoeuvering room at that location.

Today, Mobile Cartage is located on Nash Road in Hamilton's east end, where you will find the company's fleet of 32 power units, including tractors and five-ton trucks. In addition, the company operates 40 van- and flat-bed trailers.

Mobile Cartage transports general freight, everything from food products to steel on behalf of industrial and commercial clients. The firm offers truckload and less-than-truckload services to a growing customer base, within a day's drive in Ontario and Western New York State.

"We're very diversified, we do some oversized loads and we offer an expedited service – a big part of our business – for customers who need something shipped or delivered right away," notes Ed Johnson. "You have to be flexible and very service-oriented in this business to succeed," he adds.

"Hamilton is really an ideal location to run a business like this. The city is the hub of a big market area with other major centres only a short drive away," he says. "We've always been based in Hamilton – and we always will be."

• *Mobile Cartage has come a long way since it began operating out of the founder's home in 1919. Shown above is Mobile's distribution and warehousing terminal located on Nash Road in Hamilton's East End.*
*– **Photo by David Gruggen***

Chapter 9

Renaissance Project

In Italy, for thirty years under the Borgias they had warfare, terror, murder and bloodshed, but they produced Michelangelo, Leonardo Da Vinci, and the Renaissance. In Switzerland they had brotherly love, they had 500 years of democracy and peace – and what did they produce? The cuckoo clock.

– from the 1949 movie, The Third Man

In all history, there was no more enriching a period than the Renaissance; an era remembered for the artistic genius of Leonardo Da Vinci; sculptor Michelangelo's frescoes that adorn the Vatican's Sistine Chapel; the discoveries by Italian physicist and astronomer Galileo; the humanistic poetry of Milton; Elizabethan dramas, along with architecture, such as the cathedral of Florence. It was a time of quantum leaps in medicine with explorations of anatomy – not to mention intellectual freedoms, sometimes to Machiavellian heights and depths.

So, Renaissance, literally a rebirth, seemed appropriate for our city, in the throes of transition, as it were – part of a life cycle no less cataclysmic than that of convulsive labour pangs.

The Renaissance Project here in Hamilton-Wentworth, sowed the seeds of our rejuvenation by laying the groundwork for a fertile investment climate.

As the industrial revolution was, so now is the "information" era; a global eruption of seismic proportions. For the future lies not in brute strength but in sheer brainpower; in the sectors such as health, education, administration and communication.

If you're trained to interpret an X-ray, isolate a defective gene and diagnose an ailment; teach computer programming to a class of 10-year-olds; supervise a laboratory, or explain the logistics of a 500-channel TV set to the uninitiated, you will have some measure of security in the 21st century.

While nothing's guaranteed in the electronic age, excepting of course the axiomatic death and taxes, chances are good that a degree and erudition will take precedence over drudgery and routine; and no more so than in a city that was built by steel.

This concept of lifelong learning has been a quandary for the older generation who relied on manual labour rather than computer modems. In the 1950s, 55 per cent of the workforce toiled in the industrial sector; amid the whir of machinery and conveyor belts. With high-tech, that figure has been slashed by close to half. And of the 14 per cent who remain, another half would be redundant with proper, space-age production methods.

Instead of "company men" with job security and golden handshakes, many have become jobless with severance packages and antiquated skills. Not since the 19th century, when the railway criss-crossed Canada and turned farm hands into factory workers, has our economic upheaval been quite so traumatic.

There's also a multi-cultural mosaic; a country no longer the preserve of English Commonwealth descendants. In Southern

Ontario, we have greeted an average of 70,000 immigrants annually over the last half century; people from all parts of the globe, who make a rich contribution and a cosmopolitan society; not to mention the Eastern philosophy which runs contrary to a materialistic culture. Add to that the gender revolt, as women who once worked for "pin money" now compete for management jobs. The game has changed and so have the rules.

Is it any wonder that many feel they have been grabbed by their heels, spun and hurled into the next millennium?

Those trends, as radical as they might be, are overshadowed by an awareness of conservation. The future of our earth is no longer the bailiwick of fringe groups or a vocal minority. It is the mainstream mandate.

Speaking at the annual general meeting of the Rotary Club in a state-of-the-city address, Mayor Robert Morrow quoted a Canadian Geographic article which noted that a glut in steel and "cut-throat competition" had forced our hand. In a 1993 issue called "Steeltown charts a new course," the story documented how "Hamilton had to find other means of making a living."

We moved from hot mills and coke ovens, to medical sciences and environmental remediation; from assembly lines to retraining programs. We went from lunch-buckets and punching the time-clocks, to enrolling in courses at Mohawk College – mastering skills with a '90s spin.

In search of new careers, we saw workers flock to the Greater Hamilton Technology Enterprise Centre (GHTEC).

Operated by the Business Advisory Council (BAC), it acts as the incubator for entrepreneurial ideas; a nurturing ground for ventures, especially those of a high-tech nature. With shared resources, and volunteer mentors loaned by established firms, the success rate of individual companies in the GHTEC is 80 per cent; compared to the norm of less than 20 per cent. Another symbol of our modern renaissance is the Canada Centre for Inland Waters (CCIW), a beacon of environmental research.

The Canadian Geographic article waxed philosophically when it says that Hamilton as a whole may be a "lesson in untapped potential." For in the very pieces that led to the dismantling of our system – the twin malaises of the environment and the economy – lay the building blocks to construct our future. And nobody stands so tall as those who have defied the odds.

The city's propensity to turn economic tragedy into triumph is perhaps nowhere as evident as at Philip Environmental; a true modern-day success story. It's the tale of a family firm that lived up to that old motto of one person's poison is another's meat.

And it's about converting cast-offs into cash; as you will read in the profile chronicling Philip's Midas touch.

In 1994, the company earned the title of Entrepreneur of the Year, in the services category – a national award presented by Governor General Ray Hnatyshyn at Rideau Hall in Ottawa.

The contest, which was sponsored by the Toronto-based accounting firm Ernst and Young, the Bank of Montreal, Canadian Business magazine, and investment house Nesbitt Burns, marked the first event of its kind in Canada.

It went to Philip Environmental for thriving on challenge, capitalizing on risk, and setting a vision for the future. And it was no surprise to any of those in attendance.

Allen Fracassi, president, and brother Philip, vice-president, have parlayed impediments into prosperity. Now the firm is one of North America's leading integrated environmental companies.

Back in the early '80s, they launched their waste haulage firm without the apparent prerequisite of their own landfill. No matter: They diverted the material by recycling and reselling products such as concrete and steel. And the rest is history.

In 1994, Profit magazine called Philip one of Canada's fastest-growing companies. So, too, did Canadian Business magazine, which surveyed 500 publicly traded concerns.

A recent example of Philip's initiative was a pact with the region to operate water and sewage treatment plants. The 10-year partnership between its subsidiary, Philip Utilities Management Corp. (PUMC) and Hamilton-Wentworth would save taxpayers some $5 million over the duration of the contract and generate 100 jobs. PUMC would invest $15 million in new projects, and in return use the sites as technological showcases.

It would allow Canada to compete on the international market with their efficient treatment of waste water, according to PUMC president, Dr. Stuart Smith, former MPP and chair of the Science Council of Canada.

"We predict that it will be a world leader in showing how a community can export its expertise – and make money on a public utility," says Mayor Robert Morrow.

It was that kind of vintage rags-to-riches-story that was the fabric or our Renaissance Project. For ours, too, was an economic strategy crafted by those from the political, business, labour and educational sectors.

It targeted growth industries – environmental services, medicine, advanced manufacturing, tourism and town/gown partnerships (a pairing of business and university expertise). It was the collaboration of more than 100 community leaders.

• Construction in the downtown core is a positive sign for the city's future. There were several major construction jobs on the go in our sesquicentennial year, including the work on the much-awaited GO Station, facing page.
— Photos by Dennis McGreal

A mid the rattle of horse-drawn carriages, a sense of excitement filled the air as newsboys in a very young city beckoned Hamiltonians to buy copies of a very young newspaper.

It was 1846, the year in which Hamilton became a city – and a local newspaper was born, The Hamilton Spectator and Journal of Commerce.

Spectator founder Robert Smiley bought a second-hand printing press for $150 and the first four-page issue came off that press on July 15, 1846.

Mr. Smiley began publishing The Spectator twice weekly in this bustling centre in the colony of Canada, uniting former colonies Upper Canada (Ontario) and Lower Canada (Quebec).

While united as a single British colony, Canada contained two regions: Canada East (Quebec) and Canada West (Ontario), with Hamilton becoming the newest Western Canadian city.

Although he faced competition from The Hamilton Gazette and The Journal and Express, Mr. Smiley said he had assurances "another newspaper would, if carefully conducted, meet with an extend-

ed circulation and a liberal support."

Hamilton's importance as an up-and-coming centre of commerce was captured in Mr. Smiley's first editorial:

"At the head of an important inland sea, the outlet for a country that cannot be surpassed on the continent, Hamilton is unquestionably becoming the commercial capital of the West."

And he predicted more growth as "the railroad is to be brought to her assistance, and the steam car will whirl through streets where the stage coach and wagon now jog leisurely along."

While the paper was pro-Conservative, Mr. Smiley assured readers they could turn to The Spectator for "earnest advocacy of their rights upon every occasion and under all circumstances."

After Mr. Smiley died in 1855, The Spectator was owned by a succession of owners until it was purchased by William Southam and William Carey in 1877 for $10,000. The publication was still a four-page newspaper which sold for a penny.

The Spectator passed through generations of the Southam family and became the flagship of a large chain of Southam

Newspapers – the largest-circulation newspaper group in Canada. It continues to be owned by Southam Inc.

In 1897, The Spectator moved into a six-storey 'skyscraper' on James Street South between King and Main streets. An imposing structure for its day, The Spectator Printing Co. Building was a converging site for hundreds of newsboys clambering for newspapers to deliver.

After 28 years on James South, The Spectator, nicknamed The Great Family Journal, moved to larger quarters opposite the Royal Connaught Hotel on King Street East in 1921, where it would stay for the next 55 years.

In 1976, The Spectator moved to its present location on Frid Street, a huge building housing a staff of several hundred people and three presses collectively worth $7.5 million and capable of printing up to 70,000 papers per hour.

The Spectator also introduced computers to the newsroom in 1981 and upgraded in 1994. Although newsprint costs ultimately meant a slimmer paper, The Spectator began offering readers more tightly written stories in a

better-organized format providing greater visual appeal. And the paper broadened its offering of computer-connected services such as EGO Interactive.

Yet with so many changes over the years, The Spectator has retained much of the determined spirit of its first editor.

Spectator Editor Rob Austin finds much to admire in Mr. Smiley. "He was an optimistic editor," notes Mr. Austin. "He was never afraid to make bold predictions. However, I expect he would be surprised to know that we still basically enjoy the laptop information retrieval system that he called a newspaper."

"And while the wizards of tomorrow may turn it into a piece of plastic screen with silicon chips, it's comforting to know that we'll still need the reporter on the street to tell the story," adds Mr. Austin.

"Editors of today look back on editors of the past with fondness. Technology has changed but the job has stayed the same: to inform the people. Let's hope we can stay as optimistic as Mr. Smiley was regarding Hamilton and its newspaper."

Over its history, The Spectator has established itself as the truly local paper

for the Hamilton area, with a 150-years-and-counting emphasis on local news.

Managing Editor John Gibson has long identified local news as The Spectator's primary strength and source of readership appeal. Under Mr. Gibson's direction, the paper has consistently endeavoured to be the first and fullest source of information concerning local issues and events.

It's a theme that Spectator Publisher Pat Collins has taken to heart, with promises of more local content, increased coverage of education, environment, health, and local government issues, along with a "focus on delivering value to our readers and our advertisers."

"Our job . . . is to relentlessly ensure we are meeting the value expectations of all our customers within the constraints of today's reality," says Mr. Collins, who also promises that the newspaper will be "more active and more supportive of local events."

With its traditional local mandate so firmly in place, The Spectator is well-positioned to perpetuate its successful role of delivering news and views while explaining the world around us.

• After 55 years on King Street East in downtown Hamilton, The Spectator moved to its present location on Frid Street in 1976. The huge, modern building houses three presses worth millions of dollars and capable of printing up to 70,000 papers per hour.
– Photo by David Gruggen

• Executive directors Lee Kirkby of the Chamber and Carmen Rizzotto of Sesqui discuss their joint project, the official Sesqui commemorative coin.
– Photo by David Gruggen

From the beginning, Hamilton has been a thriving centre of trade and commerce. That rich commercial heritage has long been a source of inspiration and motivation for the voice of the business community, the Hamilton and District Chamber of Commerce.

In 1845 – a year before the City of Hamilton was incorporated – the bustling community had already established the Hamilton Board of Trade, the forerunner to today's Chamber. In '95, the Chamber looked back fondly on 150 years of tireless efforts to promote business and civic concerns, foster growth and develop generations of entrepreneurs.

And in 1996, the Chamber marked the city's 150th birthday with a commemorative coin, 'The Sesqui,' a joint venture between the Chamber and the Sesquicentennial Committee.

With a likeness of Hamilton's first Mayor Colin Ferrie on one side and Dundurn Castle on the other, the coin faces were designed by renowned local sculptor Elizabeth Holbrook.

The commemorative coin has a face value of $1.50. A resolution by Hamilton City Council encourages that the special Sesquicentennial coin be accepted in lieu of legal tender from June 10 through to the end of 1996.

That such a distinctive commemoration would stem from the Chamber is hardly surprising given its long history of utilizing the talents of the business community to propel the city forward.

The Chamber's role in advancing Hamilton to new levels of growth and prosperity was recognized by 1995 President Ron Foxcroft when he urged members to "renew your commitment as we move into 1996-97 under the leadership of (1996 president) Judy Marsales."

"The continued health and prosperity of our business sector and the regional community demands that you do."

The Chamber has a long history of involvement in the community. In 1903, the board of trade forerunner pushed for civic improvements such as additional drinking fountains. It also formed an alliance with Hamilton's Trades and Labour Council to help end a Teamsters strike hurting the local economy.

And in 1920 another milestone was reached when the board reconstituted itself as the Hamilton Chamber of Commerce and quickly took on such successful projects as relocating McMaster University from Toronto to Hamilton and bringing about the Chedoke Golf Course.

During the Depression, the Chamber demonstrated considerable compassion for the less fortunate in Hamilton. It initiated a system of garden plots which allowed the unemployed to grow produce. And it raised funds for the needy.

From 1939-1945, the Chamber also supported the Second World War effort by organizing massive donations of food and gifts for the City of Hamilton Tiger Squadron, a bomber squadron manned by local volunteers fighting overseas.

As Hamilton celebrated its centennial in 1946, the Chamber played its usual active role, promoting, among other major events, the first Miss Canada Pageant.

During the 1980s, the Chamber of Commerce could be found supporting the Corporate Challenge fitness and fun event, Crimestoppers and a Chinese chamber to attract Asian investment.

By the mid-1990s, Chamber membership had expanded by 18 per cent thanks to the small business sector, a vital source of commercial growth and employment.

The Chamber is maintaining its active role, speaking out on tax and government issues and community concerns. And the Chamber continues to champion its goals of promoting business development and opportunities, encouraging the development of infrastructure and emphasizing the concept of lifelong learning.

FUTURE HOMES

• *Future Homes president Phil Bozzo, shown here at the Deerview Crossing subdivision, has earned a reputation for building high-quality, larger homes.*
— ***Photo by Joe Bucci***

Phil Bozzo isn't one of the biggest home builders – but he can be ranked among the best.

Mr. Bozzo, president of Future Homes, takes pride in building large, high-quality homes costing $300,000 or more.

Most Bozzo homes feature at least 3,000 to 5,000 square feet of space and two-storey all-brick exteriors.

Interiors often boast high ceilings, ceramic and hardwood floors, plaster walls, skylights, whirlpool baths and four or more bedrooms.

"I also offer custom trim and custom kitchen cabinets, the best you can get," Mr. Bozzo says with pride.

Although many homebuyers have lowered their expectations and are buying smaller homes, Mr. Bozzo is content to serve a small but potentially lucrative niche market for large expensive homes.

"The trend now is for smaller homes costing $180,000 to $190,000, but I've specialized in the $300,000-and-up market," notes Mr. Bozzo.

"My reputation is for the larger, high-quality homes," he explains. "It's what my customers expect of me and I can't let the customers down – even if it means building fewer homes."

Born in Italy, Mr. Bozzo came to Canada at age 16 and became a skilled carpenter. After working as a carpenter for other companies, Mr. Bozzo became one of three partners who established a framing contractor firm in 1958.

Ten years later, Mr. Bozzo decided to go it alone. In 1968 he started up the home building company we know today by building just three houses.

The following year, Mr. Bozzo built 15 houses and made the pioneering move of introducing ceramic tiles into his high-quality homes. Although commonplace today, ceramic tiles were a rarity in the late 1960s "and it took a while for people to decide they liked them," he recalls.

Fortunately, many homebuyers not only liked his ceramic tiles, they liked everything about Bozzo-built homes: In

the 1970s Mr. Bozzo was building an average of 50 homes per year.

Most of those homes were built in Stoney Creek. Among his major projects, Mr. Bozzo constructed 100 homes in the Mapledene Estates subdivision located below the escarpment.

As the 1980s began, he began building in Ancaster. By the mid 1990s he was working towards completion of Deerview Crossing, a 75-home picturesque subdivision of large single-family homes near conservation lands in Ancaster.

Since the 1980s, Mr. Bozzo has witnessed a shift in consumer buying to favour smaller, less-expensive homes, a shift that is attributable in part to employment uncertainty. Rather than join this shift, he continues to serve what is now a niche market for big homes.

Although in recent years Mr. Bozzo has built just a few homes annually, he takes pride in noting that "no matter how many homes I build, they are all of the highest quality."

Vision 2020 was a long-range plan, says its mastermind, the former Regional Chairman, Reg Whynott.

"What we were looking for in the Renaissance Project was a short-range plan. We did not want to wait for 10, 15 or 20 years to put these things into place. We wanted to get some of them started immediately.

"The Renaissance Report has been a team effort," he adds. "It has been hundreds of people in this community who've worked on both Vision 2020 chaired by (Alderman) Don Ross and the Renaissance committee project. This is a typical example of how this community can pull together."

With that report as a road map, in 1995 the region's economic development department, under its current Regional Chairman, Terry Cooke, deposited a $30,000 grant into the Renaissance treasury; an amount matched by dollars from the private sector and earmarked for a community-based venture capital fund which would invest in local businesses.

Our work has only just begun. And tomorrow is another day. Few projects loom as large on the horizon as the revitalization of the downtown core.

With the modern exodus to the suburban malls, parts of King and Main streets look like an aged dowager with a tattered and musty gown; shades of Miss Havisham waiting for her betrothed in Charles Dickens' Great Expectations.

Restore the core has become a '90s rallying cry. No patch-work job will mend decades of decline. Instead, the city has patterned a whole new image, drawing up plans for a heritage district. In a courtship to woo businesses and consumers, council voted a $315,000 payment to dress up Gore Park; and install the original Victorian-era fountain that was once a nostalgic gathering spot for the citizenry.

Hand in hand with that is civic beautification, with flowers planted in the city's traffic islands and roadsides. Trainloads of commuters will make tracks for the refurbished GO station on Hunter Street, converging on the $15-million centre at the periphery of the core. Even the long arm of the law has reached into Hamilton's downtown, with plans for a $64 million regional courthouse in the restored John Street post office.

In the field of transportation, the municipality has lobbied for the completion of the north-south link of the Red Hill Creek Expressway. Next on the agenda is a drive to boost carrier traffic at the airport, with priority placed on cargo and freight arriving during daylight hours.

Some may say it all looks good on paper. Well, it sure does. Because even in the so-called "jobless recovery" of 1995 our unemployment figures, according to Statistics Canada, were the lowest in Canada at 5.9 per cent, well under the national rate of 9.6 per cent and the double-digit recessionary hardship faced by scores of communities.

And ours were not all minimum-wage jobs. The median total income for two-parent families in the sample year 1993 was $54,600 in the Hamilton region.

And so, with this Sesqui year, and 12 months of celebration, we salute the past and stand tall on the threshold of the future.

ABOVE: *A late-afternoon train arrives at the GO Centre, located on Hunter Street in downtown Hamilton.*

FACING PAGE: *Operating out of the old TH&B Station, the Hamilton GO Centre was opened for business in April. A total of $15 million was spent on the refurbishing project which transformed the crumbling Depression-era building into a modern downtown bus and train terminal.*
— **Photos by Dennis McGreal**

North America's love affair with the automobile has meant an enduring relationship for ardent car aficionado Larry Bernacci.

The owner-operator of Larry's Tire Centre has spent a lifetime caring for cars.

After arriving in Hamilton from Italy in 1950 at age 13, Mr. Bernacci became enamoured with the emerging 1950s car culture as a youngster growing up in the city's North End.

"I've loved cars for a long time," admits Mr. Bernacci, whose Ottawa and Craigmiller streets business performs general vehicle repairs and sells new tires and used cars.

By the late 1950s, a teenaged Mr. Bernacci could be seen cruising from Hamilton to Aldershot in a sporty Ford Mercury, occasionally pulling into a now-defunct A&W drive-in hamburger stand.

"Those were the cruising days," he recollects with a chuckle.

"We cruised around a lot in the Aldershot area near the Royal Botanical Gardens," recalls Mr. Bernacci who owned, at various times, a 1956 Ford Crown Victoria and 1951 and 1956 Mercury models.

As a member of the Road Runner Club, Mr. Bernacci joined fellow car enthusiasts in applying decorative trim, pinstriping and chrome to their vehicles.

The former National Steel Car worker also took advantage of company layoffs to work for Stan Miller Texaco, where he was happily in his element caring for customers' cars.

When health problems led to Mr. Miller's death, Mr. Bernacci subsequently took over the business, which was renamed Larry's Texaco Gas Station in 1960. Mr. Bernacci would operate the gas station for the next 30 years until the Ottawa Street North and Dalhousie Street business was sold in 1990.

In 1966, Mr. Bernacci opened Larry's Tire Centre, a full-service family business which also employs his wife Heidi as office manager; son Michael, 35, as a Class A mechanic and used car salesman; and son Jeffrey, 31, as general sales manager and purchaser. A third son, Robert, 33, a Grand Master Mechanic, spent several years with the family firm before going out on his own.

From the beginning, the bustling family business meant six-day work weeks and a paramount dedication to serving customers, particularly in the growing repairs and used car sales sides of the business. The company has also expanded to include a second service bay.

"You've really got to look after the customers and focus on good service and competitive price," asserts Mr. Bernacci.

• Larry and Heidi Bernacci, standing at far right, are pictured with their children and grandchildren in front of Larry's Tire, located on Ottawa Street North.
— *Photo by David Gruggen*

"We're pleased that our customers do keep coming back and refer us to their friends," he adds.

Despite a demanding work life, Mr. Bernacci and Larry's Tire Centre have still taken the time to support a men's bocce league along with minor league hockey, soccer and basketball teams.

Mr. Bernacci has served on the Men's Committee of the Venetian Club since 1972, including four years as club president, and has contributed substantially to the Hamilton community.

In 1992, he was awarded a Diploma and a Medaglia D'Oro from the Camera Di Commercio Industria Artigianato Agricoltura Treviso (Italian Chamber of Commerce) for his achievements in Canada. And in 1995 he was honoured as Man of the Year by the Venetian Club.

It all adds up to a valuable, impressive legacy of hard work and community involvement, which Mr. Bernacci intends to one day pass on to his sons. "It's a good business," he says with pride. "I'd like to see it carried on for generations."

STEEL CITY SPRING SERVICE INC.

• *Company president Ron London is shown with employees at Steel City Spring's Rowanwood Street location.*
– Photo by David Gruggen

S teel City Spring is gradually bouncing back from the recession. And that's fitting for a firm whose suspension and shock springs services smooth out the bumps in a customer's road. Now the company is travelling its own smooth road to recovery.

"We've been in a recovery mode after the recession with three years of steady sales," notes Ron London, president of Steel City Spring Service Inc.

"Given what a lot of companies have been through, we can't complain," adds Mr. London. "We're experiencing a fairly smooth recovery. It's been steady."

Located on Rowanwood Street off Beach Road, Steel City Spring employs seven people in the repair and replacement of vehicle springs for industrial and commercial customers.

The single-storey, 4,200-square-foot, concrete block building is a scene of constant activity as the company's dedicated workforce repairs and replaces springs on commercial vehicles, transport trucks, tractor trailers and excavation machines.

"We repair and replace a wide variety of springs," notes Mr. London. "It's all after-market business, and it's a pretty good business.

Mr. London founded the Hamilton company with two partners in 1978.

Then, in the 1980s, he bought out his partners and attained sole ownership of the successful company in the heart of the city's industrialized north-east end.

The demand for Steel City Spring's services has been constant.

"It's a high-volume business and we're kept pretty busy," asserts Mr. London, whose company often buys springs from a wholesaler, then customizes them for heavy industrial use by adding extra 'leaves' or sections to the spring to provide additional strength and durability.

"Sometimes it is necessary to cus-

tomize springs for the customer," adds Mr. London. "The springs have to be beefed up with extra leaves for added strength and we're fortunate to have the people and equipment capable of doing this kind of work."

Steel City Spring's expertise is relied on by a growing number of customers, including Philip Environmental, Hamilton Hydro, Ontario Hydro, Stelco Inc. and many others.

Some of the springs the company repairs and replaces also come in fairly impressive sizes. Take, for example, dump truck front springs which are about four feet long and weigh about 300 pounds each. Replacing and fixing such enormous springs is a regular task for the company's skilled employees.

The company is also dedicated to the local community, sponsoring men's league baseball teams and contributing to local charities. "We've made a home for the company here," says Mr. London, "and we're going to continue our business here for a long time to come."

HAMILTON *It's Happening*

239

• Guy Cruickshanks, shown here with
wife and company co-owner Kathy,
founded B&G Roofing & Sheet Metal
in 1986. Today, the company has a
regular workforce of 12 people.
– *Photo by Joe Bucci*

O n top. That's the most comfortable position for B&G Roofing & Sheet Metal Inc., a Hamilton firm that's adept at providing the crowning touch to some of the area's best-known buildings.

B&G Roofing was founded in 1986 by Guy Cruickshanks, then in his early 20s, after he moved to the Hamilton area following an industrious adolescence in Nova Scotia which saw him enter the roofing trade at a young age. "I've been in roofing since I was 15 years old," recalls Mr. Cruickshanks, who hopes to one day pass his thriving company on to his children, Blake and Guy.

Mr. Cruickshanks began his company with himself, co-owner wife Kathy and five employees. The couple continues to play an active role in the company on a daily basis.

B&G, which marked its 10th anniversary in 1995, today has a regular workforce of 12 people and employs as many as 25. Average annual revenue exceeds $1 million.

In the midst of a national recession, the company managed to record an annual growth of 25 per cent in its first five years of operation before this tapered off to a lower, sustainable growth rate.

B&G prides itself in its skilled workforce of highly experienced roofers, fabricators and sheet metal installers.

Specializing in asphalt and gravel rooftops for commercial and industrial customers, the company also installs residential shingle and flat roofing. It also custom fabricates and installs sheet metal flashing.

B&G is headquartered at a complex built in the early 1990s, featuring 7,000 square feet of office, warehouse and fabricating shop space on a one-acre site on Macallum Street in north-east end of Hamilton.

B&G Roofing is a fully equipped and pre-qualified contractor which regularly bids for government and school board contracts.

Evidence of the company's work can be found across Hamilton-Wentworth region and beyond. B&G's asphalt and gravel rooftops have capped the old Spectator building, Dundas Fire Hall, Canada Trust and Royal Bank branches, various Hamilton Radiator locations and numerous Tim Hortons stores.

B&G donated a roof to Jimmy Lomax's garage to help this famous Hamiltonian carry out his Operation Santa Claus.

The company regularly donates to those less fortunate through such worthwhile endeavours as Operation Santa Clause, Shriners, Hamilton-Wentworth Regional Police, Hamilton Firefighters Burn Unit, and Chedoke-McMaster Children's Hospital.

"A business should be able to help people and contribute," says Mr. Cruickshanks, "and I hope to leave this business and my values to my children one day."

Chances are it would all come out in the wash anyway – but Peter Grbavac has finally come clean about his quietly successful laundry and linen supplies business.

Mr. Grbavac is the president of Whiz-a-Top Linen, a once-tiny family firm that by 1996 had 34 employees utilizing $2 million worth of equipment and inventory and handling 2 million pounds of laundry a year for hundreds of hospitality, health care, food processing and catering customers across Ontario.

By the mid-1990s, the company was earning $1 million in annual revenue and handling 1.6 million pounds of laundry a year for hundreds of commercial customers across south-central Ontario.

Despite 23 years in business, Mr. Grbavac doesn't mind that Whiz-a-Top Linen still isn't a household name. It's enough that his company is well-known and appreciated by five-star restaurants, nursing homes and other major customers.

"My customers know me – that's what counts," smiles Mr. Grbavac, who takes pride in the relationship of service and loyalty he has with his customers. His 10,000-square-foot plant on Stapleton Avenue in Hamilton is expected to undergo yet another expansion as the company focuses on a new source of growth in servicing the health care sector.

Yet Mr. Grbavac wasn't always this prosperous. In 1963, with only $30 in his pocket, a pregnant wife and two small children, Mr. Grbavac arrived in Canada at age 30 after emigrating from what is now Slovenia in former Yugoslavia.

A metallurgist by trade, Mr. Grbavac quickly progressed to the position of superintendent of a Quebec foundry before finally settling in Hamilton with his family in 1964.

An avid outdoorsman, hunter, fisherman and gardener, Mr. Grbavac spent part of his early career taking on additional part-time work to finance his passion for sports. Ironically, in his quest for the ability to offer himself and his family the joys of the outdoors, he found himself immersed indoors – working.

His part-time laundry work ultimately led him to invest in an opportunity to work part-time at home to keep generating the cash needed for hunting and fishing. In the early 1970s, he and wife Mili were doing laundry from home to keep tavern table tops covered with tablecloths.

In 1972, Mr. Grbavac borrowed $3,000 to buy out the Whiz-a-Top Linen business – the name comes from fitted tablecloths that can be easily removed and replaced – and in six months was servicing 30 hotels with his own handmade tablecloths.

Eventually it became too crowded at

• Peter Grbavac, pictured with son Robert, is president of Whiz-a-Top Linen, a once-tiny family company that by 1996 had a total 34 employees.
— *Photo by David Gruggen*

home to continue doing laundry for a growing list of customers so Mr. Grbavac rented premises on Barton Street. The business involved Mr. and Mrs Grbavac and their children.

Within a few short years, it became a full-time business that left little time for Mr. Grbavac to continue tending his 300 colonies of honey-producing bee hives. The colonies of bees were sold, with the proceeds of the sale funding a move to larger premises on Kenilworth Avenue.

In 1980, the company made its first expansion move by buying out a laundry business in Guelph which was ultimately consolidated with the thriving business in Hamilton. Today, the business remains a

family affair. Mrs. Grbavac runs customer satisfaction and order functions while son Rob is in charge of all plant operations.

Due to its increasing growth, the company underwent a business transition in the mid-1990s which resulted in Rob Grbavac taking on more responsibility for the new direction. The Grbavacs' other two children are independent entrepreneurs involved in the laundry business.

As the new generation of Grbavacs prepares to take the business to new heights in coming decades, Mr. Grbavac's thoughts are still on the woodlands of the Great North. Until Mr. Grbavac retires, the great indoors will continue to interrupt the call of the wild.

• Located on Barton Street East in the city's East End, Frank's Tire Service is one of the oldest businesses of its kind in Hamilton. The company, featuring a 14-employee workforce, was founded in 1967 by Frank Amodio.

One of the oldest businesses of its kind in Hamilton, Frank's Tire Service also offers one of the largest selections of tires anywhere.

This vast array of tires – $1 million worth of inventory – fills most of the available space in a warehouse at the company's Barton Street East offices.

The ability to offer such an impressive assortment of tires for various vehicles, from cars to transport trucks, is a source of pride at Frank's Tire Service.

"We carry most of the major brands, including Michelin, Bridgestone, Pirelli and Dunlop," notes company owner Frank Amodio, 63. "And we sell an assortment of used tires as well," he adds.

Founded in 1967 by Mr. Amodio as essentially a one-man operation, Frank's Tire Service, located on Barton Street East between Woodward and Parkdale avenues, is today Hamilton's oldest existing tire services company retaining the original management.

It's also very much a family business, with Mr. Amodio's wife Lina contributing with customer relations work. The couple is further assisted at the business by their sons, Sam, Carmen and Frank Jr.

Frank's Tire Service never left its original location, a large, four-bay, single-storey building built for the company in 1967. The company originally specialized in truck tire services, but came to include tires for cars and other vehicles over the years, including massive, thick-walled tires for industrial dump trucks.

In addition to retailing new and used tires and installing and balancing them, Frank's Tire Service also offers mechanical repairs. The company's 14-employee workforce includes a licensed, on-staff mechanic to perform work on shocks, brakes, struts, front and rear alignment and suspension.

The company's growing workforce gained extra space in 1995, when the firm added a 2,000-square-foot addition, taking its total space to 14,000 square feet.

Frank's Tire Service also takes pride in its community involvement, as a sponsor of minor league baseball, hockey and basketball teams and as a participant in golf tournament fundraisers for local charities.

After attaining annual revenue of $6 million in the late 1980s, Frank's Tire Service joined many other companies in weathering the recession.

The company, which had revenue of approximately $4 million in 1995, is contemplating a second location in Burlington, and is gradually rebuilding ground lost to the recession.

That rebuilding process is being helped along by the many referrals the company receives from satisfied customers.

"I know a lot of people say this," Mr. Amodio admits, "but we really do emphasize our service and selection. More than anything else, our service and selection are bringing in the customers and helping us rebuild our business."

While it's true that Hamilton's best-known restaurant for fine dining is Shakespeare's Dining Lounge, how many people would know that it also serves ostrich filet mignon, buffalo steaks or wild boar?

When Chef Franco Putignano started his restaurant in 1969 it began as a steak house. But over the years, as the public's tastes changed, so did the menu. Now customers can order not only prime U.S. Choice corn fed beef steaks, but wild game which also includes caribou and venison.

Shakespeare's also provides an extensive selection of fish, including live lobster, fresh salmon, sea bass, trout and swordfish. The fish, just like everything else that is served, is personally selected each morning from Hamilton suppliers to ensure freshness.

In addition to his efforts to bring his customers the finest in dining fare, Mr. Putignano regularly travels to Europe to personally select wines for his table. Now his wine list offers the best selection in the city.

"I'm very strong on quality, freshness and service," Mr. Putignano explains. "To me, good food, good wine and good service all go together," he adds. "I want people to have the best dining experience possible, and I want them to feel at home when they're here."

Exotic dishes and quality steaks aren't the only things emphasized on Shakespeare's menu. Mr. Putignano has also devised a 'Heart Smart' selection of dishes which are low in cholesterol and salt.

It's been approved by the Heart and Stroke Foundation of Canada, and reassures diners that healthy eating need not be bland and boring.

The result of the care and service to customers means that Shakespeare's has managed to weather the recession and keep a steady clientele, a large number of which are regular customers.

In addition, celebrities such as Tom Jones, Ricardo Montalban, Harry Belafonte, Liberace, Rock Hudson, Kathleen Robertson, Wayne Gretzky and Peter Ustinov have all made their way to Shakespeare's when they were in town.

Mr. Putignano's son Leo, 27, manages the dining room and daughter Christina, 24, bartends in the restaurant while their mother, Nicole, handles the bookkeeping and weekend hosting duties. His future son-in-law, Peter Smith, also works in the dining room. The arrangement enables Mr. Putignano to see his family through the week while working from 9 a.m. until 1 a.m., Monday to Saturday.

"I don't mind the long days," he says. "I've got the business in the blood, and I love people. I work longer hours now, but I love it," he adds. "During the recession, we didn't cut back on quality – we always tried to do better. And it worked."

In 1994, Mr. Putignano was issued a certificate by the City, honouring him for his 25 years in business. Included in the many other honours in 1995 alone are his nomination as Iron Man of the Year from the Hamilton & District Chamber of Commerce and the bestowing of three Spectator Reader's Choice Awards for Best Steak House, Best Sea Food Restaurant and Best French Restaurant. The awards are fitting recognition for his dedication to providing the best to his customers for so long.

"Nothing comes easy. You have to work hard," Mr. Putignano says. "I feel proud of my family, my staff and my restaurant. And I'm proud to have been a part of Hamilton for 27 years."

• Chef Franco Putignano has a table waiting for you at Shakespeare's, one of the city's finest restaurants.
– Photo by David Gruggen

ABOVE: Hard work and positive thinking are helping to change the face of Hamilton and nowhere is the city's renaissance more evident than in the North End, an area that had fallen on some hard times. Today, with both the homes and the bay that many of the homes back onto being 'cleaned up,' the North End area is slowly being restored to its former glory.

RIGHT: A dramatically curved lookout pier, with a protected sun shelter and benches, provides a terrific vantage point for visitors to Pier 4 Park. The park also features an interactive water play area for children.
— *Photos by Dennis McGreal*

A legend assumes a dimension which is larger than life, only after years, decades or even generations of toil. Such is the saga of the Ciancone family.

And their legacy is one of fine dining in food emporiums like the Hillcrest Restaurant and the Ancaster Old Mill Inn.

But their reputation extends far beyond the confines of those two famous establishments, with their off-premises catering at the Canadian Warplane Heritage facilities; the Royal Botanical Gardens; and a smorgasbord of other venues – from an ethnic church hosting a marquee wedding to a black tie corporate ball in the tradition of the kings of industry.

The tradition began in the 1930s with the Hillcrest Dairy, in an era of milk delivery by horse and wagon. It later evolved into the family restaurant bearing the historic Hillcrest name located on a corner of Concession Street.

It is here where one matriarch, Pearl Ciancone, still supervises a culinary trade at age 80; where corporate executives assemble in the meeting rooms, or at the banquet table to break bread over delicate business negotiations; and where "Come Home To The Hill" is a popular refrain among the many loyal customers.

Today, 66 years removed from the Ciancone's ancestral venture into supplying food for the city's larder, the rhythmic clip-clop of hooves which signalled the teams of Hillcrest drivers has been replaced by the sound of buses lumbering up the Old Dundas Road to the site of the famous grist mill. Because this is the crowning glory of the Ciancone empire – The Ancaster Old Mill Inn.

Originally built in 1793, at the junction of the local watershed, the Old Mill was ravaged by fire, reconstructed in 1863, then renovated and extended in 1989.

A world-renowned landmark, the Old Mill speaks of gentler times when settlers lived by the sweat of their brow and the lay of the land. Perched on a precipice of the escarpment, it provides a panorama of streams plummeting over rocks and cascading down an embankment.

Amid a decor of floor-to-ceiling windows, hand-hewn beams, antique implements and crockery, guests can linger over a gastronomic feast – dining on home-baked breads, seafood salad bars, stir frys, prime rib, New York sirloins – with a glass of their favorite wine. They can then choose a selection from the dessert tray, enjoyed with a cup of camomile tea or freshly brewed coffee.

Visitors make the pilgrimage here from across North America and points around the globe. Much more than a major attraction, and a Town of Ancaster claim

• *The Ancaster Old Mill Inn, located in a picturesque setting in the heart of town, remains a top tourist attraction.*
– Photo by David Gruggen

to fame, it ranks with the likes of the CN Tower and Niagara Falls.

Scenery aside, "we have great chefs, a great staff and great food," say brothers Ron and Dave Ciancone, who operate the business along with their family members.

Resonating with all the romance and nostalgia of yesteryear, the Ancaster Old Mill Inn has also won the hearts of brides; many of whom tie the knot in the circular courtyard and others who will utter the words, "I do" in a newly constructed chapel by the wooded and sundappled

stream. For the reception, the matrimonial pair can choose from a range of menus, everything from casual hors d'oeuvres and canapes, to full buffet or deluxe table service in the finest French style.

The Old Mill has it all – a solarium lounge, where guests gather for cocktails by the wood-burning fireplace and baby grand piano; a third-floor sanctum which seats 125 for family gatherings, corporate functions or seminars; the gift shop with its baked goods, crafts and pottery; a main-floor interpretive centre displaying the wooden gears that once drove the mill; and the bridges and pathways that cross the thundering waterfalls.

The Ancaster Old Mill Inn and four generations of Ciancones have certainly made a mark in the heart of their town.

DOUBLE THE FUN

LEFT: *Award-winning artist Blaine, the creator of "Sesqui" the mascot, rang in 1996 with this Editorial Page drawing in The Spectator.*

BELOW: *Blaine's mascot and graphic artist Richard Freedman's logo were teamed up to create this special Sesqui postcard, which was distributed throughout Canada.*
– Card courtesy of The Postcard Factory

BELOW: *Lakeport Brewing Corp. earned its label as one of Sesqui's many corporate sponsors with financial and promotional support to promote Hamilton's 150th birthday celebrations. To mark the occasion, the Burlington Street brewery unveiled a special neck label which adorned some 9,000,000 bottles of the five Laker larger brands distributed throughout Ontario.*

ABOVE: *Canada Post put an official stamp on the Sesqui celebrations – and also made its mark with half a million cancellations per day bearing the Sesqui logo on mail processed at its Millen Road plant. This promotion delivered the Sesqui logo worldwide.*

HAMILTON 150TH BIRTHDAY 1996

• Hamiltonians were treated to many royal moments as part of Sesqui's celebrations, but none caused as much excitement as a visit by Prince Charles on April 26, 1996. Some 20,000 school children packed Copps Coliseum to see the Prince, where they were treated to a dazzling program of music and dance created by our very own Mayor Bob Morrow.

– Photos courtesy of The Spectator

– Photo above courtesy of Michael Dismatsek

ABOVE: Basketball great Isiah Thomas netted an official Sesqui sweatshirt when he visited Copps Coliseum with his Toronto Raptors. Here, Sesqui co-chair Vincenza Travale, aided by the Sesqui mascot, presents the Raptors' GM with his souvenir prior to an inter-squad game at Copps Coliseum.
– Photo by Carmen Rizzotto

LEFT: Ray Lewis, a bronze medallist in track at the 1936 L.A. Olympics, receives the first Sesqui Sports '96 commemorative poster 'Live The Dream.' The poster features Mr. Lewis and Hamilton swimmer Joanne Malar, who will compete at the 1996 Atlanta Olympics. Looking on are the Sesqui Sports '96 co-chairs Cecilia Carter-Smith and Tom Gallagher.

LEFT: Graphic artist and city employee Richard Freedman proudly shows his winning design from the Sesqui logo contest.

RIGHT: Local historian Brian Henley recited from his Sesquicentennial commemorative book, '1846 Hamilton,' during a Christmas reception at Dundurn Castle in 1995.
– Photos courtesy of The Spectator

• First Night, an alcohol-free New Year's Eve celebration of the performing and visual arts, came to Hamilton in 1995. This Sesqui event joined our city with 150 other communities across North America. The day-long family affair, included performances by Hamilton's musical ambassador Jude Johnson, who debuted her song – and the official song of Sesqui – Hamilton My Home.

– Photos courtesy of The Spectator

• Matt Hayes was among the many celebrities who helped Hamilton celebrate its numerous Sesqui events. Hayes, who co-chaired First Night with CHCH TV colleague Donna Skelly, is shown here with daughter Kyra waving to the crowd at the 1995 Santa Claus Parade. Sesqui's executive director Carmen Rizzotto and his son Adam were also along for the ride.

– Photo courtesy Lynn Wylie

LEFT: *Volunteers Edith Laidman, Jane Webster, Aline Chan, Marie White, and project manager Brenda Connell work on the Sesqui quilt at the Sesquilt Station in Jackson Square. More than 200 patches were submitted by the community for the Sesquilt.*

BELOW: *Mayor Bob Morrow initiated the Hamilton-Shawinigan Sesqui Weekend during a video conference with Mayor Lise Landry. This Sesqui event brought families from our first twin city of Shawinigan to Steeltown during the Canada Day weekend.*
– Photos courtesy of The Spectator

LEFT: *Foundry owner Archie McCoy shows off the Fountain, which he helped return to Gore Park in 1996. The Fountain restoration was a Sesqui project of the Head-of-the-Lake Historical Society.*

RIGHT: *Sesqui is escorted to the Great Costume Ball during a Mardi Gras and parade weekend staged for Sesquicentennial.*

LEFT: The city's 150th birthday plans began in earnest following the opening of the Hamilton Sesquicentennial Celebrations Inc. office in Jackson Square in early 1995. Here, Honourary Chairperson Mayor Bob Morrow cuts a special cake to open the office as Sesqui's official caterer, Peter Mercanti of Carmen's Banquet Centre, looks on.

ABOVE: There were many offerings when Sesqui asked for unique ways to mark the city's 150th. Here, chef Sulayman Grant serves up his idea, a meal Hamiltonians might have enjoyed 150 years ago, as Mayor Bob Morrow and Sesqui co-chair Milt Lewis look on.

LEFT: Sesqui's Honourary Patrons were introduced during a half-time ceremony at Ivor Wynne Stadium as the Tiger-Cats helped kick off the Sesqui celebrations.
– Photos courtesy of The Spectator

Advertising & Sales Club of Hamilton

Agrico Canada Limited

Dr. Richard C. Agro

J.F. Arsenault

Bar Hydraulics Inc.

Bell *Arte Camera

Bennett Signs Limited

Wm. & Wynn Bensen

Glen Eric Brunskill

Debbie Burch Tim Hortons

Bob Chambers Photography

Dr. Bruno A. Chiesa

Christie-Hill Contracting

Comfort Inn

Coopers & Lybrand

Mr. & Mrs. Antonino Cosoleto

Credo Books Inc.

DELCAN Corporation

De Marchi Construction Ltd.

Marvin Dyck, Barrister

Eureka Tool Steel

Fengate Real Estate Ltd.

Mr. & Mrs. W.J. Festeryga

Neil V. Finnie

Golden Financial Services

Graybar Electric (Ont.) Ltd.

David Gruggen Photography

Hamilton Boiler Works Limited

Hamilton Community Credit Union

Hamilton Construction Association

Hamilton Plastics

Hamilton Steelworkers

Hammond Metal Systems

Harvey Caron Fences Ltd.

Hayden Insurance Brokers

Healy Heating & Cooling Ltd.

Dr. & Mrs. James Hicks

J-Flo Sales Inc.

Jennings Insurance Ltd.

Joseph Photographer

Dr. & Mrs. Zenon Kiss

Lees Hamilton Limited

Lithuanian Community of Hamilton

Liuna Gardens Limited

Dr. & Mrs. D. Ian Malcolm

McGowan Insulations

McKeough Sons Company Ltd.

Mike's Auto Parts

Moffat Kinoshita Architects

Dennis McGreal Photography

William Morris

Mr. Print-All Copy Centres Inc.

Dr. & Mrs. F.A. Olivieri

Ontario Plywood Specialties

Overhead Crane Service & Supply

Leon Price

Peto MacCallum Ltd.

Radigan Bros. Limited

Rankin Architect Inc.

Raposo Limited

Rapp Pensions International

Irene Reinhold RPT

Dr. & Mrs. J.D. Richardson

Royal Canadian Legion Branch 58

The Sirloin Cellar

Skyway Lanes Ltd.

Dr. Danuta Sobczyk D.D.S.

Dr. Slawomir Sobczyk D.D.S.

Soil-Mat Engineers

Sullivan Cardiologists

Glen & Debra Swire

Taffy's OK Tire & Automotive

Herman Turkstra

United Association Local 67

U.S.W.A., Local 1005

Venetor Cranes / R&R Cranes

Victor Electric & Equipment

Western Plumbing & Heating

Yachetti, Lanza & Restivo

Yuk Yuk's Comedy Club

Zaffiro Oskroba Family

INDEX

A

A-Plus Air Systems, 27
Agriculture and Food, Ontario
  Ministry of, 43
Agro, Vince, 7
Albion Falls, 21
Alexander, The Honourable
  Lincoln M., 5, 84
algal bloom, 44
Ancaster, 8
Anderson, Terry, 7
Andres Wines, 131
Angus Employment Ltd., 91
Armour Steel Supply, 217
Around The Bay Road Race, 108-109
Art Gallery of Hamilton, 188
Ashenhurst Nouwens Ltd., 143

B

B&G Roofing & Sheet Metal Inc., 240
Bach-Elgar Choir, 141
Bank of Montreal, 196
Bank of Nova Scotia, 128
BartonAir Fabrications Inc., 216
Battle of Stoney Creek, re-enactment
  152-153
Bay, Hamilton, 42, 43, 120-121
Bay Area Restoration Council
  (BARC), 43, 45
Bayfront Park, 14, 168
Bayview Cemetery, 197
Blaine, 247
Big V Drug Stores, 55
Body Shop, 35
Bondar, Roberta, 84
Bono General Construction Ltd., 80
Brockhouse, Bertram N., 5, 78, 84, 135
Brott, Boris, 140
Browman, Dr. George, 89
Bruce Trail, 11
Brugmann, Jeb, 14
Bucci, Joe, 4
Business Advisory Council (BAC), 231

C

Canada Centre for Inland Waters
  (CCIW), 231
Canada Post, 247
Canadian Country Music Awards, 134
Canadian Christian Festival, 134
Canadian Football Hall of Fame, 188
Canadian Football League, 94
Canadian Imperial Bank of
  Commerce, 174, 175
Canadian Warplane Heritage
  Museum, 165
CANUSA Games, 122
Caplan, Marvin, 7
carcinogens, 28
carp, 28
Carter-Smith, Cecilia, 249
Cathedral of Christ the King, 183
Cattel, Eaton & Chambers
  Funeral Home, 187
Century 21, 180-181, 192
Chamber of Commerce, Hamilton, 234
Chambers, Bob, 4

Chamberlain, Brian, 165
Chan, Aline, 251
Charles, H.R.H. Prince, 165, 248
Charters, Bob, 7
CHCH TV 11, 110
Chedoke-McMaster Hospital, 54
Children's Museum, 159
CHML, Hometown Radio, 102, 103
Cody's Stores Ltd., 151
Coldwell Banker Elite Realty, 178
Collins, Chad, 7
Comtronic Computer Centre, 86, 87
Confederation Park, 158
contamination, water, 43
Connell, Brenda, 251
Contractors Machinery, 186
Cooke, Terry, 236
Cootes' Paradise, 28, 34, 44
Copps Coliseum, 101, 104-105, 112, 113,
  116, 134, 147, 180-181
Copps, Geraldine, 7, 101, 141
Copps, Sheila, 135
Copps, Victor Kennedy, 101, 140,141
Council, Hamilton City, 7, 234
Crombie, David, 42
CRS Robotics, 215

D

Davie, Michael B., 4
D'Amico, Frank, 7
DeNardis, Frank P., 5
DeSantis, A., Real Estate Ltd., 148
DeSantis, Peter, 16
Dickinson, Brock, 44
Dodsworth & Brown Funeral Home, 179
Dofasco Inc., 204-205, 206, 207, 208, 209
Dominion Castings Ltd., 210
Dominion Pattern Works, 211
Drury, Don, 7
Dundurn Castle, 135, 182, 234, 249
Dynamic & Proto Circuits Inc., 213, 215
Dynamic Steel Inc., 219

E

East Hamilton Radio, 82
ECOWISE, 45
Effort Trust, 118
Eisenberger, Fred, 7
Environment Canada, 43
Environment, Ontario Ministry of, 43
Estrabillo, Dr. Roland, 60, 61

F

Family Fitness Centres, 32, 33
Faloney, Bernie, 95, 186
Fairclough, The Right Honourable
  Ellen L., 5
Father Sean O'Sullivan Research Centre,
  St. Joseph's Hospital, 63
Fell-Fab, 215
Ferrie, Colin Campbell, 8, 234
Festitalia, 163
Firan Foundation, 22, 23
Firestone, D. Morgan, 5, 22, 23
First Night, 250
Fisheries and Oceans Canada, 43
Flek Fire Systems, 83

Fluke Transport, 114
Ford Dunn Insurance Brokers, 68
Fortinos, 24, 25
Foxcroft, Ron, 114, 234
Fracassi, Allen and Philip, 17-19, 231
Frank's Tire Service, 242
Freedman, Richard, page 2, 247, 249
Frisina Construction, 176, 177
Future Homes, 235

G

Gallagher, Tom, 249
Gennum Corporation, 70, 71, 215
George, Dr. Peter, 89
Gilbert's Big & Tall Men's Shop, 139
GO Train station, 228-229, 236, 237
Gore Park, 173
Gould Outdoor Advertising, 37
Graham Restorations & Cleaning
  Services, 166
Grant, Sulayman, 252
Greater Hamilton Technology Enterprise
  Centre (GHTEC), 231
Griffen House, 198
Griffin, W.L., Printing Ltd., 36
Gruggen, David, 4

H

Hall, John, 28, 34, 35
Hamilton Ballet ensemble, 132-133, 141
Hamilton Board of Education
  building, 188-189
Hamilton Civic Hospitals, 58
Hamilton Downtown Association, 140
Hamilton Eaton Centre, 184-185
Hamilton Entertainment and Convention
  Facilities, Inc. (HECFI), 141
Hamilton Farmers' Market, 185
Hamilton Harbour, 4, 12-13, 14, 42, 43,
  172-173
Hamilton Harbour Commission, 43
Hamilton Harbour Remedial Action Plan
  (RAP), 20, 42
Hamilton International Air Show, 165
Hamilton Mountain Bowl, 96
Hamilton Museum of Steam and
  Technology, 199
Hamilton Place, 140, 191
Hamilton Psychiatric Hospital, 64
Hamilton Region Conservation
  Authority (HRCA), 29
Hamilton Reps minor peewee
  AAA hockey team, 92-93
Hamilton Military Museum, 199
Hamilton Wire Products, 212
Hayes, Matt, 250
Henley, Brian, 249
Hermitage, The, 198
Hillcrest Restaurant, 234
Hillfield-Strathallan College, 31
Hilton Works, Stelco, 44
Hnatyshyn, The Right Honourable
  Ramon J., 5, 231
Holbrook, Elizabeth, 234
Hopcroft, Grant, 14
Hortons, Tim, 225
Hotz, Dr. Harry, 69
Hotz & Sons Co., 222

I

Indoor Games, 112
Intermetco Limited, 233
International Council on Local
Environment Initiatives (ICLEI), 14
International Network on Water,
    Environment and Health
    (McMaster University), 89
International Science and Engineering
    Fair, 134
It's Your Festival, 155, 169
Ivor Wynne Stadium, 100

J

Jackson, Tom, 7
Jinsu Productions, 136
Johnson, Jude, 250
Jones, Jack, 101

K

Kelly Auto Body Ltd., 47
Kiss, Mary, 7

L

Laidlaw Inc., 26
Laidman, Edith, 251
Lake Ontario, 28
Lakeport Brewing Corp., 98, 99, 247
Landry, Mayor Lise, 251
Langley Parisian Fabricare Services, 119
Larry's Tire Centre, 238
Leather, Sir Edwin, 5
Leppert Business Systems Inc., 97
Lethbridge, Glenn, 221
Lewis, Milton J., 4, 5, 252, 256
Lewis, Ray, 249
Link's Food Market & Delicatessen, 130
Local Agenda 21 Model Community
    Program, 14
Logo, Sesquicentennial, 2
Ludwin, David, 89

M

Macaluso, Gabe, 141
Maclean's magazine, 84
MacPherson, George, 140
Macdonald, David, 94
Malar, Joanne, 249
Man Releasing Eagles (statue), 89
Mandia, Peter, 135
Mario's Tile and Carpet, 149
Markey Family Funeral Homes Ltd., 81
Marlatt, J.B., Funeral Home Ltd., 203
Marsales, Judy, Real Estate Ltd., 90, 234
McCabe Steel, 218
McCoy, Archie, 251
McCullough, Wm. M., 7
McGreal, Dennis, 4
McKeil Marine Ltd., 40, 41
McMaster University, 52-53, 54, 76-77
McMaster University, Faculty of
    Health Sciences, 16, 57, 59, 63
McMaster University Medical Centre, 54
McNeil, Jack, 141
Mediacom Inc., 30
Mercanti Auto Body, 115
Mercanti, Peter, 252

Merling, Henry, 7
Micor Developments Inc., 142
Miller's Shoe Store, 59
Mobile Cartage, 226, 227
Mohawk College, 67, 231
Moore & Davis Ltd., 73
Morelli, Bernie, 7
Morrow, Mayor Robert (Bob) M., 4, 5, 6,
    16, 94, 100, 135, 231, 248, 251, 252
Mosca, Angelo, 95
Mountain view, Hamilton, 2-3
Municipal-Industrial Strategy
    for Abatement, 43
Munro Metal Products, 224
Murray, Anne, 135

N

Nabucco, Opera Hamilton, 134
Natural Resources, Ontario
    Ministry of, 43
Nobel Prize, 78

O

Old Mill Inn, Ancaster, 246
Ontario, Lake, 28

P

Paikin, Larry, 95
Paikin, Marnie, 95, 140
Palmese PhotoDesign Group, Inc., 138
Parkway Toyota, 126
PasWord Communications Inc., 74
Philip Environmental, 17, 18, 19, 231
Pier 4 Park, 45, 244-245
Pioneer Group, The, 156, 157
Port of Hamilton, 220-221
Procter & Gamble Inc., 117
Project Paradise, 20
Pye, Dr. Robert, 65

Q

QSI Windows & Doors, 46

R

Red Hill Creek Expressway, 236
Reeder, Susan K., 5
Renaissance Project, 230, 231, 236
Ricca's Furniture Limited, 129
Rizzotto, Carmen D., 4, 5, 138, 234, 256
Robbinex Inc., 39
Ross, Don, 7, 236
Round Table on the Environment
    and Economy, 14
Royal Bank, 72
Royal Botanical Gardens, 34, 43, 200-201
Royal Connaught Howard Johnson Hotel,
    160, 161, 194
Royal Insurance, 48, 49
Royalcrest Lifecare Group Inc., 56
Ruberto, Bruno, 4, 5

S

St. Joseph's Hospital, 63
St. Joseph's Villa, 62
St. Paul's Presbyterian Church, 183
St. Peter's Hospital, 66

Scottish Rite, 193
Sesqui coin, 234
Sesquicentennial logo, 2
Sesqui Super Home On Paradise
    Lottery, 16
Shakespeare's Dining Lounge, 243
Sheraton Hamilton Hotel, 195
Short, Martin, 95, 100, 141, 160
Silvestri Investments, 75
Skelly, Donna, 250
Sleightholm, Sherry, 4, 5, 11
Smith/McKay Florists, 39
Southside, 137
Spectator, The, 232, 233
Spencer Gorge Wilderness Area, 35
Sproule-Jones, Mark, 45
Steel City Spring Service Inc., 239
Stelco, 206, 214, 215
Stelco Tower, 180-181
Stirling Print-All & Creative
    Services Inc., 29
Stoney Creek Furniture, 106, 107
Stoney Ridge Cellars, 111
Strongman, Wayne, 141
Sutton & Son, 167

T

Tews Falls, 35
Theatre Aquarius, 135, 146
Thomas, Ian, 95
Thomas, Isiah, 249
Tiger-Cat Football Club, 11, 94
Travale, Vincenza, 4, 5, 249, 256
Turkstra Lumber Co. Ltd., 170

U

United Nations, 14
University Hall, McMaster University, 79
Upper James Toyota, 126
Urbanowicz, Ted, 5

V

Venetian Club of Hamilton, 202
Venetian Jewellers, 127,
Vineland Estates Winery, 38
Vision 2020, 14, 20, 236

W

Wark Ltd., G.S., General Contractors, 171
Waterfront Regeneration Trust, 42
Webster, Jane, 251
Webster's Falls, 35
Westinghouse Canada, 124, 125, 215
WESCAM, 144, 145, 215
West Avenue School, 162
Whitaker, Brigadier General W. Denis, 5
White, Marie, 251
Whitehern, 154, 182
Whiz-a-Top Linen, 241
Whynott, Reg, 14, 236
Wilson, Dave, 7
Wincza, Vitek, 135
World Children's Games, 123
Wright's Cleaners and Laundry, 150

Y

Yachetti, Roger, 94

– Photo by Kim Scott

Thank you, Hamilton,
for a wonderful celebration
of our 150 years!

Vincenza Travale   Milton J. Lewis, Q.C.
Carmen D. Rizzotto

• Hamilton Sesquicentennial Celebrations Inc. •